the
Bronze
Screen

the Bronze Screen

Chicana and Chicano Film Culture

Rosa Linda Fregoso

University of Minnesota Press
Minneapolis
London

Published by the University of Minnesota Press
2037 University Avenue Southeast, Minneapolis, MN 55455-3092
Printed in the United States of America on acid-free paper

Library of Congress Cataloging-in-Publication Data

Fregoso, Rosa Linda.
    The bronze screen : Chicana and Chicano film culture / Rosa Linda Fregoso.
        p.   cm.
    Includes bibliographical references and index.
    ISBN 0-8166-2135-7 (acid-free). — ISBN 0-8166-2136-5 (pbk. : acid-free)
    1. Mexican Americans in motion pictures.   I. Title.
PN1995.9.M49F74   1993
791.43'652036872—dc20   93-7755
                                                                               CIP

For my Xochitl Magaly and Sergio Emilio
and in memory of our Tio Pepe (1935-1977)

Contents

List of Photographs

Acknowledgments

This book would not have been possible without the love and encouragement of Herman S. Gray. Nor would it have been possible without the friendship and critical insights of my Bay Area *comadres*: Angie Chabram-Dernersesian, Sara García, Saidiya Hartman, Lata Mani, Norma Alarcón, expatriate Alvina Quintana, and Carmen Guerrero up in the Redwoods. Very special thanks to the great public intellectual B. Ruby Rich, who read and commented on an earlier draft of this book, leading me out of its labyrinth. I am also grateful to George Lipsitz for bringing to my attention several inconsistencies. Special thanks to Xochitl Perales for her editorial assistance. Down in Los Angeles I owe special thanks to Teshome Gabriel, Vilma Ortiz, Richard Chabran, Sonia Saldívar-Hull, and the Raza at the Chicano Studies Research Center for making L.A. my home for two years. I thank María Elena de las Carreras de Kuntz for diligently clipping and sending me every article on Chicano film from the L.A. press. I benefited greatly from Janaki Bakhle's support of my work at the University of Minnesota Press.

This project was made possible through fellowships from the Ford Foundation (NRC), the Institute of American Cultures (UCLA), and a Faculty Career Development Award (UC-Davis).

I thank my brother, Frank, and my sisters Terri, Ana, Lucy, and Angela, for lighting all kinds of candles for me in South Texas; our parents Lucia and Francisco for taking us all to "dollar-a-nights" at the Buccaneer drive-in theater; to my mother and the Tex-Mex in Corpus Christi for financially supporting my UT education.

Finally, I would like to acknowledge the presence of my Tio Pepe, whose spirit accompanies me in my life-journey and whose lifelong commitment to social justice and human rights serves as my inspiration. It is to his rebel-spirit, which lives on in my children (Xochitl Magaly and Sergio Emilio), and to these two jewels in my life that I dedicate these words.

Introduction

The Bronze Screen
Looking at Us Looking

> Our films will not merely dust off the cobwebs from
> moldy relics of our pre-Columbian past but provide a
> viable connection from the past to the present and
> beyond into the future.
>
> —Francisco X. Camplis[1]

> Write of what most links us with life, the sensation of the
> body, the expansion of the psyche in tranquility:
> moments of high intensity, its movement, sounds,
> thoughts. Even though we go hungry we are not
> impoverished of experiences.
>
> —Gloria Anzaldúa[2]

> The sign must be contradicted.
>
> —Rubén Martínez[3]

On Saint Valentine's Day, 1991, I dined with two friends, L.A.-based filmmaker Nancy de los Santos and Patricia González, a classmate from my days in journalism school at the University of Texas and now an editor for an East Coast newspaper. The subject of this book came up, and we discussed its title, which was to be something along these lines: "The Construction of the Chicano Spectator in Chicano Cinema." Unswayed, both women instead reminded me that such a title would lure only academics (specialized audiences). Why not try, "The Bronze Screen: Looking at Us Looking." Notwithstanding, I owe the first part of the title to this evening dinner on the hills of Echo Park in Los Angeles. My aim in this book is to interrupt and interrogate the terms of the critical discourse on Chicano cinema. Toward this objective, Nancy and Patricia's suggestion for a book title is as good a starting point as any: "The Bronze Screen: Looking at Us Looking."

The connection of "the Bronze Screen" with La Raza is clear. And the vague familiarity of the concept "looking at Us looking" did not distract from its poignancy. Later, I would recall these as the words that film theorist Teresa de Lauretis used to describe the "impossible place of female desire" in cinema.[4] The concept "looking at Us looking" points to the historical location of Us (Chicanas and Chicanos) behind the camera, as directors, writers, cinematographers, editors; Us as images on the screen, as subject matter, actors, actresses; and, finally, Us as spectators, as viewers seated between "the look of the camera" and "the images on the screen." Stated in different terms, my project concerns the emergence of a film culture *by*, *about*, and *for* Chicanas and Chicanos.

Project and Social Formation

A comprehensive notation of Chicano films, themes, biographies of filmmakers, and critical discourse on films is compiled in the two anthologies on the Chicano film movement, *Chicano Cinema*, edited by Gary Keller, and *Chicanos and Film*, edited by Chon Noriega.[5] As the introductions by Keller and Noriega detail, Chicano film culture developed with the Chicano Power Movement in the late 1960s. In this respect, the social formation of Chicano filmmakers is linked to early expressions of Chicano nationalism, which, in turn, demanded a certain unity of political goals out of the diversity of cultural practices and social experiences.[6]

As forms of cultural production resolutely connected to the social and political activism of the Chicano Movement, Chicano films, for the first time ever, interjected onto the social/cultural imagination Chicano countervisions of history, identity, social reality, resistance politics. Filmmakers honed their craft on the streets of East L.A., on the picket lines of farm fields, in internship programs on commercial and public television, and as students in university film schools.[7] As oppositional films, Chicano cinema emerged as an alternative film movement to what filmmaker Jesús Salvador Treviño describes as "a long history of abusive portrayals and stereotypical renderings of Chicanos and their life-styles."[8] The project of Chicano cinema may succinctly be summed up as the documentation of social reality through oppositional forms of knowledge about Chicanos. Or, as one of the early filmmakers, the visual artist Harry Gamboa, Jr., puts it, Chicano films "inexorably urge a more realistic vision of the Chicano experience."[9]

I have noted that my project explores a film culture by, for, and about Chicanas and Chicanos. Despite the fine surveys that exist about Chicano cinema, documenting its history, its context, contents and forms, details of filmmakers' formation, and so on, a certain uncertainty remains to the term Chicano cinema. The ambiguity of the term, however, is not restricted to Chicano cinema, but is often a vexed question in attempts to specify the domains of oppositional film cultures such as black and women's cinemas.[10]

Initial attempts to define the parameters of Chicano cinema connected Chicano films to a cultural politics. In 1975, Francisco X. Camplis, for instance, called on filmmakers to create "a culture by and for us."[11] Inspired by the works of Latin American filmmakers (Fernando Solanas, Jorge Sanjines, Octavio Getino, Glauber Rocha, Walter Achugar), Camplis urged the making of "revolutionary," "decolonizing films," as well as the development of a vernacular aesthetics.[12] It is in this context that Camplis expressed his vision for Chicano cinema with the words that I used to open this Introduction: "Our films will not merely dust off the cobwebs from moldy relics of our pre-Columbian past but provide a viable connection from the past to the present and beyond into the future."

In another early essay, Jason C. Johansen addressed the "nonrigorous definition of Chicano films" screened at the San Antonio film festival. Writing in the late 1970s, Johansen noted that the festival included films by, for, and about Chicanos. Yet, this all-inclusiveness elided what Johansen considered vital: the "purpose/function" of Chicano cinema, which "lies in the roots, origins, and determinants of the genre's development."[13] Like Camplis, Johansen drew his inspiration from the new Latin American cinema, outlining a general framework for Chicano cinema along similar lines:

> Chicano film as an alternative cinema requires at least some
> semblance of a theoretical foundation. Our *compañeros* in America
> Latina are way ahead of us in the game, and they provide the basis
> for the following: The demystification of film . . . The decolonization
> of minds . . . Reflective and open-ended . . . The altering of
> consciousness . . . Effect social change . . . A Chicano film
> language.[14]

These prior efforts to stake out the cultural politics of Chicano cinema thus advocated a practice of filmmaking tailored to Chicano spectators. Rooted in the politics of antiracism, early filmmakers foregrounded "communication with La Raza,"[15] as well as alternative screening venues, in order to "engage the audience by discussing our films with them after showings."[16] Camplis succinctly sums up Chicano cinema's explicit concern for its spectatorship: "Our audience is Raza. I make films for Raza because I am Raza."[17]

And so filmmakers were defining an oppositional cinema, a cinema allied to the struggle for liberation of the Chicano nation, a revolutionary cultural politics. However, as the struggle for self-determination waned with the decline of large-scale popular social mobilization, and as the cultural politics of the Chicano Power Movement retreated into more localized sites of resistance at various public and private institutions, among them universities, centros culturales, museums, and even commercial sites like the television and film industries, the definition of Chicano cinema shifted substantially. No longer was Chicano cinema defined as oppositional cinema by, for, and about Chicanos, but it came to mean films "whose major production decisions are made by Chicanos." This definition was advanced in 1991 by filmmaker Jesús Salvador Treviño at the "Chicano cinema" panel of the Society for Cinema Studies conference in Los Angeles. In Treviño's estimation, films no longer have to be about Chicanos or for Chicanos. The definitive criterion is now production, namely, films by Chicanos. And since the political upheavals of the 1960s and 1970s have reached a low point, the oppositionality of the cultural forms is no longer as strident a prerequisite for the category of Chicano cinema.

In the recent anthology *Chicanos and Film*, Noriega subscribes to filmmakers' definition of Chicano cinema, adding the criteria of theme or content:

> [A "Chicano" film is a] film (or video) by and about Chicanos. The word "by" is taken to mean that the writer, producer, or director is Chicano. The filmmakers tend to apply a third criterion when only the producer is Chicano: that he or she had significant involvement in the creative process.[18]

This definition, encompassing the by and about, according to the author, "grounds the debate in questions of production (or participation) as well as of signification."[19] On the other hand, both Keller and Noriega prefer to advance a definition of Chicano cinema against images of Chicanos in Hollywood mainstream and Mexican commercial cinemas. Keller writes:

> It is in this sense that Chicano cinema has been so painfully overdetermined. The story, the content, rests like a landscape of prominent lesions, urging us to artistic salving. What was painful in itself, "reality," had become infected by the distortive perversity of both United States and Mexican cinema.[20]

And, as Noriega adds:

> In the final analysis, "Chicanos and film" falls within the domain of two national cultures: American and Americas . . . Our representation for the most part has been limited to the commercial film and television industries of Hollywood and Mexico.[21]

Situating Chicano and Chicana filmmaking within this Mexican/American duality is understandable, because in order to examine how Chicanos make films there needs to be some consideration of the relationship Chicanos have had historically, as consumers of images, to films from both sides of the border.

The trinity "by, for, about" made sense at a particular historical moment. In its embryonic stage, Chicano films could not be defined solely by their contents, that is, in terms of the about, because historically many films dealing with the Chicano experience, produced prior and during the Movement, were inadequate in reflecting "our" experience from "our" perspective. Negative representations about Chicanos originated during the first moving pictures, beginning with the early-twentieth-century "Greaser" genre and on to the "Westerns," the "social problem" genre, up to the recent onslaught of "gangxploitation" films.[22] Keeping the "by, for, about" criteria intact prevented the kinds of distortions that have normalized Chicanos and Chicanas as images of the "other" in mainstream films. These criteria were also important, as we have seen, in the consolidation of the social formation of Chicano and Chicana filmmakers. However, if the "for" and in some cases the "about" are no longer fashionable for defining Chicano cinema, then what has in fact dropped out of the equation is the cultural politics that inspired a whole generation in the struggle for human rights and social justice. That is to say, Chicano and Chicana cultural politics has been, and continues to be, an oppositional politics. Any consideration of Chicano films as oppositional cultural forms forces us to consider their politics, their "purpose/function" (as Johansen reminded us over a decade ago), in relationship to dominant cinema, and with regard to specific contexts. If not, we are left with mechanistic or formulaic criteria where race (biology) overdetermines the cultural politics of opposition. Indeed, the relation of biology to cultural identity as one of fixed determinism resonates throughout this query of Chicano cinema. A brief digression will illustrate the complexity of what is at stake here.

Among certain cultural nationalists, the self-designation Chicano has come to mean the biological makeup (composition) of a people, i.e., the mestizo nation comprised of the racial mixture of Indian and Spanish bloods. Unwittingly reproducing the color-caste system inherited from the Spanish colonialists, Chicano nationalists often lay phylogenetic claims to the self-designation Chicano. The racial "authenticity" membership-test continues unabated in the current "second wave" of Chicano nationalism, often reaching absurd proportions, especially in light of the "mestizo" (mixed-race) claims to nationhood. So that if one has white (non-Spanish) European blood (say, one is of Anglo-Chicano parents), then one's claim to Chicanoness is open to question. Chicano rapper Kid Frost takes up the plight, or rather, the conundrum, of mixed-race mestizos (a double enigma!) in the rap song "These Stories Have To Be Told":

> . . . and this little cholito who got himself in a mess
> his plaqueazo was guero,
> and everywhere daddy went
> the batos quieren pedo.
> So as the tiempo went on,
> the hatred for guero just got more strong.
> So guero started packing the filero
> cuz the guys in the barrio, the block, the ghetto
> were all trying to get him.
> He wanted out, to forget his past,
> but they won't let him.
> So he moved out of state and changed his name . . .
> *I know this story's getting kinda old,*
> *but it has to be told.*[23]

The quandary in the self-designation Chicano undergirds the cultural category, Chicano cinema, because what to call the people of Mexican origin ("Chicano," "Latino," or "Hispanic"), or whom to consider for membership into the Chicano nation, depends on one's politics and on the context of the term's usage. As the review of the literature on Chicano/a identity and naming suggests, not only do the debates on self-designation surface with the very formation of 1960s Chicano nationalism, but they continue to this date.[24] For some (myself included), the problem is resolved by de-emphasizing the biological claims to authenticity, yet accentuating its political dimension. In this respect, Chicano refers to a political category.

Specifying that Chicano represents a category of progressive politics allows us to circumscribe further the specificity of Chicano cinema. If we recognized that Chicano cinema developed within the context of the Chicano Power Movement's struggle of antiracism (equality, self-determination, human rights, and social justice), then its cinema must somehow remain bound by these ideals. However, if we disarticulate the cultural politics from Chicano cinema, then the definition becomes too banal, too all-inclusive, too pluralistic, equating cultural forms engaged in antiracism and empowerment struggles with those informed by fascist, racist, or sexist tendencies.

As it relates to context, the political orientation of films is of singular importance. In my exploration of Chicano film culture, some of the works considered radical at the time of their production may, in our current context, strike spectators as backward and conservative. This is especially true for the male-centered nationalist films like *I Am Joaquin* and *Zoot Suit*. However, it needs to be stressed that what determines whether or not a film is reactionary or progressive depends on the configurations of power relations operating at any given historical moment. For instance, in terms of their antiracism politics, *I Am Joaquin* and *Zoot Suit* are radical by comparison to mainstream films and even to most white-Left film standards; insofar as gender and sexuality politics are concerned, they are not.

In my effort to interrupt and redefine the terms of critical discourse on Chicano films, the "for" part of the triplet bears further exploration. Does the "for" mean representing or speaking on behalf of Chicanos and Chicanas, or does it refer to something quite different? If it is the former, then there is a certain paternalism in claiming to speak for the community as though its members cannot speak on their own behalf. This is why the video artist Frances Salomé España insists (if I may paraphrase) that she speaks not *for* the Chicano community, but *from* the specificity of her experience as a Chicana in L.A.[25]

In this light, a different take on the notion of "for" refers to the dialogic/communicative tendencies inherent in cinema—the question of spectatorship so central in the critical discourse on film. In its original incarnation, the category of Chicano cinema positioned the issue of "address" on its center stage (i.e., "communication with La Raza"). For all their romanticism, Latin American guerrilla filmmakers, who in turn inspired a generation of Chicano filmmakers, stressed the politics of communicating with the "masses." The Latin Americans envisioned the spectators'/audiences' centrality to their *proyecto de concientización*, which Paul Willeman translates as a project "stressing lucidity in viewers."[26] Argentinean filmmaker/critic Fernando Birri states it clearly: the new Latin American cinema is a "nationalist, realist, critical, and popular" cinema that "trie[s] to interpret, express, and communicate with the people . . . It is a cinema of and for liberation, for economic, political and cultural liberation and also the liberation of the image, that is to say, the imagination."[27]

Drawing "some valuable suggestions" from the Latin American notion of guerrilla cinema, film critic Teresa de Lauretis reorients her examination of "women's cinema" around the problem of spectatorship, which is "central to the feminist film project." In de Lauretis's estimation, women's films qualify as "guerrilla cinema" or as "alternative" to the mainstream if they

> engage the current problems, the real issues actually at stake in feminist communities on a local scale, and which although informed by a global perspective do not assume at a universal, multinational audience, but address a particular one in its specific history of struggles and emergencies.[28]

Although the *proyecto de concientización* is, in our current historical moment, a difficult (perhaps even outmoded) enterprise, de Lauretis's observations direct us nonetheless in asking pertinent questions about the cultural politics of Chicano cinema. Does the cultural specificity of Chicano films challenge U.S. aspirations to "universality" (melting-pot-ism)? Do these cultural forms easily melt into the "American" mainstream, ignoring the oppositionality in difference? Are these films inflected by culturally specific codes of address? Do they aim at a universal, multinational audience? Do Chicano films address Chicanos and Chicanas in their specific histories of struggle? Do they engage current problems, the real issues at stake in Chicano and Chicana communities? These are some of the questions that occupy me throughout this exploration of Chicano and Chicana film culture.

Project and Social Location

In marking off the inseparability of "project" (Chicano cinema) and "social formation" (Chicano Movement), that is to say, the connection between the object of analysis and its historical context (art and society), I have indirectly named my own formation in cultural studies.[29] Before elaborating further on this "cultural studies" approach to Chicano film culture, I want to specify the place of my own location as a "positioned subject"—to quote Renato Rosaldo's oft-cited concept—who, like all cultural critics, intervenes in the cultural process.

I came to know Chicano films through a nationalist formation in South Texas. As a high-school student activist in MAYO (Mexican American Youth Organization) and MASO (Mexican American Student Organization), I first saw *I Am Joaquin* (the first Chicano film) during one of our organizing meetings. Later, I worked for three years in commercial television. It was not until I attended the University of Texas as an older single parent that I looked seriously at Chicano film. My first published article, written in 1981 on the film *Seguin*, was informed by a Marxist ideological analysis. After working two years in public radio as a radio producer (for the Longhorn Radio Network, NPR affiliate), I entered graduate school at the University of California-San Diego. There in La Jolla, I was introduced to the latest intellectual fashions of poststructuralism, postmodernism, feminism, classic Marxist political economy.[30] However, it was not until I reentered the work force that I confronted the "return of the repressed": my early nationalist formation, albeit rerouted through an "academic" training. Thoughts finally gelled for me by way of the writings of U.S. Third World feminists and the studies on race-gender-sexuality undertaken by the cultural studies group in Birmingham. Today, I re-view Chicano film texts with fresh eyes.

In embracing a cultural studies framework, I first re-claim a nationalist intellectual legacy that has a long history in the U.S. Southwest. I trace my genealogy to the nineteenth century when the population of Mexican origin first confronted Anglo-white immigrants who would later conquer the U.S. Southwestern territories. This indigenous intellectual legacy of symbolic cultural forms and practices includes written essays, folk songs, music, and poetry. I have come to understand these social symbolic acts in their mutual determinations and interrelations with historical forces, as cultural forms mixed with and within relations of power. In its nationalistic tendency to ignore questions of gender and sexuality, my legacy reaches its impasse.

Second, I draw from feminism's critical discourse on film, in particular its insights on the role of cinema in the construction of gendered subjectivities, that is, the relationship of human gender to representation. I retreat from feminist film discourse when it lodges itself

in a male/female binary, thus eliding racial, class, and sexual subjectivities: the crucial differences among women, rather than simply between men and women. Third, from poststructuralism I have learned
about subject formation and difference. Its shortcomings include the
lack of rigor in theorizing about the subject positions of non-Western
subjects. More often, in Euro-American incantations of poststructuralism, "difference" is a new word for the good ol' American concept
of pluralism. As a critique of Eurocentrism, the critical discourse on
postcoloniality has been helpful. But it too has certain drawbacks, especially when its nationalism is informed by earlier geopolitical configurations of the nation-state.[31] Postcolonial intellectual angst, say,
its sentiment of "transcendental homelessness" (to quote Saidiya
Hartman) is particularly useless for "subalterns" like myself who feel
pretty much at home in the "belly of the beast" (the U.S. of A.).

In naming these intellectual and political traditions, I hold onto
their strengths and move away from their shortcomings. In so doing,
I embrace the rebel spirits of U.S. Third World feminists who reside
"between and among" subject positions and critical cultural discourses. And so it is with these hybridized eyes that I re-view and
re-read Chicano films. For as these cultural forms are hybrid productions, so too is my cultural studies approach a mestizaje, a bricolage.

This introduction to the contents of the book requires that I specify
the terms of my writing practice. Readers will note a decisive shift in
the writing style, particularly noticeable in the different modulations
of the introduction and the conclusion from the rest of the book. In
other words, the introduction and the conclusion to this book register
a difference in voice from that of chapters 1 through 5. These key sig-
natures of my voice differ in part because the conclusion and introduction were written at a later date. I also deliberately chose to mod-
ulate the registry of my voice. In the introduction and conclusion, my
writing politics enacts the more playful, open-ended style of the Latin
American essay tradition. In contrast to most of Latin America, in the
United States this tradition is kept alive primarily by journalists and
novelists. It is virtually nonexistent among the "academic" community.

The chapters in this book are organized around problematics: for
example, the contours of Chicano film culture (chapter 1); the problem of cultural identity (chapter 2); the subversive potential of humor
(chapter 3); the border as a concept for understanding cultural processes, including the formation of subjectivity (chapter 4); en-gender-

ing subjectivities (chapter 5); and the return to spectatorship (conclusion). Unfortunately, many films (i.e., documentaries) are not included. The most glaring omission is the body of films by a pioneer in experimental Super-8 film, Willie Varela from El Paso, Texas. At the time of this writing, Varela had just completed his first narrative film, and also the first truly *noir* Chicano film, *Lonely Man*.

I chose films that exemplified a particular social formation of cultural workers: the first generation of Chicano and Chicana filmmakers. I arrived at this characterization less by the age of the filmmaker or in terms of when the film was made, but by the particularities manifest in the treatment of the subject matter. For instance, is the film inflected by a nationalist vision of community membership? Is the film guided by a particular attention to historical specificities and social conditions, positing, for example, an imaginary self-coherence? I based my decision to include a particular film text less on content than on the basis of how and why the work was made in the first place. Obviously these issues are better addressed in narrative film, which is why, save for chapters 1 and 5, I restrict my exploration to narrative films.

Much like Benedict Anderson's notion of "imagined communities," the vision of the Chicano nation captured in these films represents an "imagined community." Far from fabricating or inventing a community, Chicanas and Chicanos have reinvented (imagined anew) a "community" of Chicanos and Chicanas. In the words of Anderson, "communities are to be distinguished, not by their falsity/ genuineness, but by the style in which they are imagined."[32] There is no better place to explore this style than in cinema: the social/cultural technology of the imagination.

Finally, just as I interrupt and interrogate the terms of Chicano and Chicana film culture, I urge the younger generation of cultural critics to question, unsettle, redefine the terms I have staked out throughout this exploration. As the cultural critic Rubén Martínez, paraphrasing Father Luis Olivares quoting the Bible, puts it: "The sign must be contradicted."

Oakland, California
September 1992

Actos of "Imaginative Re-discovery"

One builds from what one has, and if these efforts are
the beginning bricks of the Chicano cinematic edifice, our
younger artists should retain them and use them for
whatever purposes they can.

—Rolando Hinojosa-Smith[1]

I begin this chapter with a quote from the Chicano novelist Rolando
Hinojosa-Smith, who writes about Chicano films as historical and cultural constructions. In order to move beyond descriptive accounts of
the early period of Chicano and Chicana cinematic production (typical
in efforts to identify the "documentary impulse" in Chicano films), I
prefer to categorize/characterize the early films symbolically, as *actos*
(or "Acts"). The short films of this early period are *actos* of "imaginative re-discovery"[2] because they work to "re-invent," "re-cover," and
"re-vision" a "lost" history for Chicanas and Chicanos. Inaugurating
discursive strategies that will reappear in later film productions, *I Am
Joaquin* (1969), *Agueda Martínez* (1977), *Chicana* (1979), and *Yo Soy Chicano* (1972) are thus treated as paradigmatic films of the "Chicano cinematic edifice."[3] In these early films the traces of an intellectual and
historical journey begin to emerge.

At stake here is the dialectics between the referential function of
cinema and its constitutive role, that is to say, art as a mediation on
the phenomenal world rather than as a simple or transparent reflection of social reality. Identifying the "documentary impulse" in Chicano films overly emphasizes the view of films as reflections of the
"real" world. Certainly the move to "document" Chicano social reality has been one of the tenets of Chicano films, but this perspective

greatly ignores their more poetic or symbolic attributes.[4] To be sure, the films *I Am Joaquin, Yo Soy Chicano*, and *Chicana* "re-construct" a history that had not been taught in public schools.[5] And, along with *Agueda Martínez*, these films "re-invent" an intellectual genealogy and a historical lineage for Chicana and Chicano cultural identity. Fernando Birri identifies similar strategies in the films of the new Latin American cinema:

> The real undertaking at hand was a quest for national identity, an identity that had been lost or alienated by a system of economic and political as well as cultural hegemony established by the dominant classes in concert first with the Spanish colonizers . . . and most recently with agents of the United States.[6]

The efforts to re-cover history are intimately connected to the re-invention of an alternative notion of Chicano cultural identity. Given that Chicanas and Chicanos were depicted as "others" according to the perverse logic of the discourse of racism, each of these films labors to dismantle the dominant system of representation.

In some instances the films trace the subjugation of Chicano cultural identity to two historical moments: the Spanish conquest of the indigenous nations and the white-American conquest of the Southwest. As responses to the violence engendered by racist, colonialist, and imperialist discursive systems, these early filmmakers propose that the re-discovery of an "authentic" identity entails recontextualizing the nativeness of Chicanos to this continent, to a space and time before the dual instances or twofold moments of conquest and domination.

This chapter is structured in a comparative framework that aims to establish the contours of Chicano cinematic practices. If the traces of an intellectual and historical journey begin to emerge in these early films, they were certainly not monolithic traces. As a corpus of early works, these films reproduce various facets of Chicano nationalism. They each are, however, gendered attempts to constitute collective memories for late-twentieth-century Chicana and Chicano political struggles. And while these films share certain affinities in their modes of expression and thematic concerns with history, identity, and social reality, they refract the diverse and embattled voices, intermingling amid diverse relations of power.

For example, one of the major differences between *I Am Joaquin* and *Chicana* derives from the fact that a decade separates the male-centered and female-centered epic films. This time span is important, for it permits us to examine stylistic and ideological differences that are attributable less to a developing "sophistication" in cinematic practices than to transformations in the social formation of cultural workers,[7] namely to the emergence of an ideological counter to the male-centeredness of Chicano nationalism. Indeed, an examination of *I Am Joaquin* and *Chicana* highlights the extent to which the discourse of Chicano nationalism, a counterdiscourse to dominant ideology, was itself a contested terrain. In fact, Chicano nationalism produced its own counterdiscourse that challenged the limitations of male-centered nationalism. On the one hand, *I Am Joaquin* represents an "instance" of counterhegemony to the racist hegemonic discourse, and *Chicana*, on the other hand, articulates a critical discursive tendency within Chicano nationalist ideology. Like the writings by women that Ramón Saldívar identifies as counterhegemonic to the second power, *Chicana* critiques dominant as well as Chicano (male) oppressive ideologies. For this reason, a comparative reading of these early films allows us to examine transformations within the social formation of Chicano Movement intellectuals as expressed in cinematic practices. Although it may be reductive to read *I Am Joaquin* and *Yo Soy Chicano* against *Chicana* and *Agueda Martínez* in a rigid male/female dichotomy, each film is nevertheless structured as male-centered and female-centered narratives of history, social reality, and identity.

The Male-centered Lineage

I Am Joaquin, directed by Luis Valdez, is the visual adaptation of the Chicano Movement poem by Rodolfo "Corky" Gonzales that narrates, in epic forms, the history of Chicanos beginning with the conquest of Mexico by Spain. Represented in the style of the popular oral tradition, the film surveys five centuries of Mexican and Chicano history. The twenty-minute film interweaves various "heroes" and "villains" of major historical periods, including the colonial era, Mexican independence from Spain, the Mexican Revolution of the early twentieth century, and the Chicano Power Movement. As depicted in cinematic form, *I Am Joaquin* is designed to "rescue the past from oblivion," to emphasize a "continuity and integration of various aspects of the Chicano experience," and to provide a "collective" historical identity for Chicanos.[8] Prior to its production into cinematic form, *I Am Joaquin* was performed in 1967 as an animated slide show by the Teatro Campesino.[9] The slide presentation, based on the still photographs of George Ballis, comprised part of the Teatro Campesino's repertoire of agitprop theater. The poem was narrated by Luis Valdez while his brother, Daniel, improvised musical accompaniment, recreating live sound effects, and troupe members dramatized select parts of the poem.[10] In general, the film follows the order of the poem's narrative, except for the omission of sixty-one lines from the published text.[11]

"Corky" Gonzales, the founder of the civil rights organization Crusade for Justice in Denver, Colorado, wrote *I Am Joaquin* in 1967, and its rapid popularity among activists stemmed from the fact that the work articulated, in poetic form, the emerging Chicano ideology of cultural nationalism. As Gonzales explains in the introduction to its book publication, the epic poem reenacts a "journey back through history, a painful self-evaluation, a wandering search for my people's and, most of all, my own identity."[12] Indeed, the poetic articulation of Gonzales's own "quest" can be read as emblematic of the Chicano student movement.

Although "Corky" was less well known to outsiders of the Movement than, for instance, César Chávez, Gonzales was one of the inner circle's most charismatic leaders. He had been a Golden Glove champion and later a professional boxer. The father of eight children, Gonzales placed an inordinate emphasis on instilling cultural awareness among young people. Described by the historian Rudy Acuña as "a well-built, beautifully tanned man, and the epitome of the *macho* [sic] (male)," Gonzales was particularly popular among the younger Chicanos for his ability to voice the sentiments of alienation prevalent among the "urban bato and barrio" youth.[13]

I Am Joaquin represents the historical emphasis of the counterdiscourse of Chicano nationalism to the dehistoricizing tendencies of racist ideology. Gonzales's Crusade for Justice and the artistic intervention embodied in his poem reflected as well a profound contravention to "the loss of identity when the Anglo teacher changes one's name from Rodolfo to Rudolph."[14] The poem resonated with the sentiments of powerlessness prevalent among young Chicanos, and located these as stemming from the distortion of Chicano history by the socialization process of institutions such as schools, the church, and media.

The opening stanzas frame the poem in the present tense in order to speak to the actual conditions of Chicanos in the United States. Although a major thrust of the poem is historical, its interpretation of history is comprised in terms of the "present-day" or "contemporary" binaries, Anglos versus Chicanos.[15] Additionally, in the present tense, the author situates "social neurosis" and the "sterilization of the soul" as by-products of "industrial progress" and "modern society," that is, features resting on the negative or Anglo side of the binary equation. The forward motion of the poem is actually cast in the past tense, propelled by a retrospective narration of a Chicano history of oppression and resistance. A dual motion thereby punctuates the poem, as expressed in the binary equation, Anglos-Chicanos, but also in the dialectics of two historical relations, oppression and struggle.[16] The significance of this latter relation rests in the function of the poem in Movement politics, for *I Am Joaquín* not only was didactic, but was fundamentally a call for a revolutionary struggle of Chicano liberation.

Thus the figuration of this dialectical couplet takes concrete form in actual historical agents. For instance, the poem recounts the actions of oppressive villains and the deeds of the heroes of revolutionary struggle. Transversing Mexican and Chicano history, the poem's duality is further exemplified in its valorization of male heroes such as Cuauhtemoc, Moctezuma, Benito Juárez, Miguel Hidalgo, Emiliano Zapata, and Joaquín Murrieta, alongside its celebration of Mexican cultural symbols and icons like the Virgen of Guadalupe and the eagle and serpent of the Aztecs. The poem's objects of scorn include Hernán Cortés, Spanish colonialists, the church, and the dictator Porfirio Díaz, along with symbols such as the Spanish crown and sword. Although it appears that the poem's movement in this case as well lapses into a binary equation of Spaniard-Indian, the poem proposes rather a fusion of contradictory historical identities.

Indeed, the quest for an "authentic" identity grounds itself precisely on this problematic. The narrative voice, I, enunciated in the first-person present tense of *I Am Joaquín*, serves to reconcile symbolically the crisis brought about by the relation between conqueror and conquered.[17] The I signifies both heroes and villains in Mexican and Chicano history; in other words, the contradiction ensuing from the fusion of the Indian with the European, a symbolic and genetic mestizaje (hybridity). Like many Chicano writers of the period, Gonzales reduces the Chicano conflict to a crisis of identity configured on this notion of mestizaje. As Rosaura Sánchez points out:

> The product of higher education, Chicano writers often view
> themselves from the perspective of postrevolutionary Mexican
> essayists seeking to explain the failure and nonrevolutionary status
> of the revolts of 1910 in terms of indigenous/Hispanic duality (which

leads to an existential crisis, à la Octavio Paz) by situating the Chicano in a similar Anglo-Mexican dichotomy.[18]

Joaquín is moreover the embodiment of that which survives a past tense of domination and oppression, namely the subject-agent of a present, reproduced culturally in spiritual and artistic forms and practices.[19] The cultural and the spiritual informs Joaquín's identity, yet the poem also posits its notion of a "collective" cultural identity that is singularly male-centered.[20] Multiple identities are subsumed into a collectivity whose narrative voice is enunciated in this historical male subject, Joaquín. The males who inform Chicano cultural identity have names (Cuauhtemoc, Moctezuma, Juan Diego, and so on), but the females are nameless abstractions.[21] Indeed, as opposed to appearing as historical subjects, women are positioned as the metaphors for the emotive side of Chicano collective cultural identity, as "faithful" wives or "suffering" Mexican mothers.

By resorting to these two strategies—on the one hand, the selective interpretation of the past, and, on the other, the fusion of contradictory identities by way of positing mestizaje—I Am Joaquin re-invents an "authentic" identity for Chicanos. Moreover, this new identity derives its basis from a "collectivity" that lies submerged in the inner psyche of the male historical subject, Joaquín. At the level of thematic concerns, the poem reveals significant continuity with Chicano Movement ideology, particularly in its emphasis on cultural identity and antiracism. Through the narrative voice of Joaquín, Gonzales transforms a countermemory of Chicano cultural resistance.

Yet in terms of form, the poem draws heavily from the popular corridos (ballads) of the oral tradition—corridos about heroes of the Mexican Revolution, like Madero, Villa, and Zapata, that are sung to this day throughout Mexico and the United States. It is the popular oral tradition that, despite the attempts by U.S. dominant culture to distort and dismember this history, kept alive a countermemory of Chicano history and struggle.[22] This intertextual quality would be taken to a new level in the cinematic rendition of the poem by Luis Valdez.

Valdez was well aware that image-making was an important arena of cultural contestation, and his adaptation of I Am Joaquin into cinematic form took place in the summer of 1969. Valdez drew heavily from multiple artistic traditions in order to render the poem into film form. Moreover, although Corky Gonzales re-invents Chicano identity, basing his construction on Mexican postrevolutionary notions of mestizaje, in the film version the figuration of cultural identity stresses the Indian side of the equation.

Valdez was one of the first Movement artists to reject the European heritage of Chicano people and to give concrete form to an explicitly indigenous legacy. As is evident in an examination of his multifaceted artistic intervention, Valdez highlighted an identity that repressed the Spanish and privileged the non-European indigenous past and the working-class history of Chicanos. In 1968, Valdez explains:

> Most of us know we are not European simply by looking in a mirror . . . the shape of the eyes, the curve of the nose, the color of the skin, the texture of the hair; these things belong to another time, another people. Together with a million little stubborn mannerisms, beliefs, myths, superstitions, words, thoughts . . . they fill our Spanish life with Indian contradictions. It is not enough to say we suffer an identity crisis, because the crisis has been our way of life for the last five hundred years.[23]

Valdez would transpose this vision of an "authentic" Chicano identity not just onto his *actos* (theater acts), but significantly onto his first filmic venture, *I Am Joaquin*, and later to his feature-length films, *Zoot Suit* and *La Bamba*.

I Am Joaquin employs an intertextual strategy of montage and improvisation. The filmmaker interweaves the poem's stanzas with photographic realism; stills of paintings by Mexican muralists Diego Rivera, David Siqueiros, and José Clemente Orozco; and music reminiscent of the corrido tradition. This intertextual basis is further accentuated by the unique improvisational style of juxtaposing images.

Like the poem, the film is framed by the present tense. This quality is rendered through photo-realism, namely stills of urban poverty and the working conditions of farm laborers that open the film, thereby evoking sentiments of dislocation and alienation prevalent among Chicanos of the period. The ending of the film dramatizes Movement activism with photographic stills of young people marching with the Farmworkers' Union flag, asserting their resistance to oppression and injustice, and affirming the "new Chicano spirit" of collective identity.[24] The fact that the film is created with stills evades the viewer, for cinematic movement is captured through the rapid montage of close-ups and long shots, and camera zooms, as well as by the skillful juxtaposition of photographic stills with images drawn from the Mexican murals.

Indeed, the film exemplifies a distinct mode of storytelling by incorporating in its sound track guitar and mariachi music from the popular corrido tradition, and the dramatic reading of the poem by Luis Valdez. This mode explodes, particularly in the middle corpus where the director contrasts photographs of the Mexican Revolution with those of Mexican mural paintings. Through an intertextual mode of storytelling, Valdez rivets attention to the relation between the past and present, the Mexican Revolution and the emergent Chicano Revolution.

Far from linear, the film is a form of memory precisely because it posits instead the location of the past in the present, both in terms of history and cultural identity. Pierre Nora explains the affective, nontemporal aspects of memory, noting that true memory "has taken refuge in gestures and habits, in skills passed down by unspoken traditions, in the body's inherent self-knowledge, in unstudied reflexes and ingrained memories." In contrast to official history, which "binds itself strictly to temporal continuities," Nora directs our attention to the "perpetually actual phenomenon" of memory.[25] In this view of memory, *I Am Joaquin* suspends time in favor of space.

The film, as well as the poem, was a call for revolutionary struggle. The film's combative, confrontational, and polemical style stems from the fact that its intended spectators were Chicana and Chicano audiences; it aimed to instruct them on their history and also to urge them to revolutionary action. And while the film generally reproduces the structural outline of the poem, the images presented to viewers skew Chicano cultural identity to the "Indian" side of mestizaje to a greater extent than is done by the poem.

On most occasions, however, the filmic process provides a synchronous rendition of the poetic form. Photographs, stills, and images drawn from the muralists Orozco, Rivera, and Siqueiros operate in a symbiotic relation to the stanzas of the poem. Moreover, Siqueiros's murals serve to illustrate alienation wrought by industrial progress; Orozco and Rivera provide pictorial details of the Mexican Revolution of 1910. In these instances Valdez transmits a stream of unambiguous messages through a standard relation of sounds and images to the extent that one could conclude that the film is merely a mimetic adaptation of the poem.

However, Valdez interrupts the symbiotic relation of both artistic practices by the calculated introduction of dissonance, exemplified in the filmmaker's heavy reliance on images from the murals of Diego Rivera. Valdez resorts to Rivera's murals in order to emphasize, on a visual plane, the grandeur of the indigenous pre-Columbian past, and the filmmaker makes extensive use of mural images that depict Spanish cruelty toward the Indian. Valdez utilizes images from Rivera's murals of bloated faces of priests, symbolic of the church, and evil faces of the *conquistadores* as cinematic devices that interrupt the narrative economy of the poem. These shots function as metaphors that disrupt the system of signification of the poem in order to signify something "other." Indeed, this strategic recourse to the Rivera murals encourages interpellation toward an indigenous and pre-Columbian notion of Chicano cultural identity.

A clear instance of Valdez's departure from Gonzales's notion of Chicano cultural identity can be grasped in a comparison of the endings of both texts. Narrative closure in both the film and poem takes place with the following stanza from the poem: "I am Aztec prince and Christian Christ. / I shall endure! / I will endure!" In the book-form publication of *I Am Joaquin*, which also contains pictorial images, these words appear on the page opposite the final photograph of the book, a depiction of the expressionless face of a young Chicanito, or as the list of illustrations to the book explains, "a Chicano boy in the barrio of El Paso, Texas."[26] The film's adaptation of this stanza presents viewers with a low-angle shot of the great Pyramid of the Sun in Teotihuacan, in effect ending the film with this image. Thus, Valdez's dramatic ending in *I Am Joaquin* moves away from the individual to the abstract, away from concrete social conditions to the realm of the mythical. In so doing, the film dis-articulates the notion of identity as fusion (mestizaje) and re-articulates its vision of Chicano cultural identity in a pre-Columbian, mythic, and heroic past.

The appropriation and reinvention of the Mexican pre-Columbian past appeared on the scene of Chicano cultural politics in the late 1960s with the consolidation of the Chicano Power Movement. Like the Mexican bourgeoisie of the early nineteenth century (and similar efforts by twentieth-century Mexican intellectuals) who turned to an indigenous past in their struggle for independence from Spain, Chicano nationalists rediscovered ancient mythic origins.[27] In a comparative study of the links between political independence movements and cultural nationalism among Chicanos, Irish, and Quebecois, Genaro Padilla makes the following point about their strong nativist impulse:

> The relationship between political upheavals and the nativist artistic projects which seek to mend a people's threatened or even shattered

cultural psyche bespeaks the lateral material and spiritual needs of a group.[28]

Drawing from Franz Fanon's *Wretched of the Earth*, Padilla underscores the "dialectical significance" of the "myth-making enterprise" clearly manifest in *I Am Joaquin*: the film provides a kind of psychic sustenance for Chicanos who began to view themselves as "dispossessed" from their own territory. Unlike the past generation of Mexican Americans who traced their lineage to the Spanish forebears, Chicanos re-affirmed their connections to their indigenous ancestors. As John R. Chávez explains:

> Chicanos increasingly saw a parallel between themselves and the native peoples of other colonized lands: all had been conquered, all had been reduced to menial labor, and all had been used to extract the natural bounty of their own land for the benefit of the conqueror.[29]

In this political project of liberation and economic self-determination, Chicano cultural workers often depicted Mexico's revolutionary heroes as symbols that strengthened their resistance to "Anglo" white domination in the United States. The appropriation of Mexican revolutionary heroes and the turn to a "spiritual link to Mexico [as] the model of language, culture and social behavior"[30] re-appears in the television documentary *Yo Soy Chicano*.

Three years after the release of *I Am Joaquin*, Jesús Salvador Treviño wrote and produced *Yo Soy Chicano* (literally, "I Am Chicano"), under the direction of Barry Nye, for KCET public television in Los Angeles.[31] The film eloquently captures the tenor of this period of political activism, orchestrating its narrative of the Chicano "nation" within a wide array of ideological impulses. For example, *Yo Soy Chicano* fuses Mexican with Chicano aspects of history. It includes the story of Aztlán as the Chicano homeland and details Chicanos' vital links to Mexico, the antiracism struggles waged by Chicanos in the nineteenth and twentieth centuries, the farmworkers' movement, and protests against the Vietnam War. The film tells its story by focusing on actual historical subjects, past Mexican revolutionary heroes and intellectuals such as Miguel Hidalgo, Pancho Villa, Emiliano Zapata, and the Flores-Magón brothers, and present-day Chicano activists/leaders such as Dolores Huerta, Reis López Tijerina, José Angel Gutiérrez, and "Corky" Gonzales.

Like Valdez's film, *Yo Soy Chicano* is a collage of photographs, stills, music, yet with an added mix of dramatic reenactment for recreating certain periods of Chicano history such as the raid in Tierra Amarilla by López Tijerina and a dialogue between the Flores-Magón brothers. The film creatively mixes stock footage, alternating between black and white, sepia, and color. Similar to *I Am Joaquin*, *Yo Soy Chicano* telescopes history, which is typical of films attempting to "tell it all" in one hour. A feature of the film's narrative is worthy of closer examination, particularly in the structural symmetries established between the Mexican "symbolic" past and the Chicano "literal" present.

The nonlinear narrative structure of *Yo Soy Chicano* ricochets between the past and the present, between history and contemporary social reality. The segments in the past focus predominantly on Mexican history whereas those in the present deal with the Chicano political struggles in the United States. The montage effect created by juxtaposing the past with the present is at stake here, for the segments on the Chicano present-day reality gain their significance from the historical segments immediately preceding the contemporary scenes. More important, filmmakers structure a distinctive narrative process of analogy, effecting a symbiosis between particular Mexican heroes and Chicano leaders.

For example, the analogy between Spain and the United States as conquering powers is established midway through the film. The past historical segment on Mexico deals with the 1810 War of Independence from Spain when "a new nation is born." This part is immediately followed by a segment on Reis López Tijerina, the Chicano leader of the Alianza Federal de Mercedes (Federal Land Grants Alliance), an association of heirs of land grants dedicated to recovering land lost by Chicanos in New Mexico after the United States-Mexico war. In addition to an interview of López Tijerina by Treviño, the film imaginatively reenacts the famous courthouse raid where in 1967 López Tijerina led twenty other armed *aliancistas* in an attack on the courthouse at Tierra Amarilla, New Mexico. They shot two deputies, freed the prisoners of the Coyote jail, and fled with two hostages. The segment ends with "on-the-scene" footage of López Tijerina lecturing to a classroom of students. If we read the scene "against the grain," or in retrospect, attending to its relation to the previous historical segment on Mexico, we grasp the rich montage effects of its narrative style, for the analogy between Spain and the United States as imperial powers becomes quite evident. Additionally, the past segment on Mexico focuses heavily on the Independence leader Miguel Hidalgo, who thus figures as the symbolic prototype for Reis López Tijerina.

This symbiosis between past heroes and present-day activists is further accentuated by the structural symmetries maintained within the film's narrative. The symbolic lineage of Raza Unida Party founder José Angel Gutiérrez is traced to the Tejano Juan N. Cortina, who led a force of dispossessed Tejanos in an unsuccessful revolt against Anglo Texas during the nineteenth century; Mexican revolutionary heroes such as Pancho Villa, Emiliano Zapata, and the Flores-Magón brothers figure as the symbolic models for "Corky" Gonzales's struggle for self-determination, liberation, and unity of the Chicano nation. There is, however, a great discrepancy in the manner in which Dolores Huerta, the sole Chicana subject in the film, is framed by the past. The vice president of the United Farmworkers' Union, Huerta is the first contemporary Chicano activist depicted in *Yo Soy Chicano*. Yet, in contrast to the male activists/leaders whose symbolic equivalents are actual historical subjects in the past, Huerta's symbiotic relation is traced to an abstraction, to an abstract identity of land and territory.

Dolores Huerta's appearance in the film is preceded by a long (roughly ten minutes) introductory portion to Chicano history, spanning five hundred years. Not only does the film draw from symbols of a popular social movement, but *Yo Soy Chicano* patterns cultural nationalism's strong nativist impulse, contextualizing Chicano history in ancient, pre-Columbian times. The film mixes actual footage with stills of the murals by Orozco, Rivera, and Siqueiros. Like *I Am Joaquin, Yo Soy Chicano* tells the untold story of Chicanos' indigenous ancestors, focusing on the Aztec accomplishments in poetry, science, and architecture. In so doing, the film reinvents a permanent tie to Indian and mestizo Mexico, particularly evident in the film's nuanced return to the "imaginary geography," Aztlán—the most powerful and lasting symbol of Chicano cultural nationalism:

> Since Aztlán had been the Aztec equivalent of Eden and Utopia,
> activists converted that ancient idealized landscape into an ideal of a
> modern homeland where they hoped to help fulfill their people's
> political, economic, and cultural destiny.[32]

Through its didactic voice-over, *Yo Soy Chicano* depicts Aztlán concretely as the U.S. Southwest. However, because this notion of Aztlán as simultaneously utopian desire and concrete land immediately precedes the segment on Dolores Huerta, woman becomes an abstract embodiment: the metaphor for Mother Earth and for masculine desire. As we have seen, the film portrays Chicano activists in terms of their continuity with concrete historical subjects, that is, each male activist/leader is symbolically equivalent to a past and actual heroic figure. López Tijerina appears as the modern-day Miguel Hidalgo; "Corky" Gonzales is the contemporary romantic revolutionary. Dolores Huerta's symbolic equivalence, however, is portrayed as an abstraction, in terms of Aztlán/land. By incorporating a narrative process of analogy the filmmakers of *Yo Soy Chicano* thereby structure a masculinist perspective on history where, unlike Chicano men, woman represents the (his) metaphor for utopian desires: Aztlán.

The Female-centered Lineage

The association of woman to "Mother Earth," "land," would not be entirely a masculine enterprise among Chicano filmmakers of this early period. Indeed, Esperanza Vásquez's film *Agueda Martínez: Our People, Our Country* portrays a woman who is passionately linked to the earth. Yet, in contrast to the totalizing abstraction of women in *I Am Joaquin* or to the discrepancy between the symbiotic depiction of the woman activist and men activists in *Yo Soy Chicano*, *Agueda Martínez* depicts a woman who simultaneously figures as historical subject and metaphor.

The significance of *Agueda Martínez* rests in its role as a counter to most male-produced documentaries, which focus on grandeur, on the important men and sometimes women in Chicano history. *Agueda Martínez* represents the life of the common everyday woman whose experience and struggle are just as heroic as those of the "exceptional" individuals. Like *Chicana*, *Agueda Martínez* challenges dominant assumptions about Chicanas as passive and subservient, for the film is an elegant portrait of a self-sufficient woman. She owns her "rancho," makes her living by working her land (which produces various crops), weaves in the winter, has raised eight children, and proudly claims sixty-seven grandchildren and forty-five great-grandchildren. Agueda lucidly instructs viewers on her various crafts, homecooking, child rearing, as well as on her views about Chicano culture, history, and tradition. Not only is Agueda resourceful, but her crafts are not at all gendered. Just as she practices traditional New Mexican cooking and weaving (woman's work), so too does she plow the field and till the soil (man's work).

The formal properties of the film mark *Agueda Martínez* as one of the most eloquently crafted films of the period. As opposed to the didactic narrative style of documentary films that use the authoritative convention of the voice-over, *Agueda Martínez* imaginatively uses direct dialogue. Because the protagonist speaks directly, the film avoids "objective" or authoritative mediation. Specifically, the film's discourse is constructed in a subjective mode, patterning a subject's stream of consciousness. And its central subject, Agueda, slips in and out of the narratives of work, cultural tradition, history, and interpretive, critical, and self-reflexive commentary.

Vásquez imbues the central subject's monologue with a dialogic quality that patterns the narrative form of oral history, a quality whose style explicitly assumes an interlocutor. The representation of Agueda's mode of address is realized in a nonlinear fashion, thereby reproducing the oral tradition, but also positioning viewers as active coparticipants in its narrative. And *Agueda Martínez*'s theme, the form of the film's imagery, articulates the matrilineal heritage of many Chicanos and Chicanas in the United States.[33]

Structurally, the film reproduces the movement of the day, beginning with sunrise and ending with the setting sun. This visual orchestration overlays onto another marker of time, the cycle of the seasons. Indeed, the cinematic representation is designed in a cyclical fashion, opening with springtime (Agueda's craft of harvesting) and closing with the winter (Agueda's craft of weaving).

Its beautiful depiction of an exemplary elderly woman may strike some as idealized and sentimental, but Esperanza Vásquez's portrayal of struggle in a woman's daily-life existence represents instead a counteraesthetics and a counterdiscourse to what Alvina Quintana terms "predominantly masculine interpretations of history and culture."[34]

Ten years would pass after the production of *I Am Joaquin* before a Chicana produced a film that patterned the tendency to tell "all" of Chicano history in one filmic statement. The first (and to this date, the only) historical film on Chicanas, Sylvia Morales's *Chicana* counters both the dominant culture and the Chicano male exclusion of the roles of Chicanas in history.

Chicana could be read as the feminist counterpart to the first Chicano film, *I Am Joaquin*. Both films are epic accounts of Chicano history: *I Am Joaquin* from a man's perspective, *Chicana* from a woman's. Similar to *I Am Joaquin*, *Chicana* renders a compilation of historical figures, but focuses instead on "vignettes of famous women."[35] Both films reproduce themes of Chicano cultural nationalism: they contest racism and provide historical accounts of conquest, domination, and struggle. As in *I Am Joaquin* and *Yo Soy Chicano*,[36] the dialectics of conquest and struggle are traced to an indigenous legacy and configured as a non-European "spirit" of resistance to domination, reconstructing a political collective memory for the struggles waged by twentieth-century Chicano activists.

The formal properties of *Chicana* reveal its likeness to *I Am Joaquin*: each makes extensive use of stills, photographs, and music and poetry drawn from an oral tradition. However, as Morales explains, other factors, beyond her intention, conditioned the film:

> The lack of photos about historical events such as the Aztec conquest or the Mexican-American War has forced us to go to classic masterworks by Mexican muralists who have depicted these events in their paintings and murals . . . We have limited resources and we must take dramatic license to convey the spirit of the time we are depicting.[37]

Thus, this likeness should not be attributed to artistic intention alone but to extratextual factors such as budget and funding constraints.[38] Nevertheless, certain intertextual factors conditioned the likenesses between both films, particularly evident in the fact that both *I Am Joaquin* and *Chicana* draw from popular oral practices based on improvisation and experimentation, as well as from a tradition of declamatory poetry.[39]

There are also important distinctions between both films. The most obvious one stems from differences in their thematic choices, namely *I Am Joaquin* tells the five-hundred-year story of male heroes, whereas *Chicana* recounts the history of female heroines. Yet, a comparison of these two films based solely on theme would lean toward a certain reductionism—a gendered binary—because their differences rest more properly in conflicts within the social formation of cultural workers.

The aesthetic discourse of Morales's film represents a rupture from that of male-centered cultural nationalism, principally because the film critiques all forms of domination, including the Chicano patriarchal lineage. Indeed, the ten-year lapse between the two films permits us to characterize *Chicana* both as the embodiment of the feminist critiques of cultural nationalist ideology and as a counterdiscursive tendency within the Chicano Movement, never before articulated in a cinematic practice.[40]

Whereas Chicano cultural nationalism was critical of "*gabacho*" society and the "*gachupín*" colonialists and landowners, it tended to idealize pre-Columbian society. *I Am Joaquin*'s epic account of conquest and domination was based on an idyllic recuperation of a glorious Aztec past. Its heroic figures were the Aztec royalty whose affront to the Spanish conquest provided the basis for tracing the legacy of struggle against oppression that twentieth-century Chicanos could draw upon. However, this recuperation was, as Genaro Padilla indicates, premised on an "outright invention of the mythic past."[41] In tracing the lineage of Chicanos to the Aztec aristocracy (i.e., Cuauhtemoc and the emperor Moctezuma), *I Am Joaquin*, and also *Yo Soy Chicano*, mystified and ignored the stratified nature of pre-Columbian society, a reality of the Chicano indigenous past whose idealization soon became untenable, even as a strategic affront to racism.[42]

Chicana was first a slide show assembled by Ana Nieto-Gómez for her Chicana history courses.[43] The slide show illustrates not just Nieto-Gómez's scholarly research, but also the important role she played as one of the first critics of sexism in the Chicano Power Movement.[44] Inscribed in Nieto-Gómez's slide show is a feminist counterdiscourse to cultural nationalism, which, however marginalized and suppressed, nonetheless emerges dialectically as a counterdiscourse to Chicano nationalism's struggle against dominant culture.[45]

Chicana includes the story of Malintzín Tenépal ("La Malinche," as she is commonly called), but takes issue with the distortions by Mexican philosophers of her historic role. La Malinche is a powerful symbol in Mexican society. Because of her role as translator for Hernán Cortés, she is considered a traitor to the Indian people, the Mexican equivalent of Benedict Arnold. This view of woman as treacherous informs the imagination of such Mexican writers as Octavio Paz and Carlos Fuentes, who have traced the pathology of Mexicans (mestizos) to La Malinche's rape by the conqueror. In their view, La Malinche facilitated the ultimate downfall, giving birth to the mestizo people. As Norma Alarcón intimates:

> Her legend and subsequent mythic dimensions as evil goddess and creator of a new race—the mestizo race—embroils her in a family quarrel, where many male members often prefer to see her as the mother-whore, bearer of illegitimate children, responsible for the foreign Spanish invasion . . . [46]

Hence, she is called *la chingada* ("the fucked one"), and her descendants, the Mexican people, *los hijos de la chingada* ("children of the fucked one"). Moreover, as Alarcón adds, among Chicano cultural nationalists, the mythology surrounding Malintzín also operates to

Filmmaker Sylvia Morales (right), assisted by Cindy Honesto during the filming of *Chicana*.

discredit critiques of sexism. Alarcón thus writes: "as Chicanas embrace feminism, they are charged with betrayal à la Malinche."[47]

Chicana intellectuals, scholars as well as creative artists, have reconfigured the Malintzín myth by drawing upon historical accounts of the conquest that disclosed the extent of her oppression in pre-Columbian Mexico.[48] In this respect, by depicting her exploitation within a stratified slave economy, the film *Chicana* rearticulates the "attempt to topple the traditional patriarchal mythology through revision and re-vision."[49]

Formally, *Chicana* draws from an intertextual tradition that combines distinct artistic practices into a new form. *Chicana* is a collage of dramatic reenactment, photographic stills, reportage, and documentary conventions. Given her work as a television producer with KABC-TV in Los Angeles, Sylvia Morales adds her expertise in television documentary and reportage to the slide show and text of Ana Nieto-Gómez, and ends the film with actual footage and interviews of Chicana community activists.

Morales also brings to the film a keen sense of irony and satire, as is evident in the opening segment. The first sequence renders a dramatic reenactment, set in contemporary time, which subverts common (mis)assumptions about Chicana passivity and subservience. Specifically she presents viewers with images of Chicanas: one making tortillas, an elderly woman sitting on a rocking chair, a woman washing clothing, and another potty-training her male child. Yet each of these images is punctuated with a voice-over that subverts the image in a humorous fashion. For example, in the potty-training image, as the mother wipes her son's rear end, the narrative voice injects: "we free men to work"—a commentary that satirically draws viewer attention to the serious issue of women's unpaid household labor.

Morales's epic account was indeed a counterdiscourse to man-centered versions of Chicano history. Through its focus on the role of "important" women like Sor Juana Inés de la Cruz, Lucy González Parsons, and Emma Tenayuca, *Chicana* re-invents a lineage for Chicanas. But the film also contests accounts that render women nameless, voiceless, and imageless in the historical process. Aesthetically and ideologically, Sylvia Morales is the first Chicana filmmaker to confront on such a grand scale what Cherríe Moraga and Gloria Anzaldúa term the "many-headed demon of oppression."[50] For the film portrays the multiple forces, internal and external, affecting the lives of women. *Chicana* stresses the Chicano nationalist concerns with equality, social justice, and freedom, yet, through its ongoing engagement of male privilege, the film goes beyond the nationalist agenda.

Conclusion

The major work of this chapter has been to pinpoint the discursive strategies undergirding Chicano and Chicana film practices. Certainly many other films were produced during this early period,[51] but in order to formulate the contours of Chicano filmmaking, the analysis has centered on four narrative films that are identified as "paradigmatic" of Chicano films in general.[52] As we will see, the discursive strategies of these four films will re-appear in subsequent Chicano narrative films.

The bilingual title of this chapter stages the multiple cultural systems that inform Chicano and Chicana cultural politics. I refer to these early films as *actos* rather than as "acts" first of all to stress their articulation with Mexican and Chicano cultural practices such as music, visual art, drama, and poetry. Beginning in this early period, Chicano filmmaking draws from a rich oral tradition of music, balladry, and performance, blending distinct cultural forms into a unique mode of visual storytelling. This quality, examined in greater detail in the next two chapters, represents the intertextual logic of Chicano cinema.

The term *actos* references the narrative style of these early films. Like the *actos* (acts/agitprop skits) of "el Teatro Campesino," their filmic style is generally direct and confrontational, reflecting the spirit and urgency of the Chicano Movement. The part of the chapter title in English punctuates the location of these films within the United States, their dialogic relation to dominant culture. Moreover, I have characterized these films as *actos* of "imaginative re-discovery" to focus on their symbolic rather than their literal labor. As Stuart Hall indicates about the films of the black diaspora, *Chicana, Agueda Martínez, Yo Soy Chicano*, and *I Am Joaquin* construct an "underlying unity" for Chicanos and Chicanas mainly by imposing an "imaginary coherence" on the experiences of dispersal and fragmentation." As Hall adds:

> Such texts restore an imaginary fullness or plenitude, to set against
> the broken rubric of our past. They are resources of resistance and
> identity, with which to confront the fragmented and pathological
> ways in which the experience has been re-constructed within the
> dominant regimes of cinematic and visual representation in the
> West.[53]

In a similar manner, the films discussed in this chapter visualize oppositional forms of knowledge and history, dialogically challenging and displacing dominant discourses about Chicanos and Chicanas. The strategy of framing Chicano political struggles in the United States within a "nativist" framework would continue to inform the cultural politics of filmmakers. For instance, long after the height of the Chicano Movement, *Chicano Park* (1988), coproduced by Mario Barrera, begins its documentary of the Chicano Park struggle in San Diego by tracing Chicano history to pre-Columbian times.

Yet, as the title of each film makes evident, often these films imposed an "imaginary coherence" on diverse Chicano communities, particularly in cases where films constructed a single lineage to Mexico. The recuperation of our indigenous ancestry collapsed into a single site, the pre-Columbian Tenochtitlan, thereby unifying us across our differences. Yet this symbolic strategy does not constitute a common origin, because the indigenous peoples constituted (and continue to re-constitute) themselves as diverse "nations." The procedure of mapping a single lineage to the central valley of Mexico elides differences of place and time, of migration patterns, language preferences, religion, gender, sexual orientation, and internal class and racial divisions among diverse indigenous peoples.[54] Indeed, the concept of the Chicano nation predicated on a single lineage to the Aztec or Mexica nation also overlooks the diverse relations of power and privilege within pre-Columbian nations. In *I Am Joaquin* (more so than in the other three films) re-covering a "lost" history often led to certain totalizing formulations about cultural identity.

For the most part, the political task of the discourse of cultural nationalism centered on the "search for an identity" (or, to re-quote "Corky," on a "journey back through history . . . a wandering search for my people's and, most of all, my own identity"). The constitution of the Chicano subject necessitated the unearthing of repressed histories, the re-discovery of a lost genealogy, and, most important, a "reversal" of the negative subject position of Chicanos and Chicanas in dominant discourse. The saliency of "identity" in the cultural politics of Chicano and Chicana artists cannot be underestimated for they formulated extensive treatises on identity in their representational practices. Whereas none of the feature-length films elaborated an overt treatment of cultural identity, the theme nonetheless figured implicitly as a subtext in some films, such as Jesús Salvador Treviño's *Raíces de Sangre* and *Seguin*, but more significantly in the films by Luis Valdez. By interweaving identity politics with other aspects of narrative discourse, Valdez's films *Zoot Suit* (1981) and *La Bamba* (1987) established themselves as major documents of Chicano cultural identity politics.

Intertextuality and Cultural Identity in *Zoot Suit* (1981) and *La Bamba* (1987)

> This is 1942 or is it 1492? . . . Something inside you
> creates the punishment, the public humiliation, the
> human sacrifice? There's no more pyramids carnal, only
> the gas chamber.
> —El Pachuco, *Zoot Suit*[1]

In *Questions of Cinema*, Stephen Heath writes: "What is film, in fact, but an elaborate time machine, a tangle of memories and times successfully rewound in the narrative as the order of the continuous time of the film?"[2] Luis Valdez's first feature film, *Zoot Suit*, appears to put into motion Heath's insights about the workings of film, surprisingly resisting the monolithic codes of dominant cinema. The unconventional style of the film confronts the viewer with an articulation of the "tangle of memories and times." Valdez deploys formal film techniques in order to represent the interplay between multiple time referents, the past in the present tense of culture. In the opening sequence, a shot in black and white of a 1940s theater house dissolves into a color shot of the present locale of *Zoot Suit*'s performance. Continuing its inflection of the past onto the present into even the smallest of prop details, an automobile of the mid-1940s is rather a vintage auto restored by contemporary Chicanos, referenced by the California license nameplate with the placa "Zoot Suiter."

Seeming to remind us of film's capacity to perform as an elaborate time machine, *Zoot Suit* further comments on the representational qualities of the medium, pushing the boundaries of conventional narrative discourse.[3] Yet Valdez's rejection of traditional narrative procedure does not in and of itself place *Zoot Suit* within the avant-garde "aesthetics of deconstruction." Rather than illuminating what Paul Willeman terms "endlessly repeated difference games," Valdez's film couples formal experimentation with a commitment to a politics of contestation. *Zoot Suit* is thus akin to Willeman's notion of the "politics of countercinema":

> A politics of deconstruction insists on the need to oppose particular institutionally dominant regimes of making particular kinds of sense, excluding or marginalizing others . . . the politics of deconstruction, then, insists on the need to say something different . . . [4]

In contrast to an avant-garde aesthetics that "emphasizes the expressive over the referential,"[5] *Zoot Suit*'s aesthetics brings to the foreground alternative ways of "making particular kinds of sense." Through the film's formal structure one encounters previously marginalized cultural traditions. Similar to the early, short dramatic films by Chicanos and Chicanas as well as to the prose writers who inflected novels and short stories with the Chicano oral corrido tradition,[6] *Zoot Suit* imbues dominant cinematic codes with those from an oppositional cultural tradition, continuing in the intertextual tradition of the early period of Chicano filmmaking.

Zoot Suit's Intertextual Logic

Zoot Suit recounts the events surrounding the "Sleepy Lagoon Case" of 1942 when members of the 38th Street Club were tried en masse and wrongfully convicted of murder in Los Angeles.[7] The club members were pachucos, urban street youth distinguished by dress (zoot suits), ducktail haircuts, and tattoos. Their appearance, which targeted them for state persecution, also made the pachucos ideal symbols of marginalization and victimization by Chicano nationalists. Decades later, Luis Valdez would recreate these events for the first Chicano feature-length studio production. At one level, the production of the film within the mainstream Hollywood industry underlines the logic of dominant hegemonic incorporation of oppositional discourses: for various historical circumstances, a corporate marketing strategy converged with a Chicano cultural politics of contestation.

In the late seventies, Coors Corporation designated the 1980s as the "Decade of the Hispanic." *Zoot Suit* was one of a series of several films within the "gang genre" financed during this period. Three others, *Boulevard Nights, Defiance,* and *Walk Proud* (previously titled

Gang), were released roughly in the same period. These films were objects of a heated controversy. In 1979 a group of students from a Los Angeles community college organized the Gang Exploitation Film Committee in order to draw public attention to negative media portrayals of Chicanos and Chicanas. Sponsored by college professor Daniel Solorzano, student research about the "gang themes" in film culminated in a picket and boycott of *Boulevard Nights*. The students were joined in their protests by other Chicano organizations, including the Chicano Cinema Coalition and the actors' guild Nosotros. Prior to the protests, other scripts for the gang genre had been in the initial pilot stages and were pending the financial outcome of *Walk Proud* and *Boulevard Nights*. However, after the "negative publicity generated by the picket and boycott," not only did Universal Studios decide against releasing *Walk Proud* in any major Latino market, but, according to Solorzano, industry plans for other films within the gang genre were dropped.[8]

It is in the context of dominant industry's corporate strategy for capitalizing on the growing Latino population (or, as Universal's executive Ned Tanen would say, "to break into the 'Hispanic' market") that *Zoot Suit* was financed by Universal Studios. The studio's interest in action-adventure films with marginal themes, like "urban violence," opened up a cultural space for the production of *Zoot Suit*. Thus, Luis Valdez obtained the modest budget (by Hollywood standards) of $2.5 million to film *Zoot Suit*. Forced to shoot the film in less than two weeks, Valdez explains much of the mise-en-scène's theatrical quality—in other words, the film's recourse to theater props for scenes—as the result of limited financial resources.

Luis Valdez negotiated total artistic control over the screenplay, but the need to reach a broader audience conditioned some of the film's narrative choices. Valdez fabricated a romance between Hank Reyna (Daniel Valdez) and the Jewish CIO activist Alice Bloomfield (Tyne Daly) for the theatrical staging, accentuating this relationship even more in the rewrite of the play for its staging in New York.[9] This element was also kept as a major subplot in the film version. Working within the dominant cinematic industry thus raises the important issue of how political artists negotiate social commitment with the exigencies of appealing to mainstream audiences.

In commenting on the adaptation from its stage performance to screen, Yolanda Broyles-González writes that *Zoot Suit* "changed from a semi-documentary dramatic narrative to a heavily melodramatic musical which obscures the play's more hard-hitting historical and social dimensions."[10] Many of the play's ideological and political problems (for instance, its "diluted historicism," "the objectification of the women-characters," "its portrayal of Chicanos and Chicanas as passive agents of history," its privileging of "White Saviors"), in Broyles-González's estimation, intensify with the film version.

Yet even if we critique the film on political/ideological grounds (Valdez's project of "mainstreaming," as Broyles-González has repeatedly maintained), the fact remains that the corporate strategy for tapping into the Latino market did not pay off. *Zoot Suit* failed to provide the expected box-office returns, in part because of the lack of corporate investment for advertising and distributing the film. In addition, the complexity of the film's format proved too difficult for mainstream audiences, especially for monocultural and monolingual viewers.

Thematically, the film critiques "official" versions of the Sleepy Lagoon case and the "Zoot Suit riots." Representing the Chicano victims of hegemonic racism as historical agents, the film subverts "objective" (media and state) accounts of these events.[11] Countermemories to official versions are provided through the agency of Chicano protagonists. At the level of content, the filmmaker enlists various visual strategies designed to contest monolithic discourse. Symbolic of dominant discourse, a full-screen spread of a newspaper is ripped apart by the Pachuco character (Edward James Olmos) who, as he walks through the front page, legitimates the countermemories behind the words of the Hearst press. At other times, *Zoot Suit*'s politics of contestation elides symbolism for directness. For instance, as the press reporter states his dateline for the news release ("City of the Angels, August 2nd, 1942"), the Pachuco interjects, "Nuestra Señora de Los Angeles de la Porciúncula, pendejo"—the original Spanish name of Los Angeles.

Zoot Suit's formal polyvocal style functions to further deconstruct dominant cinematic modes of "making particular kinds of sense" of social reality. Dominant and oppositional histories reverberate through interconnected scenes that take different forms: dramatic narrative, allegorical dialogue, and dance collage. Yet all three forms are subverted by the surreal presence of the Pachuco character.

The Pachuco's direct address to viewers is reminiscent of Brechtian theater but also of anticharacters deployed by Godard and other avant-garde filmmakers.[12] The Pachuco as narrator subverts the mimetic logic of conventional realism and the prevailing documentary paradigm for historical films. Similar to Brechtian uses of character as

Hank Reyna (Daniel Valdez) and Della (Rose Portillo) at the dance in *Zoot Suit*.
Courtesy of Universal Studios.

a distancing device, the Pachuco interrupts the narrative economy of
conventional realism. While the subversive force of this disruptive device is most apparent at the level of content, the character's more
properly formal functions intensify his effects on dramatic action.

Two formal techniques routinely used in mainstream musicals,
dance numbers and the presence of the audience in the film itself, are

extensively utilized by Valdez. *Zoot Suit*'s links to Hollywood musicals bear comparison to what critics have written about the genre. In her analysis of such musicals as *An American in Paris*, Jane Feuer writes:

> The Platonic ideal of a Hollywood film is one in which the audience perceives even the celluloid stock as the stuff of magic and the story as transcending its origin in light and shadow. The narratives of musical films exemplify this classical pattern. But the musical numbers regularly and systematically violate the smooth surface.[13]

Similarly, *Zoot Suit*'s dance vignettes and music numbers stand as formal techniques that interrupt the linear logic of dramatic narrative. In some cases, dance numbers merely supplement narrative information, particularly because the Sleepy Lagoon murder took place after the Saturday night dance. Often dance and music numbers serve a contextual function, rendering Chicano music and dance styles popular in the 1940s. At other times, highly ritualized and intensely instrumental music and dance numbers serve to heighten dramatic action. More often, dance and music numbers "violate the smooth surface" of the narrative. In moments of serious drama, for example, after the police beating of Hank Reyna, the surreal collage of dance effectively deflects sentimental "excess."

These music and dance numbers are sites of dramatic action but also of pleasure for the viewer. Dance is central to the everyday life of Chicano and Chicana working-class culture. *Zoot Suit* captures the centrality of its ritual properties, emphasizing the extent to which dance is not just an end in itself, but a means to express one's relation to the world through stylized movement. While deeply influenced by Hollywood musicals, the film's representation of dance as pleasurable and meaningful underscores as well *Zoot Suit*'s affinities to a Mexican vernacular tradition.

Zoot Suit's carefully orchestrated cluster of multiple manners of expression defies easy genre classification for the film. The film is simultaneously a filmed play, a Hollywood musical, a dramatic narrative. Like the "hybridized" films of black British filmmakers that Kobena Mercer notes "draw from a dual inheritance of First and Third World cultures,"[14] *Zoot Suit* bears polyvocal as well as multiaccentual cinematic and noncinematic codes of enunciation. *Zoot Suit* thus derives its intertextual logic from its relation to a Mexican tradition of performance, for the film's narrative style owes a great deal to Valdez's previous work in the collective ensemble El Teatro Campesino. Broyles-González's book-length study examines the performance conventions that the Teatro Campesino in turn appropriated from the Mexican tradition of the *carpa*, or tent theater:

> Prime among the generic and stylistic elements it inherited were mime, music, dance, song, dance-like movements and some acrobatic motion, *títeres* (marionettes), but, above all, the primacy of a stinging humor, and the central underdog comic figure. These combined within the Chicano *acto* of the 1960s and 70s—a direct descendant of the comic sketch and political sketch genre of the *carpa*.[15]

Thus, *Zoot Suit's* complex format derives from its biculturalism and bilingualism, simultaneously drawing both from its intertextual relation to Mexican performance tradition *and* from the dominant cinematic codes of enunciation. The film fervently syncretizes signs and codes from dual cultures. From political sketches to Hollywood musicals, Luis Valdez orchestrates cultural signs and codes from multiple meaning systems, re-creating an entirely new cultural form. In addition to this innovative, intertextual style, *Zoot Suit* is as much about cultural identity as it is about the Sleepy Lagoon case.

The "Return to the Beginning" of Cultural Identity

One way to approach the problem of "Chicano" cultural identity is to recognize from the onset what Kobena Mercer writes about the key word, "identity": "it bears not one unitary meaning but a range of competing definitions and uses as different actors invest different meanings in one and the same sign."[16] In Chicano studies, some researchers have examined "identity" as a function of the individual's identification with the cultural/ethnic group, the assumption being that there are characteristics that make the group (Chicanos) distinct from other groups (i.e., Anglos, Asians, or blacks) in the United States. Social science research on the question of identity proceeds along the following pattern. Certain cultural "markers" such as language preference, cultural values and beliefs, religion, place of origin, and generational status become features of the group's cultural distinctiveness. In some studies, the measurement or quantification of these as "cultural variables" determines the person's position in relation to the culture of the group. The higher a correlation between an individual and those "variables" deemed characteristic of the Chicano and Chicana group, the greater the degree of a person's identification with his or her cultural/ethnic group.[17] In other studies, the Mexican-

origin groups residing in the United States are subjected to question-
naires about their identification with the group or their "self-designation" preferences.[18]

The results of these studies have been quite significant, for while
Chicano intellectuals invoke a "collective identity" these studies provide evidence about the vast heterogeneity among Chicanos and Chicanas: internal differences punctuated not only by class-location and
gender, but also by regional variations, distinct patterns of language
use, religious beliefs, social values, music preferences, culinary practices, etc., etc. Moreover, Chicanos and Chicanas are dynamic social
formations whose dynamism is as much a product of endogenous
processes of social reproduction, creativity, and agency, as of exoge-
nous pressures on the group.

However, in representational discourses (visual arts, cinema, poetry, theater, music), the problem of "cultural identity" proceeds
from a different set of assumptions, more properly, abstract or ideological ones that cannot be easily quantified and measured. Chicano
cultural practices raise questions about the subject's identity and position within dominant and oppositional discourses. Insofar as cultural workers are engaged in an "identity politics," the sign, "identity," bears quite a different investment.

It is within cultural discourse that Chicano and Chicana cultural
workers experimented with alternative notions of cultural identity.
During the Chicano Movement, Chicanos produced new subject
identities by reversing their previously negative position in dominant
discourse. Cultural nationalists reclaimed as the revolutionary role
models for the new Chicano identity precisely those subjects previously devalorized by U.S. dominant culture. The desire among sub-
ordinated peoples to overturn the disparaging ways in which they
have appeared as "the Other" within the hegemonic discourses of
"Western" thought, undergirds the quest for an alternative national
or cultural identity. As Stuart Hall points out:

> The ways we have been positioned and subject-ed in the dominant
> regimes of representation were a critical exercise of cultural power
> and normalization, precisely because they were not superficial. They
> had the power to make us see and experience ourselves as
> "Other."[19]

The social and political context of the Chicano Movement opened up
a discursive space for the formulation of alternative representations of
Chicano/a cultural identity. Rather than conforming Chicano/a iden-

tity into the melting-pot ideology, Chicano Movement intellectuals rejected the assimilationism of earlier generations of Mexican Americans, affirming precisely those identities previously devalorized in relation to dominant culture, especially the identity of the pachuco (or so-called gang member).

Indeed, it is hardly surprising that when the host of a popular game show gave a contestant the clue, "They have a lot of these in East L.A.," the contestant correctly responded: "Gangs."[20] One of the major ways Chicanos become visible in public discourse is as "social problems." Part of the official race-relations narrative in the United States, the claims about "gang incidents as a major social problem" have dominated media portrayals and the social-science literature since the 1960s.[21] From greasers to bandidos to gangs, dominant culture characterizes Chicanos and Chicanas as "culturally deficient," "inherently violent," and "sexually and morally pathological." The game-show example just cited illustrates the extent to which the dominant codes of valorization have been normalized in public discourse. As we have seen earlier, the cinematic portrayal of Chicanos and Chicanas as "gang members" (short for "gangster") is neither a recent phenomenon nor one that has disappeared altogether.[22] Moreover, this positioning of the Chicano subject as a "problem" in dominant culture derives from the more general historical re-construction of the identities of non-Europeans as the negative or pathological manifestation of the Western male subject.[23] While a heterogeneous range of masculine identities is emphasized for the dominant culture, the representation of the identity of non-Western males stands out for its singular and homogeneous economy, resting entirely within the negative side of the masculine equation.[24]

The lineage for dominant culture's re-construction of the masculine identities of the Spanish-speaking Latinos has been traced to the colonial wars between the empires of England and Spain for establishing dominance in the New World.[25] Its formulation follows this common pattern: from *conquistadores* ("extremely violent" and unruly) to Indians ("bloodthirsty" Aztecs) to their twentieth-century variations in popular culture as greasers (violent revolutionaries à la Pancho Villa), Latin lovers (sexually promiscuous), and gangs (a fusion of all of the above attributes). This negative positioning of Chicanos and more broadly of Latino culture as the negative manifestation of hegemonic masculinity is clearly evident in the replacement of the term sexism with the Spanish word *machismo* in common English usage.[26]

A term that no longer requires translation, *machismo* conjures up Latinos as the model for the pathological transgressions of hegemonic masculine identities, thereby laying bare the tacit racism prevailing in dominant discourse as well as critical scholarly works.[27]

The first national Chicano youth conference, the Denver Youth Conference of 1969, exemplifies the imaginary and symbolic strategy of inversion and reversal. The conference was significant because its participants included student activists, ex-convicts, and street youth in discussions of grass-roots politics and nationalist ideology. Participants made an explicit effort to reverse the negative subject position of Chicanos within dominant discourse. In Carlos Muñoz's words:

> Conference speakers proposed that henceforth most crimes
> committed by Mexican Americans were to be interpreted as
> "revolutionary acts." The language and dress of the street youth, the
> *vatos locos*, would be emulated. *Carnalismo* (the brotherhood code of
> the Mexican American youth gangs) would mold the lives of the
> students and become a central concept in this proposed nationalist
> ideology. From the ranks of this new breed of youth would come the
> poets, the writers and the artists necessary for forging the new
> Chicano identity. This new identity would reflect a total rejection of
> *gabacho* culture—the culture of the white Anglo-Saxon Protestant.[28]

In poetry, mural paintings, film, and theater, Chicano Movement cultural workers systematically figured the pachuco (urban street youth), the pinto (ex-convict), and the indigenous (mostly Aztec) warrior as the new Chicano subjects of the counterdiscourse of Chicano liberation. In sum, cultural workers re-affirmed those repressed identities located in working-class and non-European origins. In so doing, Chicano cultural nationalists followed the pattern of strategically inverting previously negative interpellations—a common strategy among postcolonial nationalist movements.[29]

Insofar as these alternative identities are premised on the inversion/reversal of negative interpellations, claims about a newly "discovered" identity, or the "loss" of "identity on the part of a tiny minority of privileged intellectuals,"[30] require critical scrutiny. In our own historical period, the "Parmenidean principle of the identity of thought and being"[31] has been subjected to a relentless critique. Part of a long philosophical tradition of "Western" thought, the Parmenidean principle posits a homology between the subject who speaks (thought) and the subject spoken of (being). In this configuration, identity is viewed as self-identical, "persisting through time as the same, unified and internally coherent."[32]

In addressing the alternative notions of identity informing the cultural politics of subaltern groups, Stuart Hall distinguishes between two historical forms of cultural identity. The first relies on a political model of subjectivity grounded in a notion of a fixed self. In this formulation, cultural identity appears as an authentic essence, located in a core subject, whose identity is one of "being." According to this notion of cultural identity, the authentic core of the self, as Trinh T. Minh-ha explains, "remains hidden to one's consciousness and . . . requires the elimination of all that is considered foreign or not true to the self, that is to say, not I, the other."[33] It is a notion of cultural identity that, in Hall's words, is grounded in an archaeology. In other words, the re-discovery of cultural identity depends on the "unearthing of that which the colonial experience buried and overlaid, bringing to the light the hidden continuities it [hegemonic powers] suppressed."[34] Hence, the re-discovery of an "authentic" core self is predicated on the search for the "fixed *origin*" of cultural identity.

An alternative formulation of cultural identity derives from the recognition that identity is rather a mask for the self, that is to say, for the subject in process. Applying a psychoanalytic framework, Avery Gordon writes: "Our sense of ourselves and the sense we can make of others derive from this fundamental misrecognition of a masking for a singular identical self."[35] This second view consequently emphasizes a notion that privileges the concepts of *becoming* within cultural identity, rather than of being, of *process* as opposed to structure, and of *production* contrary to rediscovery or archaeology. However, the importance of Hall's theoretical insights rests in his recognition that this second notion of cultural identity "qualifies even though it does not replace the first." Cultural identity, in this second formulation, is a "strategic position" that, rather than displacing, complicates those notions that posit identity as a "fixed essence" existing "unchanged, outside history and culture." As Hall's words clearly express:

> Cultural identity, in this second sense, is a matter of "becoming" as
> well as of "being." It belongs to the future as much as to the past. It
> is not something that exists, transcending place, time, history and
> culture. Cultural identities come from somewhere, have histories.
> But like everything which is historical, they undergo constant
> transformation.[36]

If identity cannot solely be grounded in an essence but is as well a construction of ourselves as certain subjects, then one of the sites for this production is within discursive practices and forms, including cinema, for, as Hall adds, cultural identity "is always constituted within, not outside, representation."[37]

Within cultural nationalism, Luis Valdez was instrumental in the "rediscovery" of an alternative Chicano identity. Not only was he present at the Denver Youth meeting, but he took an active role in shaping the ideology of Chicano nationalism. He was one of the four authors of the Plan Espiritual de Aztlán—the blueprint of nationalist ideology for the liberation of the Chicano nation. It is thus no accident that the representation of the new "revolutionary subject" envisioned by cultural nationalists culminates in *Zoot Suit* and *La Bamba*. Indeed, the main characters of both films are reversals of the negative ways Chicanos had been positioned within the dominant regimes of representation.

The Pachuco as Desire

Zoot Suit's overt subject matter recounts the trial, incarceration, and appeals process of the 38th Street Club members, and it also exposes the racism of the police and justice system during the period. An examination of how the narrative is framed, however, discloses its implicit concern with cultural identity. The narrative in fact unfolds through a fictitious psychological struggle between two main characters. The character of Hank Reyna is based on the actual leader of the 38th Street Club, Hank Leyvas, whereas the other main protagonist, the Pachuco, is an unconventional character, a mythical figure whose presence is only accessible to Hank and to viewers of the film.[38] Together, both characters are reversals of the negative position of the Chicano "gang" member in dominant discourse. In their relation, namely, the structural contrast the film establishes between Hank and the Pachuco, Valdez theorizes the nature of cultural identity.

Earlier I cited Hall's theoretical reflections of the problem of cultural identity. In order to reverse the negative subject position in dominant culture, subaltern groups, according to Hall, usually undertake a search for "origins." Yet Hall reminds us:

> This "return to the beginning" is like the Imaginary in Lacan—it can never be fulfilled or requited, and hence is the beginning of the symbolic, of representation, the infinitely renewable source of desire,

memory, myth, search, discovery—in short, the reservoir of our cinematic narratives.[39]

Luis Valdez begins his film precisely with this recognition. *Zoot Suit* permits us to see the mechanism by which cultural identity is produced by visualizing, throughout the film, the fantasy, the myth, and the multiple registers occupying the myth, particularly as these are inscribed onto the body of the Pachuco.

The filmmaker self-reflexively depicts the audience of the theatrical performance throughout the narrative. This is especially so in the opening and closing scenes. The incorporation of the audience within the filmic material (and as audiences for the court trial) serves to interpellate film viewers in a symbiotic relation with audiences of both the play and the court trial. In the beginning of the film, the Pachuco first appears as *Zoot Suit*'s omnipresent narrator, and his words function to propel the narrative action. Using a switchblade to tear apart a full-screen newspaper, the Pachuco addresses viewers:

> "Ladies and Gentlemen. The mono [slang for "movie"] you're about to see is a construct of fact and fantasy. But relax, weigh the facts and enjoy the pretense. Our pachuco reality will only make sense if you grasp their stylization.
> It was the secret fantasy of every bato [guy] living in or out of the *pachucada* [pachuco reality] to put on the zoot suit and play the myth. *Mas chucote que la chingada, orale.*"

As the Pachuco begins his monologue, a shot/reverse-shot pattern is established between the character and audiences. Yet the only discernible audience members are rendered in a single two-shot of a seemingly father-son couple. The self-reflexivity of the film, as expressed by the Pachuco, its disclosure of the mechanism by which cultural identity is produced, signals the extent to which a masculine content governs the production of identity. This film is about men, for men. The Pachuco personifies the "myth." Displacing dominant culture's positioning of the masculinity of gang members as "inherently violent," the Pachuco systematically intervenes to halt violence among other Chicano "gang" members. In the Pachuco character, transgressions such as "sexual promiscuity" and "defiance" figure as masculine strengths rather than as marks of pathological masculinity.

Within the film's corpus of narrative action, we are privy to the way in which *Zoot Suit* foregrounds the male subject by essentializing male desire as the Pachuco. "The secret fantasy of every bato," as the opening lines indicate, is "to put on the zoot suit and play the myth."

Hank Reyna (Daniel Valdez) of *Zoot Suit* looks at himself in the mirror while the Pachuco's mirror image appears behind Hank's mirror image.

In the movie that ensues, we discover how the Pachuco in fact "plays out" a male-centered fantasy about the pachuco reality. The Pachuco functions as Hank's unconscious; he is a character that only Hank can speak to and see. If for Lacanian psychoanalysis "the other" is part of the construct of the unconscious, rather than an identity with the referent, Valdez exteriorizes "the other." The Pachuco is both a character (an identity with the referent) and Hank's "other" (the construct of his unconscious), his alter ego. As a construct of Hank's imagination and desire, the Pachuco represents the literal embodiment of Hank's unconscious.

Valdez's work is less a self-reflexive application of psychoanalytic insights about the fractured nature of identity than a result of his earlier efforts in theater. The recourse to unconventional characterization derives from Valdez's previous experience in the collective ensemble El Teatro Campesino. In its initial stages, the Teatro developed as a political theater collective, supporting the unionizing and boycotting efforts of the United Farmworkers' Union. Shortly afterward, Teatro Campesino members undertook extensive spiritual training in Mayan and Aztec philosophy.[40] The Pachuco character is taken from the Teatro's repertoire of stock characters and represents the application of Valdez's studies in Mayan and Aztec mysticism, particularly the Mayan religious principle of *In Lak'ech*, roughly translated as "you are my other self." Reminiscent of the Rastafarian notion of "I and I," *In Lak'ech* re-configures identity as inextricable from the notion of Chicano collective. Indeed, the premise behind *In Lak'ech* derives from the notion of identity as a subject that is self-identical to an "other." This other identity stands in relation to the referent as much as it is a construct of the unconscious. Valdez's narrative application of the native mystical principle to both *Zoot Suit* and *La Bamba* takes concrete form in the conflict depicted between two characters who represent two sides of the same coin, in other words, together they are one. For this reason, *Zoot Suit*'s intelligibility depends on an understanding of Valdez's application of the indigenous mystical principle, *In Lak'ech*.[41]

Thus, the notion of identity as a struggle between the self and the other is reproduced in the Pachuco (as thought) and Hank (as being). The relation is often conflict-ridden. The Pachuco is contentious with Hank, ridiculing his patriotism (i.e., Hank's plans to join the navy) and his naive optimism about a favorable outcome in the trial. As a concrete identity, Hank represents the naïveté and inexperience of the barrio youth; the Pachuco, the wisdom of an older streetwise warrior. The Pachuco is endowed with qualities of the mind (i.e., cool detachment) so that ultimately Hank turns to him for guidance, counsel, and explanation. The Pachuco signifies Hank's wish fulfillment: the Pachuco acts out and verbalizes what social codes and conventions would not sanction in Hank (for instance, making disparaging sexual comments about women, incessantly smoking a joint, or sitting when the judge enters the court chamber requiring all to stand). The Pachuco's capacity to effect cinematic transitions in time and space with the snap of a finger, his presence in multiple spaces, and his inordinate power for moving narrative action forward or backward couples him with memory. The Pachuco personifies thought, fantasy, myth; Hank represents being. Through the Pachuco's agency, Hank's accessibility to the past or to the future takes concrete actualization. Given *Zoot Suit*'s re-construction of the relation between the self/Hank (the identity with the referent) and the other/Pachuco (the construct of the unconscious) as disruptive, the film self-reflexively reveals the mechanism by which cultural identity is produced. However, this production is simultaneously regressive in nature, turning against itself.

Fundamentally, the film's production of cultural identity is grounded in an "archaeology," in a return to the pre-Columbian origins of cultural identity. During the "Marijuana Boogie" scene, for example, the Pachuco ironically states the rhetorical question, "This is 1942 or is it 1492?"—a reference to the European "discovery" of the Americas. Valdez further imbues the Pachuco with pre-Columbian significance by choosing the colors black and red for the Pachuco's zoot suit, associating him with the Aztec deity Tezcatlipoca.[42] Furthermore, the film's formulation of cultural identity in terms of a "search for origins" is illustrated in the climactic scene of the movie, the sailors' beating of the Pachuco.

In a scene with clear reference to the "Zoot Suit riots" of 1943, a group of sailors gang up on the Pachuco, violently beating him and stripping him of his zoot suit. A witness to the action, Hank approaches the Pachuco, gesturing assistance. The body of the man lying in a fetal position, weeping, turns out to be that of Hank's brother. Puzzled, Hank makes a second attempt to assist his brother. Yet the image of the Pachuco once again occupies this second shot. The Pachuco stands up defiantly. Dressed in the groin cloth of an Aztec warrior, his image moves to the foreground, toward the "Aztec" sun. A musical score of indigenous ritual sounds accompanies the over-the-shoulder shot of Hank facing the Pachuco. The superimposition of two characters (the Pachuco and Hank's brother) signifies the symbolic convergence of two historical events: the sailors' attack on pachucos (1943) and the Spanish conquest of the Aztec nation (1519). Branding first the "Zoot Suit riots" and subsequently the Conquest onto the Pachuco's body propels the notion of identity as an archaeology. The "authenticity" of the more recent historical event rests on the "authority" of the more distant Aztec past. By inscribing the Aztec warrior onto the body of the Pachuco, multiple identities are collapsed into one subject. His confinement in jail had already marked him as a pinto. In sum, the Pachuco is essentially all of the identities of the revolutionary subjects envisioned by cultural nationalism: he encapsulates the fusion of the pinto, the Aztec warrior, and the pachuco. Moreover, Valdez configures cultural identity as an inward journey to the deepest realms of the subject, as the scene prior to the sailor beatings discloses.

After a heated argument with the Pachuco, Hank spends thirty days in the solitary confinement cell. The passage of time takes place outside of the film's narrative, yet, with the help of certain visual cues (Hank's worn expression, sound cues), spectators are made aware that time has indeed passed. Thus, Hank's time in solitary confinement is located outside the process of representation. The film's narrative resumes after the passage of these thirty days in the moment Hank encounters the Pachuco again. The Pachuco takes Hank on a literal journey of the mind,[43] outside his cell of solitary confinement, where the following dialogue ensues:

HANK: Where am I? What am I doing here?
PACHUCO: You're here to learn to live with yourself, Hank.

In a tense psychological struggle with the Other, involving narrative twists and turns, Hank eventually discovers the Chicano essence buried deep within himself. His newly discovered insight is re-capitulated in the following revelation: "Sabes que ese. I got you figured out . . . I know who you are. You're the one who got me here. You're me, my worst enemy and my best friend, my self." Thus, outside the process of representation, Hank undertakes an inward journey to the psychic realm of the self. By *Zoot Suit*'s narrative closure, Hank's transformation is evident. He becomes his desire, embodies the myth, and in so doing reproduces for the film the central problematic of cultural nationalist discourse, namely that Chicano brotherhood, existing to time immemorial, involves the symbolic elevation of the Pachuco as desire.

The cultural nationalist strategy re-articulated in *Zoot Suit* thereby interpellates all subjects, Chicanas and Chicanos, into new relations, into inhabiting the brotherhood of Chicanismo by privileging the masculine. Depicting the Pachuco as desire normalizes a masculine content for Chicano cultural identity particularly because in the configuration of the film's oppositional discourse, female desire is subsumed within a universal male desire. Consequently, *Zoot Suit* ultimately offers a masculine discourse that masks itself as politics. Indeed, the film transforms the negative positioning of the Chicano male in dominant discourses into a new Chicano "positive" subject. The transgressive nature of Chicanos as "gang members," formally articulated as a pathological masculinity in dominant discourse, is re-articulated into the positive masculine attributes of brotherhood and Chicanismo. Yet by positing Chicano desire as a universal one (i.e., the final lines of the film, "The Pachuco, the myth, still lives") and by figuring the Pachuco as the singular subject of identity and struggle, *Zoot Suit* interpellates historical subjects on the basis of similarity rather than on difference. Thus the film's reversal/inversion of a previously "othered" subject offers an essential Chicano cultural identity with masculine attributes.

Valdez was not, however, isolated from more general currents in Chicano cultural politics. As Angie Chabram-Dernersesian indicates, cultural nationalists "subsume the Chicana into a universal ethnic subject that speaks with the masculine instead of the feminine and embodies itself in a Chicano male."[44] The discourse of cultural nationalism positioned the Chicana as the subject whose object of desire was also the Pachuco, subsuming the female subject within a universal Chicano male cultural identity.

To the extent that Valdez was an exponent of the ideological premises of cultural nationalism, he was also deeply motivated by broader formulations for decolonizing Chicano consciousness from dominant ideology. The cultural nationalist configuration of the new Chicano subject by way of a journey to the authority and authenticity of the pre-Columbian past led many cultural nationalists to the study of ancient Aztec and Mayan rituals.[45] The re-discovery of the authentic native traditions became not just a way of re-constructing an authentic Chicano, but also of thinking about identity as an essence. In its most extreme formulations, the true "essence" of the Chicano lay buried deep within the inner psyche, or, more significantly, in the mythic Aztlán, "the imaginary geography claimed as the true site of Chicano subjectivity."[46] As I noted in the previous chapter, Valdez was clearly a part of the project of a broader phenomenon in search of mythical origins, and he was also implicated in its essentializing strategies.

The search for the mythical origin of cultural identity continued to inform Valdez's second feature film. Whereas *Zoot Suit* universalizes an essential subject of male desire in the body of the Pachuco, in *La Bamba* Valdez re-constructs Chicano cultural identity as an "identity crisis."

Cultural Identity as "Crisis"

In his poetic essay "Pensamiento Serpentino," published in 1973, Luis Valdez makes the following prophecy:

> Y no hay que olvidar
> que según la profecía de los tiempos antiguos
> QUETZALCOATL está por volver
> al mundo.
> (Tezcatlipoca su cuate malicioso

llegó en forma de Cortés
la última vez en 1519.)
Pero por hay viene
el día y año del nacimiento
de la SERPIENTE EMPLUMADA
(según la cuenta antigua) en
el AÑO CE ACATL EN EL DIA
CE ACATL y cae el 16 de agosto de 1987.
La profecía says that the entire world will be enlightened
and so it is.[47]

And so it was that in the summer of 1987, Luis Valdez's *La Bamba* was released internationally.[48] Myth, in this instance, appears to overdetermine reality, as Valdez's prophetic date for the second coming of Quetzalcoatl coincided with the "actual" date of the release of *La Bamba*. Valdez's second feature film represents a radical departure from his earlier concerns with hard-hitting political and social issues. *La Bamba* is based on the life story of rock-and-roll star Ritchie Valens, who, at the age of seventeen, died in a plane crash along with Buddy Holly and the Big Bopper. In sharp contrast to the experimental style of *Zoot Suit*, *La Bamba* tells its story through the more conventional realist mode of commercial cinema.[49]

Part of a wider "nostalgia" trend in popular culture, *La Bamba* was also part of the phenomenon dubbed by the industry as "Hispanic Hollywood." Other films by "Hispanics" or with "Hispanic" themes include *Stand and Deliver*, *Born in East L.A.*, and *The Milagro Beanfield War*. It was *La Bamba*, however, that convinced the dominant industry of the profitability of the Latino market and the viability of Latino themes for mainstream consumption. As the first "crossover phenomenon" by a Chicano director, *La Bamba* appealed to a national and international mainstream audience. In the United States alone, the film grossed over $60 million, $15 million through its Spanish-language run of seventeen weeks and $51.5 million during its sixteen-week run in English. Its record seventy-seven Spanish-language prints provided a two-to-one return on advertising costs over that expended on the English-only mainstream audience.[50]

Undoubtedly, a great part of the film's appeal among Chicanos/ Latinos stems from the fact that Ritchie Valens was a major figure in early rock and roll who happened to be a Chicano. A rare instance in commercial cinema in which a Chicano was featured as the central subject (even though Ritchie's character was played by the Filipino-American actor Lou Diamond Phillips), *La Bamba* was a welcomed corrective to decades of bandidos, greasers, and gangs. Thus *La Bamba* provided Chicanos and Chicanas a momentary surge of cultural pride. Moreover, Valdez's bland depiction of Ritchie Valens made him very palpable to a mainstream "crossover" audience as well. This, of course, has been the major drawback of the film. The liberties taken by Valdez to give Valens mainstream appeal ended up rewriting the history of Chicano rock and roll in Los Angeles. Factual elements that would make Valens's story a bit too "ethnic" (threatening?) for a dominant audience were eliminated from the film—for instance, Valens's deep cultural roots in a Mexican working-class music tradition, or his close ties to black musicians such as Little Richard and Bo Diddley. As George Lipsitz writes about the "actual" Ritchie Valens, "His tributes to the black rhythm-and-blues singer Little Richard motivated [Valens's] admirers to start calling him 'Little Ritchie.' "[51] Not only did Valdez omit the fact that Valens "established himself as a commercial performer by playing rhythm-and-blues-styled versions of Anglo and Mexican songs for a mixed audience,"[52] but *La Bamba* distorted key details about Valens's childhood formation in Mexican music, depicting him instead as just a rock-and-roll musician.

As a result, Ritchie was both a cultural hero for Chicano/Latina audiences and a pop figure for mainstream audiences, one who happened to be a nice Mexican, a rerun of "Guess Who's Coming to Dinner?" Reproducing the dominant mode of filmmaking, *La Bamba* renders a typically conventional rags-to-riches tale. The film narrates the life of a poor barrio boy from California rising to the pinnacles of the commercial culture industry. Yet the story is not so straightforward. Underneath the narrative simplicity, Valdez imbues the film with his notion of Chicano cultural "authenticity."

At the beginning of this section I quoted from a poetic essay by Valdez published in 1973, in order to highlight the coincidence between his studies in neo-Mayan philosophy and the date of the public release of *La Bamba*. The poetic essay, whose full title is "Pensamiento Serpentino: A Chicano Approach to the Theater of Reality," according to Tony Curiel, "captures the seeds of Valdez's working aesthetics and world view."[53] Chicano and Chicana followers of contemporary neo-Mayan prophecies anticipate the coming of the "Sixth Sun" (Sexto Sol) as an epoch of universal harmony, similar to New Age views of "the coming of the Age of Aquarius."[54] It is in this context that Valdez formulates his vision of a "new world order" in "Pensamiento Serpentino." The stanzas that follow the portion already

Director Luis Valdez on the production set of *La Bamba*. Courtesy of Columbia Pictures.

cited illuminate the role Chicanos would play in this "new world order":

> LA CONQUISTA está por acabarse
> and the Chicano is part of
> that Great Spiritual ReBirth.[55]

One wonders if *La Bamba* represents the incarnation of the second coming of Quetzalcoatl, or of the Sexto Sol Valdez prophesied in 1973.

Distorting Ritchie Valens's life history allowed Valdez to depict him in a "positive" light, but also permitted the filmmaker to continue playing with the native identity principle of *In Lak'ech*. Here Ritchie's brother, Bob (Esai Morales), occupies the negative subject position previously held by the Pachuco. Moreover, Valdez figures the relation between Bob and Ritchie as similar to that of Tezcatlipoca and Quetzalcoatl, twin deities depicted on the Aztec sun calendar. As two serpents forming the outer circle of the sun calendar, their heads face each other at the bottommost part of the circle, a feature that, according to interpretations of Aztec philosophy, symbolizes the eternal struggle repeated daily between night and day.

Reading beneath the surface, the director's training in neo-Mayan and Aztec philosophy informs the plot level of the film. The plot is propelled by means of a dream sequence to the extent that the influence of neo-Mayan notions of time is exemplified by this "premonition." *La Bamba* opens with shots in slow motion, popular for dream effects. A cut to a close-up of Ritchie Valens, awakening, terrified, signals that the dream sequence was his own dream—a premonition of the future that awaits him as the film unfolds. Ritchie's dream (opening the film) foretells his death (closing the film), thereby collapsing present and future. Punctuating a biographical story with a "premonition" evokes a nonlinear notion of time. Valdez re-presents, in this manner, the Chicano folk practice of "reading the future."[56] By evoking a nonlinear or cyclical notion of time, Valdez's influence by neo-Mayan philosophy is made manifest.

Indeed, Valdez saturates the film with Chicano cultural nationalist symbols of "authenticity." Chicano "authenticity" rests in native symbols and culture (indigenismo), because for Valdez the Chicano must "find ultimate liberation in the Cosmic Vision of our Indio Ancestors."[57] This "Indio Vision" is made particularly evident in the opening scene of the film. As the credits for *La Bamba* appear, Bob rides a motorcycle at high speed down a highway. To the tune of Bo Diddley's "Who Do You Love?" a series of shots, alternating between descriptive (close-up shots of Bob and the motorcycle) and action shots (long shots of Bob riding down the highway), take effect before the viewer. Details about Bob's character are made available through close-ups of significant "motifs" on his motorcycle, from the head of an Aztec warrior on the front to the feathered Indian on the body. Additional composite shots capture "tattoo and motorcycle style of aggressive working-class masculinity"[58] such as Bob's black leather jacket, dark sunglasses, and heavy riding boots. On the one hand, Valdez enshrines a "negative" masculinity in the character of Bob, yet on the other hand Valdez's representative strategy grounds itself in the marking of two cultural systems.

The significant motifs of the cross and the snake serve to illustrate this further. An extreme close-up shot of a tattoo of a cross on Bob's hand symbolizes Catholicism. The cross as the site of Catholicism's original male, Jesus Christ, is inscribed on the body of Bob in the form of a tattoo. A subsequent shot focuses on the image of a snake on the highway. In neo-Mayan philosophy, the snake signifies "transformation." That Bob represents Chicano "authenticity" is particularly notable in the character's association with native symbolism. Yet juxtaposing both details (the cross and the snake) also effects a syncretism

Bob (Esai Morales) and his mother, Connie (Rosana De Soto), at the labor camp in
La Bamba. Courtesy of Columbia Pictures.

of two symbolic/religious/cultural systems: Catholic and neo-Mayan, that is, Valdez's notion of Jesucristo-Quetzalcoatl.

Hence, prior to the start of the film's narrative action, the opening scene reveals the extent to which identity politics informs the film. A fusion of the pinto, the Aztec warrior, and the pachuco, like the Pachuco character in *Zoot Suit*, Bob incarnates the revolutionary subject of cultural nationalism. Given that the story of Ritchie Valens is told from Bob's point of view, simultaneously, Bob's initial envelopment in Chicano cultural symbols of "authenticity" initiates the plot device structuring *La Bamba*, namely, its parallel structure for characterization and storytelling.[59]

The triangulation between the brothers and their mother (Rosana De Soto) accompanies the narrative's structure of parallel action. During the first part of the film, this cinematic strategy is intense and pronounced. In order to establish a contrast between the characters, Bob's negativity is located in a visual space separated from Ritchie's actions as a "positive" character. Making the film's intelligibility accessible through parallel action serves to punctuate the binary relation between Bob and Ritchie as different and diametrically opposed types of Chicanos.

Enveloped within the more general binary relation of the forces of darkness/lightness (i.e., Bob-Cain-Tezcatlipoca/Ritchie-Abel-Quetzalcoatl), their depiction remains consistent in terms of social and psychological attributes: bad son/good son, failure/success, abusive/supportive, irresponsible husband/good provider, and so forth. Bob occupies the "negative" side of the equation, Ritchie, the positive. Even their obsessions, substance abuse and music, respectively factor into characterization. At first glance it may appear that the binary structure of the plot provides viewers with two diametrically opposed Chicano cardboard characters. However, rendering a trivial and simplistic narrative is not the film's major ideological problem. In *La Bamba*, viewer access to "Chicano culture" mainly derives from characterization, that is, through each character's relation to dominant and subaltern cultural systems. Thus, much more informs Valdez's recourse to the binary relation established between Ritchie and Bob. In the "Tijuana episode," we learn of Bob's strong attachments to Chicano "ethnic identity," evidenced by what Valdez considers "authentic" Chicano culture. A pivotal scene, the "Tijuana episode" marks Ritchie's own transformation into both manhood and Chicanismo.

Ritchie has been unable to start up a relationship with Donna, his white schoolmate, because of racism. Frustrated, Ritchie accepts Bob's assessment of the problem ("What you need is some tail"), and both brothers end up in Tijuana. The film normalizes male payment for sex, prostitution, as an unproblematic alternative for their initiation rite into manhood. *La Bamba* offers as well a Mexican brothel as the site where inexperienced men lose their virginity. Unimpressed by the lineup of prostitutes, Ritchie is instead captivated by the Mexican musicians playing "La Bamba." Apart from the film's problematic representation of the initiation rite of masculinity, the scene across the border is invested with multiple cultural iconography, a Chicano mythmaking enterprise at work in the film.

In the scene that follows that of the Mexican brothel, Ritchie awakens in a "strange" place, a room imbued with "native" decor. He encounters an elderly curandero (shaman) and says to him, "Yo no speako español." After Bob joins the two, we learn that the curandero is Bob's spiritual father (BOB: "I've been coming here for years"). Through Bob's translation, Ritchie is instructed in neo-Mayan (Chicano) rituals: he undergoes symbolic/psychic transformation by eating a snake, and absorbs native views about reality (CURANDERO: "To live is to sleep; to die is to be born again"). Ritchie's re-discovery of his

Ritchie (Lou Diamond Phillips) and Bob (Esai Morales) in Mexico with the curandero in *La Bamba*.

cultural roots has been accessible only through Bob's agency. As the agent of cultural transmission, Bob is enveloped in notions of authenticity as much as he is by pathology.

Renato Rosaldo's discussion of the ambiguities plaguing research on assimilation begins by noting that the concept itself "usually links cultural loss to economic betterment." Rosaldo notes that assimilation "suggests, for example, that Chicanos who raise their incomes automatically lose their ethnic identity. Surely economic misery is not the only path to cultural vitality."[60] In *La Bamba*, Valdez goes one step further. Cultural vitality and retention are linked to social deviance, whereas socially mobile Chicanos like Ritchie seem to guarantee the circulation of Chicano culture on a broader scale, as the example of the recording of a popular song like "la bamba" for mass consumption indicates. The film paradoxically proposes a linear view about the process of assimilation. Ritchie's level of acculturation (cultural assimilation) is inversely related to Bob's strong attachments to his ethnic identity. In contrast to Ritchie, who embodies little "ethnicity," Bob is simultaneously characterized as socially pathological (i.e., his abusive treatment of his girlfriend, his drug dealings and substance abuse,

and his membership in gangs) and strongly identified with Chicanismo. Thus, the film's critique of melting-pot ideology is clear. Social
mobility is barred for Chicanos who, like Bob, have resisted incorporation into dominant culture, for those who have retained their ethnic
and cultural beliefs and values, their "Chicanismo." The more one is
culturally assimilated, the greater the possibility of social mobility, as
in the case of Ritchie. Unfortunately stopping short of any larger critique of dominant ideology in its multiculturalism, pluralism, or melting-pot manifestations, the film makes a diluted case for the significance of cultural affirmation, and ends by normalizing cultural
resistance as a process that engenders pathological outcomes.

Moreover, it poses Chicano culture as available not in the social
context of the U.S. Chicano community, but only in a mythical Mexico. La Bamba's plot unfolds by establishing a logical narrative sequence whereby Ritchie's experience across the border prompts his
later desire to record "La Bamba." Authentic Chicano culture, in the
film's view, is located outside of the lived experiences of Chicanos
and Chicanas in the United States. By locating the "authentic" culture
elsewhere, Valdez engages in what Renato Rosaldo terms "primitiv-
ism." Not only does La Bamba posit the authenticity of Chicano culture outside of "ongoing processes of change," but the film seems to
offer the view that culture is a "relic to be preserved just as it was."[61]

The in-between-ness of Chicano culture has been a vexed problem
for Valdez, who indicates, "It is not enough to say we suffer an identity crisis, because that crisis has been our way of life." As I have
noted earlier, this reference to the Chicano "identity crisis" is rooted
in Mexican nationalist thought of the early decades of the twentieth
century. Principally figured as an "existential crisis," Chicano identity
in this view is "torn between two cultures." The metaphor of binaries
lends credibility to this argument because Chicano identity is therein
positioned as torn first between the "Spanish" and the "Indian" (as in
views informed by Mexican existentialism), and more recently between the "Anglo" and the "Mexican." Rather than representing the
in-between-ness of Chicano culture as a site where critical insight is
made possible, La Bamba re-configures Chicano cultural identity in
either/or terms. The only space for cultural vitality and "Chicanismo"
lies on the margins. Contrary to the works of women and men engaged in the creative processes of Chicano cultural reproduction, cultural workers whose practices attest to the regenerative potentiality of
the margin, La Bamba represents marginality (Bob's position) as a
space of deviance and social pathology. Kobena Mercer makes a sim-

ilar observation about films of the black diaspora that frame identity politics in terms of the thesis of pathology, indicating that the films retell "stories of identity . . . within a code or language that positions that identity as a 'problem.' "[62]

Valdez was not the only Chicano filmmaker that positioned identity as a "problem." Jesús Treviño's film *Seguin* (1981) similarly represents Chicano identity as a crisis. In *Seguin*, Treviño recounts the story of the landed Tejano (Chicanos from Texas) aristocracy who fought on the side of the Texas Anglos in the nineteenth-century war with Mexico. After the war, during the initial stages of the newly formed Texas Republic, racism among Anglo-Texans effectively denied access to equality to the Tejanos. The film's retelling of the story from the perspective of the landowner Juan Seguin ultimately positions identity as a crisis grounded in betrayal.[63] Although *Seguin* is clear about its contestation of the racist attitudes among individual Anglo-Texans, the film ends by positioning Chicano identity as an individual dis-illusion, the privileged intellectual's problem, which, as Mercer explains, "is generalized and universalized as something everybody is supposed to be worried about."[64] Certainly the identity positions of Anglo versus Mexican, or Spanish versus Indian, are not the only options for Chicanas and Chicanos of the late twentieth century. Nor does identity politics, as in the works of Luis Valdez, need to be grounded in an archaeology, or in the "symbolic construction of an other."

As Angie Chabram-Dernersesian explains, this definition of identity "was deceptive, since Chicano nationalism was also predicated on the necessity of mimesis: a one-on-one correspondence between the subject and its reflection in a mirrorlike duplication."[65] As we have seen, *Zoot Suit* practices the kind of distortions and deceptions typical of Chicano nationalists who "only required their own self-reflection in order to know themselves and are privileged enough to encounter that image in a seemingly unmediated fashion."[66] It is a cultural politics that, as Stuart Hall instructs us, ignores the site/location from where the subject (he/she) speaks, the positions of enunciation:

> What recent theories of enunciation suggest is that, though we
> speak, so to say "in our own name," of ourselves and from our own
> experience, nevertheless who speaks, and the subject who is spoken
> of, are never identical, never exactly in the same place. Identity is
> not as transparent or unproblematic as we think.[67]

The central contradiction informing the cultural politics of Chicano

cultural nationalism has been that, contrary to the attempts to redis-
cover identity in the "authority" of the past, cultural identity could
only be constituted in the present and, more important, within representational forms such as poetry, art, drama, and cinema. Indeed,
while alternative notions of identity are available through practices
and memories of resistance, the process of its constitution requires a
"retelling," performed in the present. There is no Chicano core-es-
sence, awaiting that inward journey of discovery, without a language, codes, or location outside of history. Cultural identity, as Hall
indicates, is "always constituted within, not outside, representation."[68] The positive feature of cultural nationalism is the fact that
Movement intellectuals excavated a historical past and constructed
and reconstructed memories of a Mexican culture of struggle and resistance in order to develop a cohesive group identity that would
shield them from racist ideology and oppression. Often, however,
their retelling of stories re-constructed Chicano identity in a debilitat-
ing fashion, as the site of crisis and pathology. Given that cultural
identities are not handed down as essences, the task remains for an
identity politics able to re-construct subjectivities in ways that em-
power people as creative subjects of history. Cinematic representation plays a formidable role in such a project, for cultural identity is
not an "already accomplished fact" but a "production which is never
complete."[69] One of the sites for its production is representational
forms such as cinema.

Humor as Subversive De-construction
Born in East L.A. (1987)

In Cheech Marin's *Born in East L.A.* (1987), a skimpily clad French woman appears in the opening and closing portions of the film. Her image is enigmatic. Residing outside the corpus of narrative action, her *red* hair, *white* body, and *green* dress—the colors of the Mexican flag—frame the film's story. In the beginning of the film, the red-white-green body of a French woman is obsessively stalked throughout the barrio by the main character of the film, Rudy (Cheech Marin). Her final appearance during the Cinco de Mayo parade scene stages the narrative's closure, literally halting the Cinco de Mayo parade in East Los Angeles. In both instances, the eyes of all characters are upon her. What does this image mean?[1]

As this "red-white-green" French woman interrupts the brown economy of East L.A., every male notices her body. Eroticized close-ups of legs, hips, breasts reveal the objects of Rudy's (and Chicanos') voyeuristic desires. Insofar as her body is sexualized, this "red-white-green" image of a French woman directs our laughter against a universal (essential) voyeurism in Chicanos. Viewers familiar with Cheech Marin's earlier films (*Up in Smoke*, 1978; *Cheech & Chong's Next Movie*, 1980; *Nice Dreams*, 1981; *Cheech & Chong Still Smoking*, 1983), codirected with Thomas Chong, are able to read this scene against their previous knowledge about Cheech and Chong's improvisational style of parody. Their characters are always satirical portraits of various ethnic/racial groups and subcultures in California (surfers, dopers, hippies, mystics, nationalists, motorcycle club members, and so on). An imaging strategy displaying Cheech and Chong's trenchant wit, these characters are usually depicted in absurd or inordinate circumstances. In light of Marin's early work, the scene of

The red-haired French woman dressed in green walking through the streets of East Los Angeles in *Born in East L.A.* A mural depicting the Mexican and U.S. flags appears in the background.

the "red-white-green" French woman serves to parody Chicano voyeurism, and Rudy figures as the emblem of the Chicano voyeur.

Born in East L.A. was Marin's first film directed without his sidekick, Thomas Chong.[2] The film deals with a serious political issue, namely, the indiscriminate deportation of Chicanos (U.S. citizens) to Mexico by border-patrol agents, on the basis of skin color, symbolizing a new threshold for Marin's repertoire but also in the domain of Chicano cultural politics.[3] With the exception of *Zoot Suit*, "political" and "social problem" films directed by Chicanos fashioned their stories around a serious approach to dramatic narrative or what some may choose to call the prevalence of "social realism." The thematic focus had been on the political emphasis or on "getting the message across" through downbeat (depressing) narrative closure.[4] In contrast, Marin renders a depiction of Chicano social reality through humor as opposed to the more serious political style. The film's recourse to parody nonetheless provides a powerful indictment of dominant society.

Prior to *Born in East L.A.*, Cheech and Chong had been "cult" heroes of sorts, principally among Chicanos and countercultural youth. In commercially successful LP recordings and Hollywood films, Marin perfected what Christine List has termed "self-derogatory ethnic humor."[5] Marin attempted to identify specific U.S. comedians as influences in his work, citing Charlie Chaplin as his predecessor.[6] While this parallel to Chaplin's films has undoubtedly helped to legitimate Marin in the eyes of some, the bicultural flavor of his humor roots him as well in Chicano vernacular traditions. In fact, *Born in East L.A.* illustrates the extent to which Chicanos draw from an alternative tradition of inquiry into the politics of representation.

Grotesque Realism

We have seen the extent to which Marin deploys the enigmatic image of the French woman in order to universalize the parody of Chicano voyeurism. Yet because the filmmaker ironically inflects the French woman's body with Chicano symbols and iconography in both the opening and closing scenes,[7] film critic Chon Noriega reads her image in relation to a major subtext in the film, its subtle critique of the claims about "America" as the "land of opportunity."[8] For Noriega, the image of the French woman operates as a parody of the Statue of Liberty. Yet, Marin creates a fusion between the Statue of Liberty as emblematic of immigrants' desire for a better life in the United States (hence, Neil Diamond's tune "They Come to America," which closes the film) and the white woman as emblematic of Chicano desire for social mobility. Thus the French woman functions not simply as a parody of the Statue of Liberty but on a different register as well. Her image serves a dual function, as an allegory for the Statue of Liberty and as a sign of the construction of Chicano sexual desire for a "white woman." The polyvocal style and multiaccentuality of *Born in East L.A.* is evident in its playfulness with various levels of meaning. By making this analogy, Marin parodies the illusory nature of desires, whether for a better life or for social mobility.

But, in certain respects, the process of encoding particular social and cultural meanings onto images/language/sound does not correspond neatly with decoding strategies. Viewers may or may not get the point, so the problem of equivocation surfaces.[9] To be sure, objections may be raised about the objectifying impulse in the image of the French woman, yet, because a comedic mode predominates in the film, images and scenes in *Born in East L.A.* simply cannot be taken literally or at face value. Further understanding of the enigmatic image of the French woman requires that we situate Marin's imaging strategy within a representational style more properly associated with manifestations of grotesque realism in a Mexican popular tradition of humor.

Emily Hicks underscores the centrality of the "grotesque" in the works of borderlands writers, indicating, "what Mikhail Bakhtin in *Rabelais and His World* calls 'the grotesque' has not been homogenized out of the metaphors deployed in border writing."[10] Bakhtin's observations about the popular tradition of grotesque realism, even though based on research in another context, are especially helpful in locating the mechanism of humor operative in *Born in East L.A.*

Bakhtin's discussion of the privileged space of laughter and the relationship between popular traditions and artistic expression sets the stage for contextualizing *Born in East L.A.* within the popular aesthetics of grotesque realism. A tradition that was "suppressed in the nineteenth-century European novel," it nonetheless continues to inform the representational politics of many Latin American writers, whose works, according to Hicks, have "given the grotesque a place from which to speak."[11] As Bakhtin indicates about this popular aesthetics:

> For thousands of years, folk culture strove at every stage of its
> development to overcome by laughter, render sober and express in
> the language of material bodily lower stratum (in an ambivalent
> sense) all the central ideas, images, and symbols of official culture.[12]

Bakhtin's insight on the strategy of expression "in the language of the lower stratum" parallels Marin's imaging strategy of sexually objectifying the French woman. Yet, in today's context, the allegorical relation of the French woman to the "Statue of Liberty" also means something else as well.

If the analogy between the French woman as signifier for sexual desire and the Statue of Liberty as a symbol of desire for a better life is properly grasped, then the strategy of sexually objectifying the French woman spills over onto the Statue of Liberty, effecting a critique of the hypocrisy of dominant culture. Yet this potential—the subversion of a revered icon of dominant culture—may also turn against itself, normalizing the general objectification of women in dominant cinema. As the image functions to parody male voyeurism, directing its critique against the subjects of the gaze, the inscription of sexual desire onto the French woman simultaneously reproduces dominant imaging strategies. Thus the ambivalence of the imaging strategy interpellates viewers in contradictory positions, as coproducers of the objectifying impulse and as coparticipants of ironic excess.

Marin further attempts to couple social critique with imagery characteristic of grotesque realism. The jail scene's affinities with grotesque realism stem from its use of degradation for comedic effect. According to Bakhtin, "the essential principle of grotesque realism is degradation, that is, the lowering all that is high, spiritual, ideal, abstract; it is a transfer to the material level, to the sphere of earth and body in their indissoluble unity."[13] Moreover, the principle of degradation takes various forms. The artistic expression of this principle, according to Bakhtin, may assume a verbal form of abuse, for instance, what the writer characterizes as the dual tone of "praise/abuse in language," or a visual form, as images that are "ugly, monstrous, hideous from the point of view of 'classic' aesthetics."[14]

During a brief stay in jail, Rudy disfigures a tattoo of a Chicana "home-girl" on the chest of an estranged inmate. A misogynistic humor, rendered through elements of absurdity, predominates throughout the scene. The opening shots depict Rudy's hand on a circuit breaker followed by a shot of a prison inmate strapped on an electric chair, screaming in pain, thereby giving the impression that we are witnessing an execution. However, Rudy was actually turning on the electrical current, and the inmate was accidentally sitting on top of the tattoo instrument. Ironic and satirical excess reverberates through the contrast between the "ugly" and "hideous" features of the inmate and Rudy's "normal" composure.

The tattoo on the chest of the inmate depicts the image of his beloved wife. In this respect, the tattoo is to be read as an honor symbolizing "ideal love," similar to that of the wedding vows " 'til death do us part." The inmate's wife has left him for his brother, however, and Rudy is asked to remove the tattoo. Given that tattoos are permanent, Rudy suggests altering the image. His distasteful ideas for disfiguring the image ("Let's give her a black eye"; "break her nose"; "Draw a gun on one side and her brains splattering on the other") are enthusiastically received by the inmate. A shot/reverse-shot pattern is established between Rudy, disfiguring the tattoo, and the hideous facial expressions of the inmate, in simultaneous pain and pleasure. The act of violence is of course figurative, that is, directed onto the inscription of a face on the body of a male. The scene humorously privileges the therapeutic value of "mental" violence as a substitute for "concrete" acts, rendering the inmate's desire for revenge onto a figure and thus deflecting brutalization and violence from the body of a real person onto that of an image.

My focus on Marin's imaging strategy in these scenes of the jail and of the French woman directs attention to two moments of significa- tion, the meanings of the images in the context of the narrative and the cinematic effects of this process. This distinction is crucial be- cause, as Stephen Heath reminds us, "meaning is not just con- structed 'in' the particular film, meanings circulate between social for- mation, spectator and film."[15] However grotesque its realism may be, the scenes of the tattoo and the French woman are nonetheless prob- lematic precisely because violence against women is so prevalent in this society, outside cinematic representation, in the "real" world, so to speak. The objectification of the French woman, even in light of its comedic intention, normalizes the general derision of women in the social world as well.

Apart from its ambivalent treatment of women, *Born in East L.A.* nonetheless stages an effective indictment of dominant official dis- course, furthering its connection to vernacular culture. The praise/ abuse aspect of popular speech, according to Bakhtin, "was waged in a popular struggle against the stabilizing tendencies of the official monotone."[16] Similar to *Zoot Suit*, *Born in East L.A.* liberates a space from dominant culture, deriving its intertextual logic from its relation to a Mexican tradition of performance.

Popularized throughout the Southwest and Mexico via both film and *carpas* (tent theater), comedians such as Mario Moreno "Cantin- flas" and Germán Valdez "Tin-Tan" (among others) surfaced as the prime exponents of a uniquely flavored style of Mexican parody and satire that drew its strength from a critique of power.[17] The narrative emphasis was in many cases on maneuver and improvisation through a comedic role reversal of the protagonist.[18] In theater and *carpa* per- formances, Cantinflas emerges as the master of *cábula*, the subversive (and pleasurable) play with language.[19] Through the practice of *cábu- la*, Cantinflas satirized and parodied a rhetorical tendency of Mexi- can politicians known as *"puro palabrerío,"* or the excessive usage of words that said either "nothing" or very little, or signified the "un- said" or unsayable.[20] During the 1940s in northern Mexico, Tin-Tan blended working-class forms of expression and dress and came up with a Mexican version of the U.S.-Mexico border character type: the pachuco. Tin-Tan's parodic characterization of the pachuco provided a critique both of U.S. treatment of Chicanos and of Mexico's neglect of its emigrants to the United States. Foregrounding questions of bilingualism and biculturalism within the context of class,[21] Tin-Tan also problematized the increasingly unsettling issue of "Mexican" identity—an issue that the Mexican philosopher Octavio Paz in his existential outlook would later distort.[22]

Through performance, Tin-Tan and Cantinflas, along with Palillo and Viruta y Capulina,[23] thus refashioned the persistent popular expressions of resistance by a strategic artistic intervention. Here we have a critique of power in its institutional and propertied forms that ultimately was able to configure a space for unscrambling and reshaping mestizaje. This skillful intervention would transform Tin-Tan and Cantinflas into prolific as well as popular comedians among Chicano/a and Mexican audiences. Outside the politics of the Chicano Movement, Cheech Marin had inflected a linguistic and cultural code-switching practice drawn from two semiotic systems onto his more properly commercial "mass" culture ventures, the Cheech and Chong series. Marin would perfect his version of Chicano vernacular aesthetic in *Born in East L.A.*

Lo popular and Collectivity

In 1987, *Born in East L.A.* received the award for "Best Script" at the New Latin American Cinema festival in Havana, in part because of its unique satirical, political criticism. Marin's representation of the repatriation problem through humor deepens and extends the spatial boundaries for social criticism within commodified popular culture. His concurrent sensitivity to *lo popular* (everyday popular culture) and to commodified popular culture as axes of identity is what in fact makes Marin's cultural politics so effective. Determined to render an alternative image of the barrio, the opening scene of *Born in East L.A.* depicts its dignity with a shot of a neatly kept "house," in sharp contrast to the images of Chicano neighborhoods in dominant commercial films (i.e., graffiti-ridden walls, unkempt gardens, and dilapidated homes, replete with violent urban gangs), combining a sensibility for *lo popular* with an equally brilliant acuity for the meaning of popular commodified culture in the everyday lives of people.

As the title makes evident, the unifying motif of the film is the parody of Bruce Springsteen's rock hit "Born in the USA." This expression of commodified popular culture functions to frame the central problematic of *Born in East L.A.* Springsteen's song intervenes in each movement of the narrative, and the task of the plot is to solve the central disruption: how will Rudy (Cheech), a Chicano born in East L.A.

who has been illegally deported, return home? The film poses an even more scathing question: what type of society deports its citizens merely on the basis of the color of their skin? To answer, or to be willing to accept the film's response, one must recognize the pervasiveness of institutional racism in this country.

However, it is not simply Springsteen's song that transverses the film, for the authorial intention in this case was to promote the celebration of working-class culture and resistance in the United States. Marin in fact parodies not Springsteen's intentionality, but rather another level of social meaning manifest by the song's reception. At this second level, "Born in the USA" had indeed been disarticulated from its signifying elements of working-class discourse and rearticulated as an expression of racist and patriotic discourse, that is to say, the song was reappropriated hegemonically to signify "foreigners (or non-whites) go home."[24] The strategic brilliance of Marin's intervention has been the effectiveness with which he parodied the song's ethnophobic/xenophobic seizure. The film enters the symbolic level, infusing popular discourse with precisely those elements that are inimical to U.S. dominant culture. If "Born in the USA" signifies "U.S. for non-*others* (white Anglo-Americans)," then Cheech Marin ingeniously dismantles the patriotic significance of this ideology through his cultural creation—the music video as well as the film—*Born in East L.A.*

In this manner, the parodic elements of both cultural forms reflect a more significant symbolic elaboration of the contradiction of white-American nativism, because as Marin exemplifies through humor, brown people are natives too. *Born in East L.A.* becomes an alternative way of saying America for Americans. Yet, contrary to the official versions of history taught in U.S. public schools and circulated in the media, certainly in the Southwest, the Mexican-origin population predates Anglo immigration. As such, the film reclaims a counter-memory of struggle for Chicano/as. It elevates to the level of mainstream discourse that which, from the perspective of Chicana/os, has been silenced from "popular" mainstream memory: the conquest of the Southwest by Anglo-Americans. A further pun to Californians who, displaying the "California Native" bumper sticker, arrogantly view Chicanos as recent arrivals, it is not gratuitous that as Rudy is arrested by *la migra*, his words echo at a distance, "I'm a U.S. citizen, I was born in East L.A., my mother was born in East L.A., my grandmother was born in East L.A." Literally tracing this lineage, Rudy's family has been in Los Angeles at least since the early twentieth century.

The narrative disruption is generated through a role reversal on the part of the film's Chicano protagonist, Rudy. Narrative action begins with Rudy's carrying out his mother's request to meet his cousin Javier (Paul Rodríguez), an undocumented worker from Mexico, at the toy factory in downtown Los Angeles. Upon Rudy's arrival at the toy factory, U.S. immigration agents raid the factory. A core signifying element that interlaces the entire text, the "play of appearances," is introduced in this early film sequence. From the perspective of the white agent, Rudy looks or "appears" to be "Mexican." Despite his insistence that he was born in East L.A., the clarity of his enunciation in English, his Chicano-style dress and mannerism, Rudy is forcefully deported to Mexico along with the Mexican workers employed in the toy factory. His cousin Javier, however, arrives at the factory moments after the raid and is later taken by the factory owner to Rudy's home—the space where Javier is to remain throughout the film. From this narrative instance, the role reversals of Rudy and Javier motivate the primary desire of the film's subject: Rudy's quest to return to East L.A. from Mexico (Tijuana). The task of the plot thus becomes the demonstration of the protagonist's ability to resolve those conflicts necessary for the final narrative equilibrium or closure. In the process, the subject's skills at maneuvering and improvising are sharply illustrated.

The film spotlights role reversal through a visual-spatial contrast between the subject's quest to return and the object of his desire: the space occupied by his cousin, Javier. In other words, the film confines Javier to the space of Rudy's desire (his home in East L.A.) whereas Rudy inhabits the conflict-ridden space where Javier should be (Tijuana). Parody punctuates these dual spaces, humorously converting the "play of appearances" into a subversion of images. In the initial sequence (the factory raid) spatial contradiction is depicted through comical role reversal, a strategy that subsequently permits a number of signifying elements to materialize as cinematic tensions. Anchoring the tale in double entendre, *Born in East L.A.* de-constructs dominant images and codes and offers powerful instances of social critique.

Rudy's fate is sealed at the moment he is asked by the *migra* to prove his citizenship by answering the question, "Who's the president of the United States?" The double entendre in Rudy's response is ingenious: "That's easy. That guy who used to be on *Death Valley*. John Wayne." In the eyes of the INS agent (who speaks in a typically southern drawl), Rudy has failed to revere properly an American icon, dooming him to deportation. But the subversiveness of Rudy's response lies in the truth behind the joke. Rudy's wrong answer was in fact a "right" one. In voting for Ronald Reagan, Americans were voting for John Wayne and for everything these two icons of mainstream culture represent.[25]

The text of the film generally upholds cinematic realism, but several sequences interrupt the linear narrative flow and thereby alter the referential illusion commonly ascribed to a Hollywood mainstream film. This effect is first established by the back-to-back visual-narrative contrast in the film's opening pair of sequences. Marin renders cinematic realism its due in the first mise-en-scène at his home but follows with a voyeurism played as grotesque comedy in the subsequent "Chicano pursuit of a white woman in the barrio" scene.[26] Throughout the film, Marin employs mainstream cinematic codes of realism only to splice them with absurd elements. During the *migra* chase scene, for instance, where Rudy attempts to cross the border several times but fails, the filmmaker introduces a collage of absurd dramatic action and music in place of dramatic realism.

By scoring what dominant culture believes to be a favorite tune among Mexicans, the "Mexican Hat Dance" ("El Jarabe Tapatio"), the film ritualizes the *migra* chase scene as a hide-and-seek game. To the "Jarabe Tapatio," Rudy "dances" with *la Migra*, whether camouflaging himself as a shrub or teaching the Mexicanos the art of tag football. The playfulness of the film's formal techniques subverts, disrupts, and ritualizes the logic of fictional realism, reclaiming a pleasurable cinematic experience through humor. Other playful scenes further confirm Marin's acumen for capturing the significance of popular commercial culture in shaping everyday lives.

The most subversive quality of *Born in East L.A.* is the effectiveness with which the film reverses the dominant society's codes of positive/negative value embodied in such binary systems of representation as the white as good/black as evil polarity, or the view of the flag as a value of patriotism and an upside-down flag as unpatriotism. Rudy is the viewers' object of identification yet he is also the central subject of the film's discourse. Consequently his actions and attitudes elicit identification by the spectator. By re-constructing Rudy as the object of our identification, the film challenges our viewing habits in a number of ways.

The drug-smuggling sequence depicts two elderly white people traveling from Mexico in an RV and returning home through the border crossing. Without their knowledge, Rudy has hidden inside the camper. As the couple talks with the border-patrol guard, they relate their enjoyment of the sights as well as the fact that the "Mexican people are wonderful . . . we love the people." In dominant discourse, an elderly couple traveling around in a recreational vehicle is positively valorized or coded as a "harmless" retired couple—perhaps even as signifying an easy prey for thieves (i.e., "Mexicans"). Moreover, in dominant practices of representation, the differential relation between Rudy and the retired couple would certainly be constituted in the following equation: Rudy signifies a "sleazy," "greasy," dark-skinned, Medellín-cartel drug runner,[27] whereas the elderly couple is a signifier for "innocent" American tourists, an innocence/guilt binarism. Furthermore, the cultural code of vacationing in a luxurious camper signifies that they are naturally enjoying their hard-earned life savings.

The film discourse, however, de-constructs precisely these dominant social codes and constructs an entirely new significance. As it turns out, the drug-sniffing dogs discover the elderly couple is smuggling a van full of marijuana back to the United States, while Rudy is actually a harmless guy hiding in the RV, simply attempting, in whatever way possible, to return home. Because the film maps viewer identification with Rudy, it also re-codifies a new meaning for the image of a Chicano. As opposed to the barrage of media images, not all drug smugglers are of Latino extraction. The film forces viewers to engage dominant codes of valorization and, in so doing, positions viewers in the unsettling role of questioning hegemonic racist signs.

Besides subverting the binary system of representation, the film re-articulates an internationalism among people of color in the United States.[28] One of the many jobs that Rudy has to take in order to save money for his return to Los Angeles is that of "tutoring" a group of Asians on how to look and act "American." At first glance, the tutoring sequences seem to render a Chicana/o stereotype of Asians; however, a deeper reading of the scenes reveals a more important strategy driving this representation. From the perspective of the white businessman who had hired Rudy to "Americanize" the Asians, their ethnicity was indiscernible. He tells Rudy that they are either "Chinese," "Indians," or "something." The film's background music, however, encodes them as ethnically Asian. Rudy proceeds to teach them the style, mannerism, talk, and dress of a Chicano from East Los Angeles. At the end of the film, Rudy, his Salvadoreña girlfriend, and the undocumented Asians finally reach East L.A., by entering a street in the midst of a Cinco de Mayo parade through a "man"hole. Passing as Chicanos, the Asians, when they spot a police officer, immediately assume the East L.A. youth posture and manner of walking, give the officer a "high five" hand slap, and say, "Go Raiders."

The film thereby critiques the dominant social discourse of racism that fixes a binary system of representation between native-born and foreign-born in terms of the figurative markers of skin color, or "white" as native and "dark" as foreigner. Constructed within the film is a dominant perspective that is unable to differentiate an Asian from an Indian, or a Mexican immigrant from a Chicano native. However, the film itself dismantles this inscription for its viewers. The very cinematic fact that the film allows spectators a knowledge of its narrative truth, that Rudy is U.S.-born and that the Asians are not Indian, problematizes dominant ideology's racist notion of *nativeness*. If the figurative marker of the dominant culture is the color of one's skin, then Cheech Marin pushes this hegemonic distinction to its ultimate consequences. Because all people of color "look alike," then Asians can be taught to act like Chicanos and vice versa. Ultimately the filmmaker's critique of dominant culture illustrates the opacity of racism.

Marin's appreciation for commercial popular culture as an axis of identity is equally brilliant in this part of the film. In their masquerade as Chicanos, the Asians are required to pay homage to the most revered football team for L.A. Chicanos, the L.A. Raiders. The Raiders are favorites not just because they are the Los Angeles home team, but because this was the first pro-football team with a Chicano coach (Tom Flores) and a Chicano quarterback (Jim Plunkett).

Marin also represents the syncretism of commercial popular culture with Chicano/Mexican music tradition. When Rudy spots a Mexican trio in the cantina, he decides to join them by playing "Summertime Blues," a song recorded by Ritchie Valens's best friend, Eddie Cochran.[29] One of the trio's members is played by Chicano conjunto musician Steve Jordan, whose accordion-music recordings effectively syncretize Tejano conjunto and rock-and-roll musics. Later, Rudy attempts to teach the trio "Twist and Shout," a song by white songwriters, which the trio hears and plays back to Rudy as "La Bamba."[30] Blending music from Jimi Hendrix and Carlos Santana, Rudy and the trio perform "Purple Haze" in their debut as a newly formed band, the "Nuevos Huevos Rancheros"—an interlingual pun between "new wave" and "huevos rancheros."

Rudy (Cheech Marin) leads hundreds of immigrants across the Mexican border into the United States at the end of *Born in East L.A.*

The film's finale offers a utopian vision for cultural politics. In the scene prior to the narrative's closure, Rudy had finally earned enough money to purchase his way back, or to be smuggled into the United States by a coyote. The penultimate sequence depicts an intense encounter between the coyote and a husband who did not have enough money to cover his wife's fare on the contraband journey. The emotional good-bye between the wife and husband provokes Rudy's decision to give his own space on the truck to the woman. Ultimately, this sacrificial act on the part of an individual leads to a collective resolution for the narrative. Determined to return home, Rudy, along with hundreds of thousands of undocumented "brown" people, descends from the mountaintop upon two unsuspecting border agents. Through evoking this political/religious metaphor of struggle, *Born in East L.A.* resists ideology of individual heroism at the same time that the film reaffirms the sense of collectivity.

In their book *Camera Politica*, Michael Ryan and Douglas Kellner entertain the political significance of experimenting within Hollywood through the "recoding of conventional formulas that transcend some of their ideological limitations."[31] The authors therefore call on oppositional filmmakers to create a different sense of progressive cinema, a politics that "rather than conceive of the Hollywood representational system as being inherently ideological . . . would assume instead that what matters are the *effects* representations have."[32] One of the effects we can attribute to Cheech Marin's recent intervention within the Hollywood system is certainly that his cultural form transcends "social expectations" and "normative assumptions" regarding what shape Chicano/a symbolic creations should take. He does so by liberating the "image" from the constraints of the dominant cultural codes and the "correct" mode for political cinema. In this manner, Marin injects a liberating imagination back onto social and cultural discourses. He re-inscribes a Chicano political space that ruptures both the notion of Hollywood hegemony and borders of political correctness in Chicano cinema. At the very least, Marin gives us an alternative form for a Chicano/a activist aesthetics, one that draws from a vernacular tradition and re-constitutes, albeit in the ideal, a new social world through collective strength. In its narrative closure, *Born in East L.A.* embraces a consciousness of the social and symbolic struggle that the Chicano artist Gronk best evokes with the following spatial and temporal metaphor: "Borders don't apply now. East L.A. is everywhere."

Conclusion: Mestizaje (Hybridity) in Cultural Politics

Exemplifying the extent to which Chicanos have their own tradition of inquiry into the politics of representation, *Born in East L.A.* is a mestizaje of cultural codes. Like the hybridized mode of enunciation of black diaspora filmmaking in Britain,[33] and the Latin American cinema, *Born in East L.A.* extracts from an aesthetic tradition that is indigenous to the American continent. As I have noted elsewhere, the cultural configurations of the continent led to profound renovations in the conceptualization of culture to the extent that Latin American filmmakers, for instance, logically re-formulated a new aesthetics from the indigenous tendencies.[34] Moreover, for the New Latin American Cinema movement, the emphasis has been on the theoretical and political space of *lo popular*.[35] Since 1958, the three components of the New Latin American Cinema have been expressed in terms of "nationalist, critical, and realist" films.[36] Because its filmmakers also sought to "interpret, express, and communicate" with the people, *lo popular* progressively formed a central theoretical and political tenet of the movement. In other words, a significant project has begun to emerge that links cultural politics to a "re-discovery" of *lo popular*. This space is not manifest transhistorically, but can only be discernible within the historical dynamic, and mestizaje is the term that refers to this process. Similar to the "creole" or "hybrid" articulations of British blacks, in Latin America mestizaje construes, in the words of Jesús Martín-Barbero, "the intermingling, the impurity of relations between ethnic group and class, of domination and complicity."[37]

To these cultural configurations, the Chicana/o experience contributes an additional layer of complexity: the historical circumstance that the now-discarded model "internal colonialism" attempted to explain.[38] The social history of the population of Mexican origin includes both the loss of a large part of Mexico's territory during the Mexican-American War of 1848 (conquest) and the subsequent waves of immigration to the United States during this century. Consequently, the Chicano/a collective memory articulates, in addition to the histories of colonialism and imperialism, those of conquest, marginalization, and domination within territories that, for many Chicana/os, are considered native (the Southwest). The formal expression of this historical development can be clearly recognized in the deliberate affirmation of bilingualism and biculturalism in Chicano/a vernacular aesthetics. It is precisely these multiaccentual forms and practices of "resistance" that are modulated by the "politics of representation" of Cheech Marin's *Born in East L.A.*

Yet *Born in East L.A.* goes one step further: its intertextuality refashions *lo popular* with commodified popular culture, centering both as axes of identity for late-twentieth-century Chicanas and Chicanos. In the music-video promo for the film ("Born in East L.A."), one of the ways Marin tries to make it back to East Los Angeles is through a sewer tunnel. As he looks into the tunnel his horrified facial expression evokes the laughter of viewers familiar with the film *El Norte*, where two immigrants came into the United States through a tunnel and were bitten by rats. In instances such as this parody the film offers a way out of cultural nationalism's disdain for dominant commercial culture and its tendency to fix meaning in one "true" path. Shuttling in between vernacular aesthetics and commodified popular culture, the filmmaker's acuity for the meaning of commodified culture in the everyday lives of Chicanos empowers those marginalized from the centers of power. In the words of Trinh T. Minh-ha:

This shuttling in-between frontiers is a working out of and an appeal to another sensibility, another consciousness of the condition of marginality: that in which marginality is the condition of the center.[39]

Indeed, contrary to the nihilism of certain strands of bourgeois avant-garde, Cheech Marin's popular aesthetic style affirms a profound respect for life, a humanism that so often radiates from the symbolic elaboration of everyday tragedies. After all, what is left after a day's hard work for below-subsistence wages but the laughter at the comedic reenactments of one's misfortunes and the momentary pleasure gained from commodified popular culture, or from the tradition of performance in the *carpas* and the dance halls? Yet in the film, as George Lipsitz recently reminded me, popular culture is both "affirmative and more a part of life than an escape from it." How does one transform this humor, this creative energy, into collective will and political action? *Born in East L.A.* uses comedy effectively, providing a cinematic experience whose pleasure derives from humor. At the very least, in its critique of dominant racist discourse about Chicanos, *Born in East L.A.* teaches us that the cultural struggle must also be fought and won on the commercial screen.

4

From Il(l)egal to Legal Subject Border Construction and Re-construction

> As soon as you move from the position of a named
> subject into the position of a naming subject, you have to
> remain alive to the renewed dangers of arrested
> meanings and fixed categories—in other words, of
> occupying the position of a sovereign subject.
>
> —Trinh T. Minh-ha[1]

From borderlands to border texts, border conflict and border crossings to border writing, border pedagogy and border feminism, the concept of "border" enjoys wide currency as a "paradigm of transcultural experience."[2] Representing an alternative way of conceptualizing cultural process in the late twentieth century—a time when people, media images, and information journey across the world at unprecedented rates—the category of border directs our attention to the spaces "within and between" what were once sanctified as "homogeneous" communities.[3]

Its recent popularity among intellectuals may lead us to conclude, as Henry Giroux notes about postmodernism, that border is perhaps the new "buzzword for the latest intellectual fashions."[4] For Chicanas and Chicanos (border residents, artists, and researchers) and also for Mexicans living on the borderlands, the concept has a longer history and a more politically charged meaning, referring to geopolitical configurations of power and to power relations within a cultural process. In this view, the border figures as an intrusive or invasive border, the division established after the Mexican-American War of 1848, that is, an illegitimately imposed separation. If we translate the Spanish word for border, *frontera*, literally into the English "frontier," we open up its equally older usage in the Anglo-American imaginary.[5] A central trope of Anglo-American desire for conquest and westward expansion, "frontier" metaphorically signifies "no-man's-land" (better yet, "no-white-man's-land," as in the Western genre), namely territories outside of white men's jurisdiction and, therefore, land available for private appropriation. In these two older historical forms, the border refers to a physical division between territories, divisions that were a consequence of material processes, including the westward expansion of capitalism through conquest and war. Thus, we are talking about historically and socially constructed physical borders, usually between geopolitical entities.

In Américo Paredes's account of "border-conflict" corridos and Gloria Anzaldúa's poetic meditations on border subjectivity, we are reminded that military conquest of Mexican-held territories transformed the Rio Grande region from a place of peaceful coexistence into a barbed line of demarcation.[6] Writing in 1958, Américo Paredes indicates:

> It was the Treaty of Guadalupe [1848] that added the final element of
> Rio Grande society, a border. The river, which had been a focal
> point, became a dividing line. Men were expected to consider their
> relatives and closest neighbors, the people just across the river, as
> foreigners in a foreign land.[7]

Whether this separation takes the form of a natural marker, like the Rio Grande, or an artificial one like the *alambre* (barbed wire), it is a historically imposed borderline that separates the United States from Mexico. Films such as *Raíces de Sangre* (1977) by Jesús Salvador Treviño, which deals with the maquiladoras (border assembly plants) on the U.S.-Mexico border, are guided by a concern with the effects of this illegitimate and artificial geopolitical border.

In the writings of cultural critics, the concept of border draws attention to the historically and socially constructed borders and spaces we inherit and that frame our discourses and social relations. For Sonia Saldívar-Hull, Chicana writer Gloria Anzaldúa's use of border deconstructs the exclusionary boundaries of white hegemonic feminism: "[Anzaldúa's] is a feminism that exists in a borderland not limited to geopolitical space, a feminism not acknowledged by hegemonic culture."[8] Similarly, Mexican performance artist Guillermo Gómez-Peña writes about the concept as a paradigm of transcultural experience in the following words: "Whenever or wherever two or more cultures meet—peacefully or violently—there is a border experience."[9] This usage of border pinpoints not just the spaces where cultures intersect but also the experience of "crossing," either as literal migration, that is, as the spatial movement of people across borders, or crossing as an effect of the cultural process of "mixing." In James Clifford's estimation, this sense of border crossing as mixing "represents aspects of interactive cultural process, of the power-charged, always-unequal entanglements of different populations in what Mary Louise Pratt has called 'contact zones.' "[10]

There are multiple ways of applying the concept of border in a study of Chicano and Chicana cinema, just as there are various manners in which Chicano films have themselves deployed borders. Features of this "interactive cultural process" especially pertinent for my initial discussion of border construction and re-construction included the mixing of cultural forms and practices and of the subject identities of border crossers. The films *Born in East L.A.* and *La Bamba* depict an alignment of multiple senses of the concept of borders, including the physical border (borderline between United States and Mexico), the spatial movement of border crossing, and border crossing as the mixing of cultural forms and subjectivities.

Border Re-construction

Whereas, as we have seen, the stories of *Born in East L.A.* and *La Bamba* differ, both films depict the border geopolitically, as the borderline between the United States and Mexico that the main characters, Rudy in *Born*, and Ritchie in *La Bamba*, are forced to cross. In contrast to Mexican immigrants whose spatial movement of crossing takes the form of a south to north pattern, the main subjects of these films cross in an inverse pattern, from north to south, and back again. Yet the border crossing south is, for Rudy and Ritchie, similar to the border crossing south (or deportation) of undocumented immigrants because neither Rudy nor Ritchie chooses to cross to Mexico voluntarily. In *Born in East L.A.*, Rudy is forced to cross the border through deportation by the dominant order, the INS; the familial order, embodied in Ritchie's older brother, Bob, compels Ritchie's border crossing.

The spatial movement of border crossings is implicated in climactic moments, and the journey south is crucial to the plot's development. For example, Ritchie Valens first hears the folk song "La Bamba" in a brothel in Tijuana; Rudy suffers firsthand the hardships of the border crossers in Tijuana. The circuitous nature of the border crossing (north to south to north), however, interrupts the homogeneity of the narrative economy. In other words, the circuitous spatial movement problematizes a simple reading of *La Bamba* as a film solely about the rise to fame and the death of Ritchie Valens, or of *Born in East L.A.* as a comedy about how a character makes it back home. The border crossing marks the subjects in important ways.

The changes in subject positioning that take place in both Rudy and Ritchie suggest that Chicano subjectivity resides in the space "between and among" cultural systems/orders—in a situation that Trinh T. Minh-ha describes as "the space in between, the interval to which established rules of boundaries never quite apply."[11] For instance, in various places *Born in East L.A.* sets up scenarios for its main character to affirm his distinctiveness from Mexicans. In the early part of the film, Rudy makes clear his difference from his cousin (whom he calls the "illegal"), and by extension his difference from immigrants across the border. From the point of view of *la migra*, as noted in the previous chapter, Rudy looks like one of "them" (the others). Rudy, in fact, attempts to convince the custom agent of his citizenship ("Americanness"), by referring to his cousin as an "illegal"—a ploy that fails because for the agent, Rudy "looks" more like them (Mexicans) than like US (Americans). His forced residence in Tijuana effects a transformation in Rudy's subject position. By living like an immigrant, experiencing the difficulties of trying to make it across, Rudy gains a new awareness. His transformation has a symbolic resonance at the level of political consciousness. The narrative resolution of the film, when Rudy returns not alone but accompanied by hundreds of undocumented immigrants, is, as I have argued, a "collective resolution." Yet the changes in Rudy, particularly in terms of his new political identity, signal the extent to which one's identity is fragile as it moves into borderlands that are crisscrossed with a variety of languages and experiences. The subject who first crossed over is not the same subject who returns across the borderline. In *Born in East L.A.*, the subject crosses back as a collective subject, as a people, thereby translating the ambivalence of cultural identity into a politics of political identification. Such a symbolic resolution is in most cases a difficult process, as the complexity of *La Bamba*'s narrative makes evident.

Ritchie figures as an accomplice with the dominant U.S. culture: he changes his name from Valenzuela to Valens, dates a young white woman, doesn't speak Spanish. Ritchie is the typical *agringado*, that is, he represents assimilation or the symbolic incorporation on dominant culture's terms. Bob (Ritchie's brother) embodies continuity with

a Mexican alternative knowledge system: he has been a frequent
"border crosser" to Mexico where his spiritual father (a curandero or
shaman) resides. Bob symbolizes the familial order that coerces Ritchie's own border crossing. Through this familial order, the traces of an
alternative countermemory are resurrected in Ritchie. By clothing Bob
in Chicano "authenticity," as a nonassimilated cultural resister who is
also marginalized by dominant society, and by figuring "authentic"
culture in a mythic elsewhere in Mexico, the film reproduces cultural
nationalism's tendency to return to the source.[12] Yet, the implicit con-
ceptual demand of this border crossing rests in the symbolic transformation of subject positioning because the journey signals a reconcili-
ation with a prior loss or a rupture. Crossing the border disrupts the
previously assimilated Ritchie, resurrecting a countermemory of Mexican music.[13] In the brothel, Ritchie displays more interest in the musicians playing "la bamba" than in the prostitutes Bob has lined up for
his pleasure. Later Ritchie returns to the United States determined to
record a rock version of the folk song.

The narrative resolution of *La Bamba* is cast in poetic irony: Ritchie,
the model success story who has attempted to assimilate, that is, the
brown version of whites, dies. Read poetically, assimilation metaphorically "kills" cultural tradition. His brother, the sign for marginal
yet "authentic" subjectivity, survives to tell the story.[14] Yet the product or the cultural form created from the instance of border crossing
survives the individual subject. In its hybridized and even appropriated rock and roll form, "La Bamba" exemplifies the cultural process
of transculturation—a term used by Cuban Fernando Ortiz and Uru-
guayan Angel Rama to refer to the multidirectionality of cultural influences.[15] In this sense borderlands represent the sites of crossing
that James Clifford indicates "assume circuits of regular interconnec-
tions: people, things, expressive cultural forms (music, food, etc.)."[16]

In terms of the subject positioning of its main characters, Rudy and
Ritchie, both films play with the precarious space of in-between-ness,
the border, thereby positing forms of transgression in which existing
borders forged in domination can be redefined. Figuratively, Chicano
subjectivity is located in the difference from dominant white (U.S.)
and Mexican cultures, but also in the similarities with both systems.
Thus, *Born in East L.A.* and *La Bamba* portray the border as a site
where identities and cultures intersect productively. Both films create
the conditions for their main subjects, but also for their spectator subjects, to become border crossers. Historical subjects become border
crossers, according to Henry Giroux, "in order to understand other-

ness in its own terms, and to further create borderlands in which diverse cultural resources allow for the fashioning of new identities within existing configurations of power."[17] *La Bamba* and *Born in East L.A.* deploy and align the concept of border to fashion Chicano subject positions productively, whereas *The Ballad of Gregorio Cortez* creates a new border between subjects, cultural discourses, and social orders.

Constructing the Border

The Ballad of Gregorio Cortez (1984) is a film about the persecution by Anglo-Texans of Gregorio Cortez at the turn of the century. Cortez was wrongfully accused of stealing a horse. His attempted arrest led to a shoot-out that claimed the lives of Sheriff Glover and Romaldo Cortez. After shooting the sheriff in self-defense, Gregorio Cortez eluded an inflamed posse of hundreds of Texas Rangers. The film shows how the newly constituted Anglo-Texan legal and police systems reacted to native Mexicans. In its critical portrayal of Anglo-Texans, their lynching tactics, and the racism of the judicial system against Mexicans, *The Ballad of Gregorio Cortez* captures the "intrusive border," namely, the political apparatus, instituted after the Mexican-American War of 1848 by Anglo immigrants (intruders to the region) to police the native Tejanos.

The film draws from Américo Paredes's classic account of the "corrido de Gregorio Cortez," a ballad that memorialized the heroic tale of a peaceful man "fighting for his right with his pistol in his hand."[18] Based on the original script written by Victor Villaseñor, later rewritten as a screenplay by Robert Young and Villaseñor, the film is an adaptation of the actual events recounted in chapter 3 of Paredes's book-length study. The film then speaks about and to the experience of racism that affected (and continues to affect) the public life of Chicanos/as in this country. Despite Young's self-reflexive antiracism politics, the most striking feature of the film is the subordination of Cortez within narrative discourse. The character hardly speaks on screen. Rather, he is segregated from spaces where dramatic dialogue predominates. Cortez's silence is moreover significant because the film privileges Anglo-Texans as the subjects of verbal discourse, thus relegating Cortez to the status of a mute-silent Other. Several Chicano critics have been uniformly negative in their assessment of the implications of this cinematic choice. We have argued that Gregorio Cortez's marginality from the verbal part of cinematic discourse directly corresponds to the elision of the Chicano point of view in the film.[19]

How is it that a film that denounces the illegality of the legislative frontier created by Anglo-Texans to subjugate Mexicans ultimately ends up denying a subject voice in the narrative to the central agent of the historical event on which the film is based? A partial answer can easily be deduced from the title of the film. In other words, as the title makes evident, the film is not entirely about Gregorio Cortez, but rather about the ballad of the hero, and hence about the problem of representation or more precisely about the problem of "translation." Cortez is a pretext for the critical question of translation that informs the film from beginning to end. As Carl Gutiérrez-Jones explains, the film sets up its plot in terms of the problem of "how to account for translation between Mexican and Anglo-Texan culture in an Anglo-Texan legal framework."[20] Because the legal framework of Anglo-Texans derived from the "implicit whiteness and maleness" of the original U.S. Constitution,[21] there is no way to account for the legal position of a culture that is "nonwhite." Therefore, undergirding Cortez's position as the object of cinematic discourse is this very illegality of Mexican society within dominant culture's discursive framework. The very structuring principles of the film stage a modernist "system of power that authorizes certain representations while blocking, prohibiting and invalidating others."[22] Gregorio Cortez is an object of narrative discourse because the film stages a border between cultural systems. This border is reinforced by certain contradictions that the experimental documentary style of the film perhaps unwittingly enacts.

The Ballad of Gregorio Cortez was shot on location in Gonzalez, Texas. Prior to this film, director Robert Young was best known for a series of hard-hitting political films. Young's affinity for the cinema verité tradition of interest in ordinary people is evident from the themes of his films as well as from his casting choices. Many local residents played minor roles in The Ballad. From Angola to Alambrista to Short Eyes, Young blends cinema verité techniques with realist codes, poignantly treating topical issues within a cinema of open commitment and analysis. Young's experience in the documentary tradition is clearly brought to bear in The Ballad of Gregorio Cortez.

Instrumental in the development of its plot is the appropriation of codes from the documentary form. Hayden White defines plot as the "structure of relationships by which the events contained in the account are endowed with meaning by being identified as parts of an integrated whole."[23] In the first part of the film, the plot follows a discontinuous, bifurcating path, evoking the flavor of a Western as the early scenes suggest the classic crime and horse chase. Certain experimental documentary techniques undergird the structure of relationships in the film: the journalist character, the interview mode, and active counterpointing in the text.

The events contained in the account, namely its story line, deal with the chase of Gregorio Cortez by posses of Anglo-Texans, the witnesses' accounts of the event that led to the chase, and the trial/conviction of Cortez. The film opens dramatically, moving swiftly from one short scene to another: the chase on horseback of Cortez by Texas Rangers; a group of Anglo-Texans meeting the arrival of two bodies pulled on a wagon; the lynching of a Mexican-Texan by Anglo-Texans. Following this series of establishing scenes, the dramatic action slows down, allowing us to tie together the narrative threads: Texas Rangers are chasing Gregorio Cortez; two men have been shot; Anglos, fueled by racism, retaliate against Mexicans.

From the beginning, *The Ballad of Gregorio Cortez* explicitly adopts a political perspective in favor of Gregorio Cortez. Even as the opening intertitle states that what follows are "different versions of the same event," the resort to experimental documentary techniques effectively discredits certain versions of the event while privileging that of Cortez. The scene immediately following the shorter establishing scenes, which shows a Texas Ranger reading the newspaper aloud, calls attention to press distortions of the events. The Ranger quotes from the newspaper account, "suspects are headed for the Rio Grande," whereas the visual imagery shifts to a shot of a lone man on horseback. Thus, the newspaper account of the events differs dramatically from the visual portrayal of the events.

As the outline of the sequence of narrative action illustrates, the story unfolds in a nonlinear pattern, ricocheting back and forth between different narrative spaces and times. It is precisely this nonlinearity that buttresses the major narrative strategy of the film, its attentiveness to the reconstructed nature of verbal discourse. As characters tell an account of reality, the film deconstructs the mechanisms operative in the construction of that account. The interrelationship of three elements from the documentary form in the service of this strategy is especially worthy of closer examination.

Contrary to viewer expectation, character identification does not rest with Gregorio Cortez. The film draws heavily from the neorealist experimental narrative form of Orson Welles's *Citizen Kane*, where the journalist character literally stands in for the critical eye of the filmmaker/camera. Moreover, the film reproduces the form of bond-

ing most common in commercial cinema: character-viewer identification with the journalist, Bill Blakely. The representation of the journalist character functions as a plot device in the service of truth or
objectivity. The film positions Bill Blakely, a reporter for the *San Antonio Express*, as a distant "objective" observer. Our identification
rests with the journalist, we weigh the facts, evaluate different versions of reality as recounted by the witnesses. In his capacity as an
impartial observer, Blakely symbolizes the discourse of objectivity en-
grained in modern journalism.[24] In many respects, the deliberate imaging of the journalist character in the process of fact-gathering provides a "factual" basis for the film.

The veracity of the film's factual basis is further accentuated by the
effective use of another important convention taken from the documentary form: the interviewing technique, a primary artifact of audiovisual culture here used to structure the narrative discourse of the
film. The image of the journalist is inseparable from the function he
performs within the text, namely, reportage through observation and
interview. Significant segments of narrative action move forward in
those segments where the journalist is depicted in the process of
gathering facts, thereby further wedding viewer identification with
Blakely. As Blakely conducts his interviews with members of the
Texas Rangers, past events visually unfold before the viewer. Consequently, through the intervention of the objective impartial journalist,
conducting interviews of witnesses, the limits of memory and witness
testimony as "objective source" become increasingly evident.[25]

Blakely's interviews raise viewer doubts about the credibility of
some of the Anglo-Texan witnesses. As Blakely questions one of the
Rangers, we learn about excessive drinking by the Texas Rangers during their raid of the Robledo home, forcing us to conclude that the
Rangers' carelessness (and not Cortez's gun) resulted in the death of
one of their own. Blakely's interviews also reveal the racist sentiments
of Anglo-Texans. For example, to Blakely's question about a lynching
at the Robledo home, Boone Choate responds: "Sure, we had a little
necktie party. But we didn't croak him." More important, the use of
these two staples of reportage, fact-gathering and interviewing,
within the narrative is further accentuated by skillful editing and camera work.

In the style of the politically committed film documentary, *The Ballad of Gregorio Cortez* visually counterpoints verbal claims of the witnesses interviewed by Blakely. The filmmaker deploys evocative
counterpoint, calling attention to the gaps between what witnesses

say and the "truth" the film puts forward. Ranger Frank Fly's statement "Tracks don't lie" (which sounds like "facts") re-affirms in verbal discourse the film's visual imagery: that there was no gang of Mexicans, only the solitary Cortez. In several places within the film, the juxtaposition of visual images as counterpoint to Anglo-Texan claims effectively discredits their accounts. We have already noted the subversive discrepancy between the Ranger's reading of the newspaper and the visually contradictory evidence of the lone Cortez.

The nuanced counterpoint between verbal and visual discourse is rendered especially effective by the repeated rendition of a single scene with slight variations in camera angles, editing, and duration of shots. Earlier I described the scene depicting a group of Anglo-white characters who witness the arrival of two Rangers who are pulling a horse-drawn wagon that carries two bodies. The same scene is depicted again as a flashback-recall during Bill Blakely's interview of Boone Choate. In the first depiction of the scene, the Ranger's comments to the Anglos ("I'm sick and tired of all this senseless violence. What are we going to do about it?") are followed by the scene depicting the lynching of a Mexican-Texan who is clearly innocent. The editing of these two events in a linear-causal sequence within the narrative draws attention to the vengeful violence on the part of Anglo-Texans. Yet, in the repeated depiction of this scene, during Choate's flashback-recall, the scene is altered, for it is rendered in longer shots, from different angles, and edited in different places. More important, the discrepancy between the "actual" narrative event (in real time) and its recollection by Boone is further accentuated by the following omission. Boone does not mention his inflammatory words or the lynching. This nuanced counterpoint thus underscores for viewers the selective nature of testimony, for the truth of Boone Choate's spoken comments collide with the truth the filmmakers permit us to see visually.

The major work of the film, then, is to discredit the verbal discourse of Anglo-Texans. The neorealist codes of experimental documentary form, investigative journalism, interviewing, and active counterpointing in the text deconstruct verbal/spoken accounts, leading spectators to interrogate critically the process of constructing the "truth." This self-reflexive strategy underscores the limits of testimony and memory as a source of objective truth, particularly as it is written (newspaper) or spoken (witnesses) within existing configurations of power and privilege. By "analyzing the process by which

Gregorio Cortez (Edward James Olmos) leaves the Gonzalez jail to serve his prison sentence in *The Ballad of Gregorio Cortez*. Courtesy of Embassy Pictures.

judgments are made"[26] the filmmakers deconstruct offensive regimes of racism and call attention to the reconstructed nature of reality. The filmmakers' interest in how dominant culture normalizes the truth explains *The Ballad of Gregorio Cortez*'s overwhelming focus on the Anglo-Texan characters—a political project that also explains the reason why Cortez is not centered as the subject of the film. Carl Gutiérrez-Jones makes the following observation about the narrative structure of the film:

> By allowing the different stories to be told and not, for instance, presenting the film solely from Cortez's point of view, the film's makers were creating a structure explicitly opposed to the mock-dialogue between Cortez and Sheriff Morris, in which Boone's ventriloquism eliminated Cortez's voice, metaphorically killing him long before the sheriff had a chance.[27]

Gutiérrez-Jones correctly points to the structural asymmetries between two modes of translation or representation of events: the film permits (authorizes) the presence of multiple voices; Boone's account prohibits (outlaws) the presence of Cortez's voice. However, the asymmetries are valid for the verbal/textual part of cinematic discourse. Unlike written text, point of view in cinema depends heavily on the "look," and on both visual and verbal systems of representation. It is in this intersection between multiple points of view (including Cortez's) and Cortez's visual depiction where the filmmakers in fact stage a structure explicitly symmetrical to Boone's ventriloquism. In this case, the filmmakers function as stand-ins for Boone's ventriloquism. Specifically, the procedure of decentering Cortez's verbal point of view from the main subject position cannot be disassociated from the ways in which his image is visually made present. The film's ventriloquism of the Western colonial gaze "metaphorically" kills Cortez's subjectivity.

From a "Figure of Masculine Heroics" to an "Infantilized Other"[28]

The film maps the historicity of its account by opening with an intertitle that locates its basis in historical fact: "At the turn of the century, Anglos and Mexicans lived side by side in a state of fear and tension." From this referential level that includes historical figures, *The Ballad of Gregorio Cortez* moves to the metaphorical level: the train corrido. The superimposition of the corrido (the actual singing of the ballad off-screen and a translation of its stanzas on screen) onto the frontal image of the train functions as a figurative border between two cultures. Given its role as a technology that facilitated the expansion of capitalism and white immigrant conquest of the West, the train is a major trope in Anglo culture. The corrido is a trope for Mexican-Tejanos because it was a symbolic form of resistance to white supremacy in the nineteenth and early twentieth centuries.[29] The border between two cultures is thus established literally and figuratively, that is to say, in historical fact and with symbolic motifs such as the train and the corrido.

This border is then fixed in narrative discourse in the first dramatic scene of the film. A shot of Gregorio Cortez, chased by men on horseback, culminates with a close-up shot of a man with a badge. This scene stages the border between the Law and the Outlaw. Yet what is at stake here is more than a reference to physical borders. Henry Giroux states the issue clearly:

> These are not only physical borders, they are cultural borders
> historically constructed and socially organized within rules and
> regulations that limit and enable particular identities, individual
> capacities, and social forms.[30]

The film reproduces the very borders it seeks to undermine. The physical border between groups (Anglos and Mexicans), the symbolic (train and corrido), the legal (Law and Outlaw), the linguistic (English and Spanish) are all buttressed by an aesthetic border or divide between the "rules and regulations" that enable the identities of white-Anglo characters and contain or prohibit the identities of Cortez and the Mexican community.

Early criticism of the film centered on its failure to render the Mexican community in any meaningful way. Historian Tatcho Mindiola writes:

> The audience does not come away from the film with a sense of how
> Mexicans in South Texas lived in 1901 and more importantly, how
> they felt and reacted to the events involving Gregorio Cortez. A
> sense of injustice against Mexicans is conveyed but again it comes
> from Anglos and the manner in which they acted and talked about
> Mexicans. How the Mexican community feels about the injustices
> they encounter is never present.[31]

The Ballad of Gregorio Cortez has also been faulted for omitting the role of the Mexican community in the defense of Cortez. Guillermo Hernández notes that "the public is thus deprived of essential knowledge to understand the extent of support for Cortez in the Mexican community. The absence of any references to the journalist Pablo G. Cruz, who through his newspaper, 'El Regidor,' waged a spirited and effective campaign on behalf of Cortez is inexcusable."[32] Hernández further draws attention to the omission of details about Cortez's "questionable personal life," including his divorce, love affairs, and support for the Mexican dictator Huerta during the Mexican revolution.[33] Indicating that Cortez was a "competent bilingual," Hernández ironically comments on Cortez's language proficiency:

> Whatever the reason and intention of the filmmakers might have been, the consequence of this dramatic choice is the representation of Gregorio as an inarticulate and stoic victim whose tragedy would not have occurred had he enjoyed the benefits of bilingual education.[34]

One could characterize the omission of certain factual events as minor—the stuff that usually plagues artistic adaptations of historical events. (How often have many of us heard or said, "The novel or history was more accurate than the film?") However, given the historical absence of Chicanos in the regimes of representation, the film's omission of the Mexican perspective reinforces a border of power relations where Mexicans are generalized out of existence.

In this respect, Paredes's study is noteworthy for its re-covery of Texas-Mexicans as the voices and agents of socially symbolic discourse. Paredes's study is more than a history of Gregorio Cortez and the corrido. Although *With His Pistol in His Hand* does provide readers a penetrating historical account of racism at the turn of the century, Paredes establishes the contours for forms of resistance embodied in the artistic practices of the Mexican community, exploring the interrelationship of hegemonic domination and counterhegemonic resistance. Because ballads like "el corrido de Gregorio Cortez" emerge during the period of intense racial conflict between Anglos/white intruders and the native Mexican population, Chicano scholars such as José Limón characterize the corrido as the first artistic expression of social protest by Chicanos.[35] Literary theorist Ramón Saldívar notes the import of Paredes's work in the following words:

> With impeccable scholarship and imaginative subtlety, Paredes' study of the border ballads that concern the historical figure of Gregorio Cortez and his solitary armed resistance to the injustices Mexicans faced in Anglo Texas, may be said to have invented the very possibility of a narrative community, a complete and legitimate Mexican American persona, whose life of struggle and discord was worthy of being told.[36]

The point raised by this appreciation of Paredes's work is that corridos privileged the voice and the sentiments protesting the injustices Mexicans faced in Anglo Texas. Corridos are thus symbolic forms of cultural and political resistance that articulate the narrative point of view of the Mexican community at large.

The "border conflict" corridos express the Tejano (Mexicano) point of view, but *The Ballad of Gregorio Cortez* is faulted precisely for inverting this relation. In Tatcho Mindiola's estimation, the film deals primarily "with the Anglo community and its reaction to the killing of an Anglo sheriff by Gregorio Cortez." *The Ballad of Gregorio Cortez* is "not told through the eyes of the Mexican community," but is instead "slanted toward Anglo point of view."[37] As we have seen, this emphasis on Anglo-white characters partially corresponds to the film's deconstructive thrust. Taken on their own terms, however, "el corrido de Gregorio Cortez" and Paredes's account of its history function as points of departure for the film, deployed strategically: they inform the film's political perspective in favor of Gregorio Cortez. For one, the corrido's melody serves as the major aural motif of the film. Even though the conventional disclaimer is included at the beginning of the film, *The Ballad of Gregorio Cortez* does not contest Cortez's version of the events. As we have seen, the primary impetus of the plot is to discredit the Anglo-Texans' points of view. The film privileges Cortez's account of the event as the film's final point of view, but the major evidence in favor of Cortez has already been established through visual discourse.

In an audiovisual culture, the image is regarded as primary, as the ultimate guarantee of truth. The filmmaker's desire to represent the "truth" visually derives from the potency of this ideological claim. In the textual system of *The Ballad of Gregorio Cortez*, verbal discourse is contradictory and opaque whereas visual images assume the transparency generally attributed to classic fictional cinema. Visual discourse therefore possesses an ontological priority over verbal discourse. Offering a more "adequate picture of reality" than spoken discourse, visual representation appears to unfold as an unmediated event before our eyes. Rather than countering verbal/spoken accounts verbally, the filmmakers pay a great deal of attention to visual images. Slavoj Zizek's comments about zero-degree filmmaking are especially pertinent for the film: "We remain captive of the illusion that we witness a homogeneous continuity of action registered by the 'neutral' camera."[38] The images that contest verbal discourse are rendered in a neorealist aesthetic that "presupposes the reality of the world prior to its documentation."[39] Given that the opacity of verbal discourse is unraveled by visual evidence, the film reproduces the "effect of natural-ness" embedded in cinematic realism. The images function as the film's "ultimate guarantee of truth." On this side of the aesthetic di-vide where the image as truth resides, we find Gregorio Cortez as the visible but silent subject, therefore, the image-object of cinematic dis-course. Because we accompany quite literally Blakely's perspective, Cortez's existence depends heavily upon the "look" and the "read-ing" of the white journalist. The nearly total portrayal of Cortez as pure image forces us, in the words of Henry Giroux, to "interrogate how the colonizing of differences by dominant groups is expressed and sustained through representations in which the humanity of the Other is either ideologically disparaged or ruthlessly denied."[40] In sharp contrast to the film, the humanity of Mexican culture has been celebrated and authorized in the writings of Chicano and Chicana critics of Anglo Texas. Paredes, for example, positioned Cortez as the agent of the historical event and as the embodiment of the sentiments of people who were central subjects of narrative and historical dis-courses.

Although the concept of the hero of border corridos was certainly patriarchal, Gregorio Cortez nonetheless epitomized the feature that Renato Rosaldo terms the "warrior hero as figure of resistance." As Rosaldo adds, the warrior hero "enables Paredes to develop a concep-tion of manhood rhetorically endowed with the mythic capacity to combat Anglo-Texan anti-Mexican prejudice."[41] This valiant "figure of masculine heroics and resistance to white supremacy," riding on a horse with a "pistol in his hand," made sense during a particular mo-ment in history when the patriarchal orientation of Chicano scholar-ship remained hegemonic and uncontested. By the late 1970s, Chi-cana writers and critics provided alternative visions of resistance that were certainly less male-centered, thereby rendering obsolete the epic hero. Ramón Saldívar adds that "the corrido is decisively linked to the heroic past of cultural resistance"—an insight that allows us to pin-point the historical impossibility of an epic male hero after a certain historical moment in time.[42] By re-affirming this impossibility, I do not mean to imply that it could not be done, or that it has not been attempted. I am simply drawing attention to the regressive aspect of this type of hero. Reworking the forms of cultural resistance into more viable alternatives for the present demands that we critically in-terrogate the limitations of the epic heroic figure. For some critics, *The Ballad of Gregorio Cortez* seems to do just that.[43] The film's departure from the male-hero concept of a previous era of Chicano cultural pol-

itics weighed heavily in Edward James Olmos's motives for portraying Cortez differently. During the discussion after the screening of
the film at UCLA in 1983, Olmos stated that in his characterization he
"intended to portray Gregorio Cortez as a 'human being' rather than
as a 'macho.' "[44]

In efforts to downplay the excessive masculinity of the "warrior
hero," the filmmakers ultimately fashion a textual strategy with certain "colonial overtones." The observations by Ella Shohat on West-
ern-produced films on the "Orient" are equally applicable to the positioning of Mexicans as Others. Citing Edward Said, Shohat indicates
that non-Occident cultures are portrayed as "simple, unself-con-
scious and susceptible to facile apprehension." Shohat adds:

> Any possibility of dialogic interaction and dialectical representation
> of the East/West relation is excluded from the outset. The films
> reproduce a colonialist mechanism by which the Orient, rendered
> devoid of any active historical or narrative role, becomes the object of
> study and spectacle.[45]

The neorealist experimental form of *The Ballad of Gregorio Cortez* constructs a modernist border predicated on the division between nature
and culture. Similar to films about the Orient, the symbolic economies
of race derive heavily from this division between nature and culture.
Even sympathetic portrayals of non-Western "natives" are for the
most part premised on their proximity to nature, to a prior, infantlike
innocence that is disturbed by the parental violence of "Western civilization."[46] *The Ballad of Gregorio Cortez* likewise celebrates the "noble
savage." In the film, Mexicans are "rendered devoid of any active historical or narrative role" and are depicted as the victims of a violent
"intrusive" civilization.

With colonial overtones, the filmmakers visually portray Cortez as
"close to the earth," as the "noble savage" who confronts the domes-
ticating technology of Anglo civilization. The climactic scene of the
Texas Rangers' chasing Cortez both on horseback and on train best
exemplifies this strategy. In this scene, the confrontation is literal and
metaphorical. The train's powerful image (Anglo culture) confronts
the equally potent sound track of the melody to "el corrido de Gregorio Cortez" (Mexican culture). In a triumphant denouement, Cortez
(Mexicans) out"foxes" the posse of hundreds of Texas Rangers but
also the metaphorical symbol of Western "civilization." Cortez's ani-
mallike closeness to nature is captured in the imagery of his bond
with horses, which serve as his sole sources of meaningful interaction

in the film. The Western colonial gaze is further accentuated by images of Cortez's cunning ability to survive in the wilderness of the
Texas wastelands. One scene in particular captures Cortez's innocence as the noble savage.

Midway into the film, Cortez encounters a lone cowboy who
shares his campsite meal with Cortez. Clearly hungry and tired, Cortez devours the meat, at first ravenously but then shifting to the cowboy's command, "Slow down." In the telescoped passage of time we
see that Cortez has decided to stay the night. The entire dialogue in
the scene is rather a monologue by the cowboy, who reveals his various exploits with women. Even though Cortez is obviously fatigued,
he remains awake during this fireside monologue. At the end of the
scene, Cortez shows his appreciation by giving the cowboy a knife
and, in an infantile innocence, pronounces his only utterance of the
entire scene: "Gracias."

The Ballad of Gregorio Cortez's deconstruction of the legislative frontier of Anglo Texas is plagued by a certain liberal nostalgia for the "noble savage" prior to Anglo penetration. The film reproduces a master
narrative and hegemonic discourse in which Gregorio Cortez suffers
the fate of being generalized out of existence by virtue of his visible
yet silent presence. The Western colonialist inclination to project the
non-West as feminine is equally applicable to the positioning of Gregorio Cortez on the nature side of a Western binary opposition between nature and culture.

As we have seen, the single locus of subjectivity in the film is the
journalist Bill Blakely, who is in the final instance dialectically linked
to the camera, the Western colonial gaze. In its marginalization of
Gregorio Cortez's voice and the subordination of his point of view,
The Ballad of Gregorio Cortez is complicit with Eurocentric articulations
of power that historically construct and socially organize borders
where dominant culture owns the language and in which the Other
remains outside of language. In the final analysis, like its title, *The Ballad of Gregorio Cortez* is a "translation" of Mexican culture by the white
colonial gaze.

Crossing the Geopolitical Border

The rigorous application of border, border crossing, and borderlands
as concepts of transcultural experiences has not translated well for the
analysis of the actual social conditions of the vast majority of "border
crossers," the undocumented immigrants who cross the U.S.-Mexico

border daily, nor has it done so for the actual border inhabitants who literally live on the borderlands on a day-to-day basis.[47] Indeed, one finds a great deal of "fantasy" in the theoretical application of border in that the concept seems more like a kind of privileged "tourism" practiced by those who are not subjected to the deplorable living and working conditions on the borderlands. A case in point is Emily Hicks's otherwise eloquent study of border writing. Defining border writing as "the differences in reference codes between two or more cultures," Hicks adds, "It depicts, therefore, a kind of realism that approaches the experience of border crossers, those who live in a bilingual, bicultural, biconceptual reality."[48] Among the historical subjects of this bicultural experience whom Hicks privileges are the coyotes (persons who smuggle undocumented immigrants across the border) because "their lives depend on their ability to survive in the interstices of two cultures."[49]

Border writing for Hicks is thus a framework for the analysis of cultural process, that is, cultural and not physical borders, in the works of such Latin American writers as Gabriel García Márquez and Luisa Valenzuela, and Chicano and Chicana writers such as Alurista, Gloria Anzaldúa, Rubén Medina, and Gina Valdés. While I am well aware of the allegorical thrust of Hicks's project, the fantasy operative stems from her choice of analogies, namely, her radical attempt to read the coyote as "shaman" or "psychic healer."[50]

Hicks reads the coyote's transgression of the Law as smuggler as a metaphor for writers. Similar to coyotes, according to Hicks, writers operate like "bicultural smugglers"; the coyote/shaman serves as an allegorical figure for a writing process that performs a "psychic healing" of the reader.[51] This imaginative procedure can only be sustained through the erasure of the coyote's actual entanglements in regimes of physical violence and exploitation. The coyote's transgression before U.S. (and Mexican) Law and his (most coyotes are male) ability to maneuver outside legal jurisdiction also grant him absolute/ inordinate power over the subjects he smuggles across. Coyotes are often accused of unrelenting violence against immigrants, of rape, of abandoning people in desolate places without food or water. Films about the experience of border crossing, such as *Born in East L.A.* and *El Norte*, have tended to emphasize the more negative underside of coyotes.

Rather than celebrating the coyote's transgression of the Law or romanticizing his role as smuggler, in *Raíces de Sangre* (directed by Jesús Salvador Treviño) the coyote appears as the figure of exploitation and abuse on the borderlands. In an innovative, fragmented, nonlinear narrative structure, where the ambiguity of the opening sequence must be read against the ominous certainty of the film's narrative closure, *Raíces de Sangre* tells parallel stories. On the Mexican side, the film deals with the working conditions of Mexican workers at a U.S.-owned maquiladora (garment assembly plant) and focuses on the lives of Rosa and Adolfo Mejía. Another story unfolds on the U.S. side of the border, where Chicana and Chicano activists of "Barrio Unido" work to unionize the employees of the Morris Garment Factory, the maquiladora across the border.[52]

A divergent characterization of coyotes to that of Emily Hicks is made available by the opening and closing scenes of *Raíces de Sangre*. Here the coyote is neither a shaman nor a romantic transgressor before the Law, but an absolute and unrelenting violator of human rights. The opening shot depicts a truck followed by a car, riding on a dimly lit road. The truck pulls over, a man walks to the back and unlocks a padlock, leaving the door sealed. As he walks away, voices are heard coming from the inside. The following scene portrays two U.S. policemen opening the back of the truck and discovering several dead passengers. We learn in the subsequent scene, through a radio broadcast, that over twenty undocumented immigrants have been found asphyxiated after they were abandoned on a hot desert road on the U.S. side of the border.[53] Yet not until the end of the film do spectators grasp the solemn impact of the coyote's transgressions.

The couple in Mexico, Rosa and Adolfo Mejía, have lost their jobs at the Morris maquiladora and decide to cross the border into the United States, leaving their children in Mexico. Prior to this decision, the narrative deals with the Mejías' working environment at the assembly plant and their contacts with union organizers, for which they were fired by the plant foreman. In crossing to the United States, they unknowingly contract with the coyote (who is also the foreman at the Morris assembly plant), and they enter the same truck portrayed at the beginning of the film. When the foreman/coyote closes the door of the truck, spectators are positioned in a privileged place for, unlike the Mejías, we know that his action literally and figuratively seals the fate of the couple. This nonlinearity of the opening and closing scenes of the film intensifies the effects of its narrative closure. The final shots of the scene portray the last moments in the lives of the Mejías, the painful drama inside the truck, which earlier had appeared as disembodied voices hidden from our view by the shots of the exterior.

In this gruesome manner, *Raíces de Sangre* provides a stunning indictment of the fate of immigrants in the hands of coyotes. Undoubtedly, a coyote's biculturalism, as Hicks has indicated, stems from his "ability to survive in the interstices of two cultures." There is, however, a dual side to this border culture, which James Clifford describes as its "deep utopic/distopic tension."[54] If we consider the political dimension of this "interstice" and not simply its metaphorical/allegorical quality, as the material domain or space that must also guarantee human rights indiscriminately, then its distopic elements become more evident. Coyotes' livelihoods depend not just on their ability to live on the border of two cultures, but more precisely on the fact that they exist beyond the legislative frontiers of both. The fact that coyotes are not subjected to any Law, but instead operate outside of legal jurisdiction, requires that we trust wholeheartedly in the individual coyote's self-regulation and respect for human rights. *Raíces de Sangre* was based on the many actual cases where coyotes have shown total disregard for human lives. In the summer of 1992, the *New York Times* published a report about some of these incidents. The creation of a special Mexican police group called the Beta Team in Baja California, to protect the human rights of immigrants on the borderlands, responds to the abuses perpetrated by both the U.S. border patrol and coyotes. These abuses include beatings, murder, theft, and the raping of women.[55]

From Il(l)egal to Legal Subject

Raíces de Sangre deploys the concept of the border literally (an actual image) in order to focus on its illegitimacy, thereby making problematic the dominant notion of citizenship. The film is noteworthy for its attempts to expand "citizenship," particularly evident by its narrative strategy of contrasting ambiguous (disembodied and unidentified voices from a truck) at the beginning of the film with the certainty of their identity in the closing scene (i.e., images of the Mejías, dying inside the truck). This common form of character-spectator identification forces us to confront the humanity of the narrative subjects. In other words, spectator identification with the Mejías, secured through a fairly typical mode of narration, positions us critically. For all its conventionality, this narrative strategy nevertheless forces us to "look at mutual respect," as Mary G. Dietz argues about citizenship in general, "as a model of the kind of bond we might expect from, or hope to nurture in, democratic citizens," and in which respect for human lives is certainly a central tenet.[56] Yet the conventional code of spectator-character identification is moreover a viable strategy in the film because it gives subject voice to undocumented immigrants. In securing this identification with subjects who happen not to have legal documents of residency, *Raíces de Sangre* undermines and critiques dominant culture's terms for Mexican immigrants, "illegal aliens." James Cockford points to the racist underpinnings of this term by writing:

> If so many employers and all consumers depend so heavily on these people, then why is it that they are viewed as a "problem" or as "illegals"? Human beings can *do* illegal things, but can a human being actually *be* illegal?[57]

In many ways, the narrative closure of the film, depicting Mexicans and Chicanos in a protest march, as subjects from both sides of the border who are unified yet divided by barbed wire, interrogates the fundamental illegality, not just of human beings ("illegal" aliens) but of that very borderline constructing their illegality. This literal image of the border, where both groups confront each other with clenched fists, figuratively makes visible the filmmaker's refusal of the distinction between Chicanos/as and Mexicans—a distinction brought about by the illegal imposition of the barbed wire. The parallel story lines, divided geopolitically by a literal border (*el alambre*), intersect in the political and ideological borderlands staged by the film. Its visual rendition of Chicanos/as and Mexicans unified against the border assembly plants captures the extent to which both groups are entangled in regimes of economic inequality and political exploitation. In so doing, the film maps a "distinctly political consciousness." Dietz makes very clear the connection between political consciousness and citizenship:

> The only practice that can generate and reinforce such a consciousness is . . . the practice of acting politically, of engaging with other citizens in determining and pursuing individual and common interests for the public good.[58]

By portraying Mexicans and Chicanos/as together, "acting politically" and "pursuing common interests," *Raíces de Sangre* critically challenges the legitimacy of the "American" political-economic constitution of citizenship. The film's interrogation of the dominant notion of citizenship is similar to Chicano and other Latino political and cultural movements of the past two decades whose works, according to Kathleen Newman, have centered on rearticulating the "national redefinition of citizenship as citizenship in a multicultural society."[59] *Raíces de Sangre* speaks to an alternative notion of citizenship, one that is premised not on "white male embodiment" or on "property ownership,"[60] but on Chantal Mouffe and Ernesto Laclau's notion of citizenship as a "form of political identity."[61]

The reference to the "border" in films such as *El Norte* (1983, directed by Gregory Nava), *Alambrista* (1977, directed by Robert Young), and *Esperanza* (1985, directed by Sylvia Morales), which focus on the lives of border crossers on the U.S. side, similarly questions the purported illegality of immigrants. Filmed from the point of view of immigrants, *El Norte*, *Alambrista*, and *Esperanza* give subject voice to immigrants from south of the border, recounting the obstacles they confront on a daily basis. The films portray immigrants' own perspectives on issues ranging from economic exploitation and impoverished living conditions to their relentless persecution by the *migra* (INS). Each of these films deals with the social condition of inequality, but *Break of Dawn* (1988, directed by Isaac Artenstein) confronts more explicitly the muddled entanglement of geopolitical border and citizenship.[62]

Break of Dawn tells the true story of Pedro J. Gonzalez (played by Mexican singer/actor Oscar Chavez), a telegraph operator for the general Pancho Villa who crossed the border with his wife (played by Mexican actress María Rojo) in 1928.[63] Gonzalez lands a job with an English radio station in Los Angeles, reading commercials in Spanish, and later becomes the show host of a "block-time" program in Spanish, "Los Madrugadores" ("The Early Risers"). As the first Spanish-language radio personality in Los Angeles, Gonzalez becomes an instant hit with the large Mexican population of L.A. during the thirties. Yet his on-air opposition to "Operation Deportation"—the U.S. Department of Labor's project for deporting Mexicans during the Depression—and his activism on behalf of the Mexican Mutual Aid Society's efforts to assist the victims of U.S. repatriation get him into trouble with the white power structure of Los Angeles. Gonzalez is framed for the rape of a minor and sentenced to twenty-five years in prison. After the appeal deadline has passed, the young woman confesses to the frame-up. The Mexican community wages a grass-roots campaign to free Gonzalez, and, after spending six years in San Quentin, Gonzalez is paroled and deported to Mexico in 1940. In 1972, Pedro and Maria Gonzalez were permitted to return to the United States and become U.S. citizens. However, a formal petition for pardon was denied by Governor Deukemejian of California in 1985.

Break of Dawn depicts these strands of the story, orchestrating its narrative structure through various forms of the opposition Outlaw-Law: subject identities, cultural and social forms, and property. In other words, the narrative proceeds by contrasting the experiences of subject identities who are Outlaws/illegal subjects (Mexicans on one side of the binary) before the Law (white power structure on the other side); the prohibition of Spanish language and Mexican music in the public sphere (English radio) and the policing of language in prison (by the white warden); the sanctions waged against Mexicans for unionizing efforts and for political mobilization by the Department of Labor and the District Attorney's office. Undergirding the structural opposition between "legality" and "illegality" resides a nuanced focus on the dialectic between property ownership and citizenship.

The film is well crafted, shot in muted sepia tones. Through its carefully selected colorized archival footage, the film ingeniously establishes its historical reference point in the 1930s. *Break of Dawn* begins with a scene that is hauntingly contemporary. The film opens in San Quentin prison with the heated struggle between Gonzalez (Outlaw) and the warden (guardian of the Law) to define the borders between cultures through language and territory/land. Accompanied by two prison guards, Gonzalez is brought before the warden, who sits behind a desk, examining a stack of letters. In a shot/reverse-shot pattern, the following exchange takes place:

WARDEN: Did you write these letters?
GONZALEZ: I did it for some guys who can't read or write.
WARDEN: Why did you write them in Mexican?
GONZALEZ: Because they only speak Spanish.
WARDEN: Pedro, can you tell me where we are?
GONZALEZ: In San Quentin.
WARDEN: And where is San Quentin?
GONZALEZ: [in a heavy-inflected Spanish pronunciation] California.
WARDEN: Right. U.S. of A. And as long as this is the United States you're gonna write in American, understood?

In a melodramatic denouement, Pedro strikes the warden, an act that lands him in "solitary confinement," where the film narrative proceeds in the form of a flashback-recall, reminiscent of film noir. Yet the point to emphasize is the way in which the scene replicates the problem of the English-only amendment, which, as Gutiérrez-Jones indicates, serves as a "nodal point of our society's search for its own definition,"[64] and where Spanish language represents the problem. It is a problem particularly from the conservative definition of "Americanness," a perspective that prohibits (outlaws) Mexicans from that national identity. Enunciating the exclusionary notion of identity, the warden clearly marks the border between the United States and the Other, between a language that is "legal" and one that is "illegal." Yet, Gonzalez's inflection of "California" in Spanish signals the very illegality of that exclusion, for the Spanish pronunciation is, after all, the proper (legal) one. Because California was once a Mexicanheld territory, attempts to prohibit "Mexican" are, from a historical standpoint, the "illegitimate" ones. The illegality of actions against Mexicans by whites, whether these take the form of repatriation, denial of citizen rights, or the bogus rape charge, is repeatedly reaffirmed throughout the narrative, and it is also inflected in the intimate connection between citizenship and property/land.

Feminist legal theorists have critiqued the "implicit whiteness and maleness of the Original American citizen," directing our focus to the historicity of "abstract citizenship." In her stunning analysis of three versions of *Imitations of Life* (the novel by Fannie Hurst and the films of John Stahl and Douglas Sirk), Lauren Berlant draws from feminist legal scholars and makes the following observation:

> The Constitution's framers constructed the "person" as the unit of political membership in the American nation; in so doing, they did not simply set up the public standard of abstract legitimation on behalf of an implicit standard of white male embodiment—technically, in the beginning, property ownership was as much a factor in citizenship as any corporeal schema.[65]

Thus, if the Constitution's framers initially constructed property ownership as a factor in citizenship, then the illegal seizure of territory from Mexico (the War of 1848) clearly makes problematic a notion of national identity premised on the denial of constitutional citizenship to Mexicans. Even though property ownership is no longer a factor in the legal constitution of citizenship, the centrality of land ownership continues as an ideological reference point for "American" identity.[66] The inclusion of a scene where one of the "Californio" families (the original, pre-nineteenth-century Mexican settlers of California) sponsors a fund-raiser for the victims of repatriation cements the image of Anglo-whites as more recent immigrants than Mexicans.[67]

Indeed, *Break of Dawn* contests the illegitimacy of the exclusionary (white) "American" identity by underscoring the fundamental contradiction between "legal" citizenship and "illegally" seized property. In a scene midway through the film, the filmmaker explicitly establishes his counterviews on citizenship during Pedro Gonzalez's address to his Mexican radio audience:

> They say that this deportation campaign is to secure jobs for North American citizens. It's a trick. It's really nothing more than a racist attack against all Mexicans. We are neither illegals nor undesirables. They say that we came to this house and it is not our home. It's the complete opposite. Like it or not, this is our home and we have every right to stay here.

Gonzalez's on-air editorial strikes a familiar and contemporary chord with those of us living in the Southwest where the "illegal" problem is consistently deployed by public officials to scapegoat undocumented immigrants during economic recessions. Because the film narrative unfolds in layers of complex asymmetries, it meticulously forces us to contend point by point with the contradictions between the fabricated criminality of its main subject, the prohibition of Spanish, the illegality of Mexicans, and a Law based on the fundamental illegitimacy of white-Americans' claims to California. In contrast to Gregorio Cortez, who does not "own the language," Pedro J. Gonzalez is portrayed as the righteous proprietor of the Spanish language. Finally, in the face of the persistent exclusion of Mexicans from full citizenship, Gonzalez figures as the embodiment of those legitimate heirs to human rights in a land that was once owned by Mexicans.

Conclusion: Subjectivity across the Borderlands

In writing about the subject on the border/crossroads, Renato Rosaldo indicates: "Creative processes of transculturation center themselves along literal and figurative borders where the 'person' is crisscrossed by multiple identities."[68] The notion of multiple identities on the borderland has been examined in the writings of Chicanas, especially Gloria Anzaldúa, principally because Anzaldúa "seeks out the many-stranded possibilities of the borderlands."[69] As Sonia Saldívar-Hull explains, the notion of multiple identities is central in Anzaldúa's poem "To Live in the Borderlands Means You":

> She is one who "carries" five races, not Hispanic, Indian, black, Spanish, or Anglo, but the mixture of the five which results in the

mestiza, mulata. She's also "a new gender," "both woman and man, neither." While not rejecting any part of herself, Anzaldúa's new mestiza becomes a survivor because of her ability to "live sin fronteras [without borders]/be a crossroads."[70]

The voice, then, of a text/body on the borderlands refers back not to a single locus of subjectivity, but to the voice of multiple subject identities.

Break of Dawn and *Raíces de Sangre* carefully resist homogenizing the differences between Chicano and Mexican identities, maintaining the finer subtleties of language, gesture, and mannerism between Chicanos and Mexicans. However, *Break of Dawn*'s attention to the political dimensions of a border crosser's life proceeds textually with scant attention to the subject identity of the border crosser. *Raíces de Sangre* focuses on the social conditions of existence on the borderland, but it too shares this problem. Consequently, though both films are about the border experience, their main characters radically depart from the multiple subject identities of characters we find in border texts. In contrast to the multiple-voiced subjectivity of border writings, for example, the main character of *Break of Dawn* shares a striking resemblance to the "subject as defined by European-based philosophy" who, as Emily Hicks adds, "labors under the illusion of acting [and thinking] on its own."[71] The textual focus is on Gonzalez's victimization rather than on how, if at all, the character's crossing of the literal border maps a transformation in his subject position. Instead of depicting a "person" crisscrossed by multiple identities, *Break of Dawn* portrays a stable, unified identity. The Pedro J. Gonzalez who first crossed the border remains, after over a decade in the United States, the unified subject who, by the film's end, occupies what Trinh T. Minh-ha calls the "position of a sovereign subject."[72]

It is because of the "dangers" of "fixed categories" that Trinh T. Minh-ha insists on attending to the productive qualities of the interstice, the border space. Read as a unit, that is to say, as a corpus of Chicano cinematic narratives created from an "insider's" perspective, these various films contribute to our understanding of the literal and figurative border-crossing experience. Viewed separately, in isolation from each other, as meditations on the borderlands, each film paints a partial portrait of the border experience.

The main subjects of *Born in East L.A.* and *La Bamba*, Rudy and Ritchie respectively, "thrive on this fragile ground" of the border, which as Trinh T. Minh-ha explains is "the space in between, the interval to which established rules of boundaries never quite apply."[73] Yet in sharp contrast to *Break of Dawn*, for instance, *La Bamba* downplays the geopolitical signification of the border. The fundamental illegitimacy of that imposed separation (*la línea*) is alluded to humorously in Cheech Marin's film, but it is totally absent in Luis Valdez's *La Bamba*. And whereas *The Ballad of Gregorio Cortez* denies Cortez a meaningful subject position, the main characters of *Break of Dawn* and *Raíces de Sangre* tend to occupy the problematic "position of a sovereign subject." Following in the nineteenth-century Chicano tradition of social-symbolic resistance, it is ultimately *Raíces de Sangre* that represents *la frontera*, literally, as an embattled terrain, as the violent illegitimate dividing line: *la línea*.

5

Nepantla in Gendered Subjectivity

> Differential consciousness is the expression of the new
> subject position called for by Althusser—it permits
> functioning within yet beyond the demands of dominant
> ideology. This differential consciousness has been
> enacted in the practice of U.S. Third World feminism
> since the 1960s.
>
> —Chela Sandoval[1]

> I believe, however, as Bernice Zamora so succinctly
> expressed it, that our complexities are infinite: that we
> have grown up and survived along the edges, along the
> borders of so many languages, worlds, cultures and
> social systems that we constantly fix and focus on the
> spaces in between, Nepantla as Sor Juana would have
> seen it.
>
> —Tey Diana Rebolledo[2]

Introduction

During the Christmas season of 1991, Luis Valdez's made-for-televi-
sion film *The Pastorela: A Shepherd's Play* aired on PBS.[3] For the first
time in the history of Chicano cinema, a film directed by a Chicano
featured a Chicana as the central subject of its narrative.[4] Not that
women have not played major parts in Chicano films, but usually
they are portrayed in terms of timeworn stereotypes: as virgins or as
whores in Valdez's films *Zoot Suit* and *La Bamba*; as sidekicks of the
main characters (supportive wives) in Jesús Treviño's *Raíces de Sangre*
and *Seguin* and in Isaac Artenstein's *Break of Dawn*; as translators (ma-
linches) between cultures, as in Robert Young's *The Ballad of Gregorio*

Cortez; as enigmas, as in Cheech Marin's tattoo of the "home-girl" in *Born in East L.A.* and so on.[5]

In *Zoot Suit* and *La Bamba*, the Chicana subject is the object rather than the subject of the male gaze. Even though Chicanas have not been constructed in a demeaning fashion in *Seguin, Break of Dawn, Raíces de Sangre*, and *The Ballad of Gregorio Cortez*, the women of these films are nevertheless denied any active role in discourse. As we have seen, in Chicano-directed films the male subject is allowed to occupy the position of the speaking subject whereas the female subject is excluded from positions of authority both inside and outside the fictional universe of film.[6] In fact, Treviño's film about the maquiladoras in the border region was ripe for depicting a woman as the central subject of the narrative particularly because the majority (70 percent in the 1970s) of employees in these assembly plants are women, and union activism is largely dominated by women organizers.[7] In this light, Valdez's *Pastorela* appears, on the surface, as a corrective to the marginalization of Chicanas from the main subject position in Chicano films.

The film tells the story of the *pastorela*, the traditional Catholic play, through the eyes of a young, rebellious Chicana who is tired of babysitting her brother (she berates her mother for having too many babies) and is embarrassed by her family's Mexican cultural values and life-style. Basically, this young woman just wants to be a normal "American" teenager. Here we have Richard Rodriguez's *Hunger of Memory* incarnate in a young Chicana. The dramatic possibilities are incredible. Conflicts between dominant culture (white) and nondominant culture (rural Chicano) could have been accentuated. Her gender/sexual subordination within both dominant and Chicano cultures could have added a nuanced twist to our knowledge of male privilege, that is, to how Chicanas experience multiple forms of oppression in the late twentieth century.

Instead, this new female subject reluctantly attends Catholic mass with her family, and is accidentally hit on the head during the service, thereby entering an unconscious state, where the main portion of the story takes place. In her dream state, she becomes one of the shepherds who, as recounted in the original *pastorela*, search for Baby Jesus. She awakens a new subject, repentant, rehabilitated, and reformed from the "*rebelde*" into the obedient daughter, willingly re-inhabiting her "proper" place within the symbolic order of Chicano patriarchy: the embodiment of male (parental) desire. This young Chicana may be the main subject/character of the film, but she is not the speaking subject. Rather, she is confined to the same place within the story and within cultural orders (Chicano and dominant), to a position that comes under the eventual range of male vision, authority, and discourse.

The demand, therefore, is not so much for "positive" images of Chicanas, because, except for a few films, Chicano filmmakers have not spent a great deal of energy objectifying, reifying, or demeaning their women characters even though in most cases Chicanas have been excluded from participating in the "discursive fellowships" of power that Michel Foucault speaks of.[8] Several years ago, the Cuban filmmaker Humberto Solás was asked about the "feminist" orientation of his films, particularly because he cast women as the central subjects in *Lucia* and *Manuela*. This is his response:

> My point of departure was . . . that the effects of social
> transformation on a woman's life are more transparent. Because they
> are traditionally assigned to a submissive role, women have suffered
> more from society's contradictions and are thus more sensitive to
> them and more hungry for change. From this perspective, I feel that
> the female character has a great deal of dramatic potential through
> which I can express the entire social phenomenon I want to portray.
> This is a very personal and very practical position. It has nothing to
> do with feminism per se.[9]

Indeed, feminism in Latin American politics has a very different resonance. The point to underscore is that if one genuinely desires to address the full range of society's contradictions, then the gender contradiction cannot be brushed aside so easily. Filmmakers who elide women's "sensitivity to society's contradictions" and their "hunger for change" are complicitous with gender domination and male privilege in this society. In male-directed Chicano films, we see how commercial, aesthetic, and political contingencies, circumscribed by male privilege, coalesced in that moment, making it literally impossible to frame the woman as the central subject of cinematic discourse, and thereby tailoring a socially pertinent discourse to the problem of the Chicano male-subject.

The films discussed in this chapter are unique in that they position gender and subjectivity as central problems in narrative discourse, addressing the submissive position traditionally assigned to women that Solás speaks about. *Después del Terremoto* maps Chela Sandoval's notion of "differential consciousness" onto its main character, visualizing a Latina's subjectivity, that is to say, her "sensitivity to social contradictions" and "hunger for change." *El Norte* is unusual in that cofilmmakers Gregory Nava and Anna Thomas attempt to address cultural difference from the position of its woman character. In this case, gender subjectivity slides or collapses into Indian identity, positing woman as "mystery," "Nature," the "magical." The film *La Ofrenda* and the experimental films of Frances Salomé España center questions of subjectivity, desire, and gender in an entirely new light. These films offer their spectators a different way of knowing and a different vision, and here I mean vision as a socially constructed way of locating oneself in the world, a tactical positioning, rather than simply a different way of seeing or looking.

"Differential Consciousness" in *Después del Terremoto*

Después del Terremoto (*After the Earthquake*) (1979), by Lourdes Portillo and Nina Serrano, begins with an angular, stationary shot of a modest bedroom dresser. A woman enters the room, opens a drawer, and reaches for a book entitled *Vida Sexual Prematrimonial* (Premarital sexual life). Clearly a self-help book for the "modern" single Latina, stored between its pages is a stack of dollar bills, which the woman takes from the book and places in her wallet. Dressed in the attire of a domestic housekeeper, Irene (Vilma Coronado) leaves the workplace for the streets of San Francisco to purchase a television set with her savings. This establishing sequence initiates the slippage of desires that thematize the narrative. A Latina's emancipation, signified by the book about sex before marriage, visually coheres with her desire for the ideologically charged commodity, the television. As the narrative unfolds, this young Latina immigrant overinvests in the value of the television set.

Influenced by the Third World internationalist spirit of Bay Area Chicano/Latino artists and activists, Lourdes Portillo and Nina Serrano made this film about a Nicaraguan woman who migrates to San Francisco after the Nicaraguan earthquake of 1976.[10] The filmmakers decided to make a different kind of film, one that was less straightforward, didactic, and programmatic—a film that thematized the liberation of a Latina immigrant in the United States, shifting toward the attitude of "differential consciousness" that Chela Sandoval speaks of.[11] *Después del Terremoto* indeed enacts the "unique form of U.S. Third World feminism, active over the past thirty years."[12]

Despite its black-and-white format, the film's inordinate concern with detail colorfully visualizes the interstices of Latino culture in

Director Lourdes Portillo, eight months pregnant, talks with one of the actors during the shooting of *Después del Terremoto*. Courtesy of Lourdes Portillo.

dominant U.S. culture. Not only does the film position Latino (Nicaraguan) immigrants as central subjects of narrative discourse, but figuring similarities in language, religion, and ritual *Después del Terremoto* poignantly provides viewers with generalizable insights about Latinos and Latinas, and the transactions between two cultural systems, namely, U.S. and Latino cultures.

Although initially it appears that *Después del Terremoto* stages the theme of gender politics in male/female binarism, its emphasis on the multiplicity of female subjectivity refreshingly undermines this simple opposition. As we have seen from my description of the establishing sequence, the film's politics are complicated by the tension between two forms of independence: sexual freedom and freedom to consume. The film's subversion of male/female binarism derives from Irene's embodiment of a "differential consciousness." As Sandoval explains it:

> U.S. Third World feminists . . . have long understood that one's race, culture, or class often denies comfortable or easy access to either [male/female] category, that the interactions between social categories produce other genders within the social hierarchy.[13]

The theme of gender conflict is represented in terms of the tension between male and female discourses, that is to say, between formal politics (the idea of oppression as framed by the discourse of anti-imperialism) and an informal politics (the actual experience of oppression in the daily life of a woman). Indeed, the richness of the film stems from its refusal of binary categories and ideologies, illustrating well the "praxis of U.S. Third World feminism." Sandoval points out that

> what U.S. Third World feminism demands is a new subjectivity, a political revision that denies any one ideology as the final answer, while instead positing a *tactical subjectivity* with the capacity to recenter depending upon the kinds of oppression to be confronted.[14]

Irene's "tactical subjectivity" pivots on the way in which Portillo and Serrano choreograph her desires within the tension between internal and external spaces, the domestic sphere of traditional "Latino" culture and the public sphere of production. Irene is a woman who works outside the home, a woman who moves between cultures, languages, the public and the private, possessing the ability to act on multiple levels. In this respect, Irene is a prime candidate for the "kinetic and self-conscious mobility" that according to Sandoval "is utilized by U.S. Third World feminists as they identify oppositional subject positions and enact them *differentially*."[15] More important, the film depicts a range of women in various domestic situations, thus drawing attention to the fact that Latina subjectivity is informed by a range of discourses. Spectator identification with the multiplicity of Latina identities derives from the film's meticulous imaging of cultural motifs, particularly in the domestic sphere's emphasis on ritual as a mechanism of both repression and female bonding.

The narrative action in this short twenty-four minute film takes place mainly within interior spaces. The tension between antagonistic cultural systems is captured in the spatial contrast the film sets up between younger and older generations of Latinas, as seen in three key sequential scenes. Irene anxiously anticipates an encounter with her boyfriend, who has just arrived from Nicaragua where he was imprisoned and tortured by the Somoza regime for political activism. In the first scene, Irene and her friend, Maria Amanda, are visualized in the bedroom—the site of consummation for libidinal desires. Within this sexually charged space the younger women begin a conversation about Irene's impending meeting with her boyfriend as well as the possibility of marriage. The bed and the dresser mirror function as focal points for character action. Their conversation explores poverty in

Nicaragua and the impact of the earthquake on relatives, then feelings of alienation in the United States and women's autonomy as wage earners, and finally culminates in their discussion of the likelihood of marriage for Irene. The visual emphasis at this point comes to rest on a dual framing of Irene's image. While the conversation is taking place, the fractured image of Irene's backside on the screen and her mirror reflection as she is brushing her hair accentuates the extent to which internal conflicts occupy the character's thoughts. A voice calling Irene from offscreen interrupts the tension.

Walking toward the kitchen space, Irene observes one of her aunts praying to Saint Anthony for a husband for Irene. The aunt places Saint Anthony in an upside-down position on the home altar—a religious practice designed to ensure that the saint will grant the request. When the aunt leaves, Irene returns Saint Anthony to his upright position. She returns to the bedroom but not before glancing at the image of the Virgen de Guadalupe. Irene's facial expressions disclose an uncertainty about her relation to religious rituals and icons. Entering the bedroom again, Irene asks her friend, "¿Qué piensas de la virgen?" ("What do you think about the Virgin?"). Her friend responds, "Nada interesante, la verdad" ("The truth is, nothing interesting"). The details in this scene illuminate the range of cultural conflicts that Irene is struggling with. In contrast to Maria Amanda, Irene exhibits an ambiguity toward religious and cultural traditions. Yet, rather than rejecting cultural tradition and ritual wholeheartedly, Irene undermines their effects. Turning the saint to its upright position captures the character's ambiguous relation, not just toward the aunt's desire for a husband for her, but also in terms of her belief in the miracle of saints. For if she simply rejected cultural ritual as superstitious, Irene would not have intervened or altered her aunt's action.

The filmmakers locate the more traditional desires in the domestic space of the kitchen. In contrast to the libidinal bedroom, the kitchen represents the familial domestic space where older women are confined to the ritual of making tamales. As in the bedroom, the kitchen conversation centers on gender and politics, but in this case "las tías solteronas" or spinster aunts project their desires for marriage onto Irene. In marked contrast to the bedroom, visual imagery is more static. The frontal, stationary shots of the aunts sitting at the kitchen table connote cultural tradition, particularly because the conversation revolves around the institution of marriage. However, even this contained kitchen space is fraught with an ambiguous tension.

Irene (Vilma Coronado) pauses before the image of Saint Anthony, the patron saint of singles, at the beginning of *Después del Terremoto*. Courtesy of Lourdes Portillo.

While they are making tamales, one of the aunts resorts to a refrain in Spanish: "No se vaya a quedar a vestir santos" (literally, "she should not end up dressing saints")—commonly used to reference nuns and spinsters who, in the absence of conjugal relationship, give their services to the Catholic church. In a second breath, an aunt responds with another common refrain, "Más vale vestir santos que borrachos" ("better to dress saints than drunks"). However subtle, this self-reflexive response demystifies the institution of marriage, directing our attention to its subjugating underside. Thus inflecting proverbs with Catholicism unmasks a contradiction, by upholding traditional patriarchal values and then subverting the discourse that prescribes women's position in marriage. The ritual of tamale-making opens up a space within the familial kitchen for both containment and subversion.

The liminal division between two generations of Latinas located in two distinct spaces thus accentuates difference within female subjectivity. The film attends to the task of negotiating between cultural systems by focusing on differences in linguistic use across generations. Spanish-language use predominates in these sequences, punctuated by moments of "code-switching" between English and Spanish, but a third space depicts two younger Latinas who speak only English. In this scene the two Latinas cannot communicate with Irene's boyfriend because they ask him questions in English, yet he only speaks and understands Spanish. Insofar as *Después del Terremoto* depicts a range of Latina characters (young Latinas who are completely inside a U.S. cultural system; elderly *tías* who are inside Latino culture; and Irene, who occupies the intermediary position), the film undermines spectator notions of a singular Latina identity and subjectivity. Irene's position within these multiple narrative spaces directs our attention to the subject's production of her own identity in the world.

Resisting patriarchal discourse and tradition requires a conscious act of defiance and agency. Although it is clear that Irene is subject-ed to oppressive cultural and religious discourses, she also performs a significant action that turns out to have a transforming effect. Irene's situation is fraught with tensions; straddling the border, as Sonia Saldívar-Hull reminds us, means negotiating two, often antagonistic, cultural systems.[16] In *Después del Terremoto*, two events in particular suggest the complexity of negotiating between two cultural systems: the *cumpleaños* and the purchase of the television.

The climactic scene of the grandmother's *cumpleaños* (birthday party) articulates the tension between cultures, genders, political ideology, cultural tradition. The strands of the narrative converge here because the *cumpleaños* ritual operates as the culminating scene for making sense of the previous character actions: Irene and Maria

Amanda dressing up for this event, *las tías* making tamales for the party, Irene's impending meeting with Roberto. Different genders, generations, ideological positions are depicted in one scene, dancing, eating, and celebrating the birthday of the matriarchal elderly Latina. The significance of the *cumpleaños* transcends its literal level, for the ritual-performance serves as the pretext for the articulation of more fundamental discursive positions.

The scene culminates when Roberto, who has just returned from Nicaragua, is asked to show his slides of the aftermath of the earthquake. In the first series of slides, Roberto provides general information about the earthquake, its effects on people, the casualties, the devastation of homes and schools, and so on. Roberto's tone and demeanor change from a neutral account of the events to a more political analysis of the corruption of the dictator Somoza and the repression of political activists. As we learn, he was imprisoned for stealing food from the government and giving it to the poor. As Roberto voices condemnation of U.S. support for the dictatorship, one of the tamale-making *tías* intervenes. As she stands up before Roberto, the slide show is transposed from the makeshift screen to her white apron, projecting images of Nicaragua onto her body. She says, "Stop this slide show. I don't want to hear anymore."

A film decidedly sympathetic to anti-imperialist struggles, *Después del Terremoto* opts for depicting conflict and divisions within the Nicaraguan immigrant community. As this pivotal moment of the film demonstrates, peoples from the diaspora, displaced and uprooted from their homeland, are affected individually in variable ways. An elderly woman's daily life ("I'm afraid," she adds) forces her to be conservative and cautious in a foreign context, whereas a recently arrived younger man is more inclined to engage in revolutionary political activism. This didactic moment in the film masks a more complex strategy, however, namely to envision the extent to which a formalized political discourse elides the question of gender.

As Irene and Roberto leave the party, walking outdoors, she broaches her uncertainty about marriage by bringing up the subject of the purchase of a television set. In order to understand broader implications of this event, and the conflicts between these individuals, it is important to examine Roberto's positioning in the film. His resistance to Irene's desire stems from two sites: his location in traditional Latino culture and his position as the subject of a formalized discourse of radical politics. From the perspective of Third World internationalism, especially during this period, the problem of cultural imperialism transverses the television. Given the widespread dissemination of U.S. programming in Latin America, "Third World" internationalism defined the TV as the icon of U.S. imperialism. As media critics often indicate, the world comes to know and to desire the United States primarily through the international marketing and distribution of U.S. advertising and television programs.[17]

In Latin America, then, the television represents U.S. cultural imperialism. Within the United States, though, the television is known historically for assimilating and acculturating immigrant communities. Domestically, the television functions instrumentally, instilling American values, homogenizing audiences, organizing viewers as markets for the culture of consumption. What television programming and advertising do most efficiently is to inculcate immigrant communities with the ethic and logic of consumerism as a route to becoming "American." For many lower-income workers, earning enough wages to purchase a television registers their successful incorporation into U.S. culture as consumers. Because success or "making it" in this country is measured by consumption, access to television discourse symbolically marks the effective incorporation of immigrants in the naturalized and commodified world of consumerism offered by television.

For an informed political activist like Roberto, the television signifies the primary mechanism in the reproduction of capitalist propaganda, securing passivity and conformity among viewers. From this politically informed ideology Roberto reacts negatively to Irene's purchase of a television set. Yet the television's embodiment of the illusion of freedom through commodities magnifies the form of complex transactions between two cultural systems. Earlier I noted the contradictory location, the slippage of desires between sexual freedom and freedom to consume, embodied in the television. The filmmakers brilliantly use the television, transforming it into an icon of gender conflict. In the logic of the film's narrative the television appears as a polymorphous object, signifying something else for the main subject. Irene transforms the television into the emblem of her independence and autonomy. She strategically invokes the television purchase as a way to mark her distance from Roberto, displaying that she is well aware of its multiple significations:

IRENE: I bought a television set.
ROBERTO: How much did it cost you?
IRENE: Four hundred dollars.

Irene (Vilma Coronado) signs the installment contract for the television in
Después del Terremoto. Courtesy of Lourdes Portillo.

ROBERTO: That's enough money to feed two families for one year in
Nicaragua!
IRENE: I live in the U.S.

It is precisely this contradictory subject who draws attention to what Norma Alarcón terms the preference for "multiple-voiced subjectivity."[18] *Después del Terremoto* assigns multiple discursive registers to the female subject's quest for her identity as a woman, enacting a "politics of identity that is flexible enough to encompass the ironies and contradiction of the modern world system."[19] This is what Chela Sandoval identifies as U.S. Third World feminism's "differential consciousness":

> Differential consciousness requires grace, flexibility, and strength: enough strength to confidently commit to a well-defined structure of identity for one hour, day, week, month, year; enough flexibility to self-consciously transform that identity according to the requisites of another oppositional ideological tactic if readings of power formation require it; enough grace to recognize alliance with others committed to egalitarian social relations of race, gender, and class justice, when readings of power call for alternative oppositional stands.[20]

Living in the United States, Irene operates in the public sphere, working as a domestic housekeeper, as a wage earner within an advanced capitalist economy. Her other option is clear: her marriage to Roberto may very well signal her dependency as a wife within traditional Latino culture. However uncomfortably, the filmmakers raise the question of gender politics from a Latina's position in the dynamics between two cultural systems, visualizing the informal discourse of a counterpoised consciousness resulting from a woman's daily-lived experience of oppression. *Después del Terremoto* visualizes a woman who is aware of the sexual, gender, and cultural structures that formed her and who has made a decisive and deliberate break with those structures.

By giving narrative voice to a contradictory Latina subject, Portillo and Serrano image the process that recognizes that knowledge of Latina subjectivity, as Norma Alarcón indicates, "cannot be arrived at through a single discursive register."[21] Formally refusing to tie up the fiction's threads, to achieve narrative closure, opting instead for the ending with the intertitle, "y empezó así . . . " ("and so it began . . ."), filmmakers Portillo and Serrano open a critical space for the viewer to weave his or her own ending to this ongoing struggle of gender politics. Roberto, the masculinist proponent of revolutionary ideology, and Irene, the corporeal image of a budding feminist counterdiscourse, decide to discuss their conflicts over "un cafecito."

Female Subjectivity as Allegory in *El Norte*

Four years after *Después del Terremoto*, Gregory Nava and Anna Thomas made a feature-length film depicting another Latin American couple. In this case, *El Norte* (1983) deals with the story of a brother and a sister from Guatemala who are forced to leave their homeland after their father is brutally killed for land-rights activism and their mother is "disappeared" by the military death squad.[22] Rosa (Zaide Silvia Gutiérrez) and Enrique (David Villalpando) migrate to Mexico en route to their final destination: Los Angeles. Using intertitles to signal transitions in narrative space, the filmmakers also resort to cinematic style shifts, from panoramic as well as lyrical long shots and diffused lighting for scenes in the Guatemala part of the film, to more conventionally edited patterns of narration and brightly lit scenes for the parts set in Mexico and the United States. In order to recreate the homeland in the United States, the filmmakers maintain diffused lighting only for scenes shot in the domestic interior of the main characters' home in Los Angeles. Differences between locales are rendered visually to the extent that the cultural relocation and displacement of immigrants is captured in the contrast the film maintains between the homeland of origin (Guatemala) and the "new" life in Los Angeles.

The depiction of the homeland, San Pedro Guatemala, leans toward the idyllic, and in many respects acquires an air of exotic strangeness. Despite the repression of Indian workers, the filmmakers render a quintessentially breathtaking Guatemalan natural landscape surrounding the village of a native people whose culture, rituals, music, dress, and daily life appear as though from another time and space. Rosa and Enrique have unwillingly left a world impregnated with non-Western traditions, traveling through poverty-infested Mexico and into the artificiality of Los Angeles.

At the thematic level, *El Norte* presumes an articulation between political repression in Guatemala and the plight of undocumented Latino immigrants. Broadly speaking, this articulation is conditioned through various subplots contained within specific geographic locations by the intertitles: "Arturo Xuncax," "El Coyote," and "El Norte." For example, "Arturo Xuncax" takes place in Guatemala where the theme of landowner/military repression of indigenous land-rights activists dominates. In Mexico, the segment entitled "El Coyote" deals with the attitudes of "mestizos" against Indians, as well as the exploitation of immigrants in the underground economy.

In the United States ("El Norte"), the focus of the film is on the everyday lives of Rosa and Enrique as undocumented workers. Together, the various subplots orchestrate a sympathetic portrait of Guatemalan refugees in the United States.[23]

Rather than reading *El Norte* entirely as a political film about the plight of Guatemalan refugees, the glaring difference in character depiction forces us to attend to other registers in the film, specifically the subtext of cultural difference and gendered subjectivity. The articulation of a female subjectivity with the "poetic imagination" surfaces in the film's nuanced attention to character difference. Moreover, certain formal mechanisms privilege a reading of events in terms of the surreal or the supernatural order of things.

The film borrows certain artistic conventions from the aesthetic style of the "marvelous real," more commonly known as "magic realism." Latin American writers such as Julio Cortázar and Gabriel García Márquez subverted the conventions of sequential history by figuring the "surreal" and the "magical" reality within artistic discourse because, as Cortázar explains, "Latin America has the obligation to be outside European historical time."[24] *El Norte* uses supernatural images to interrupt the seamless logic of realism, re-configuring in this fashion a narrative reality distinct from rational political discourse and from most commercial films. Like the marvelous-real aesthetics, surreal segments strategically inserted within cinematic realism produce a multivalence of effects. The strategy privileges the impact of supernatural forces on the lives of its characters, in sharp contrast to a social realist depiction that would tend to foreground the significance of historical forces.

According to the filmmaker, Gregory Nava, the film's recourse to the marvelous-real aesthetics was designed to render reality as his Guatemalan informants in Los Angeles described it.[25] Consequently, the story is driven by a logic that transcends human agency and psychological motives, privileging a non-Western understanding of the order of things. What governs relations in the world of *El Norte* has less to do with human actions and more with the realm outside of bourgeois reason and rationality. The film's notion of temporality leans away from the linear, toward a more properly circular conception of existence.

The narrative closure of the film best illustrates this distinct notion of historical time. Rosa's death shatters the dreams and illusions about "el norte" forever for both characters. Enrique has lost his job, his opportunity for a "green card" in Chicago, his sister. In sum, he has lost his hopes. Earlier in the film, Enrique's father, Arturo, warns Enrique with these words: "Let me tell you, Enrique, something life has taught me. I have worked in the farms of Mexico and Guatemala. I have learned that for the rich, we [the poor] are only arms." In the scene after Rosa's death at the hospital, Enrique stands outside with the other immigrant workers waiting for day work. A truck arrives with a man yelling, "I need strong arms to work," and Enrique eagerly responds, "Me sir, I have strong arms"—a response ironically fulfilling his father's warning. The future of Enrique's life in the United States is thus sealed at the beginning of the film by his father's prophecy.

Narrative moments loaded with the uncanny and characteristic of the aesthetic style of practitioners of the marvelous real will figure predominantly in Rosa's, rather than Enrique's, experience of cultural dislocation and displacement in Los Angeles. To a greater extent, a non-Western logic is even more pronounced in the case of Rosa. Her death is enveloped in symbolism; for example, like her father, Rosa dies during a full moon. In many other instances, the story foregrounds the survival of Guatemalan culture in the United States around Rosa. Therefore, it is not simply the presence of non-Western modes for understanding reality within the content of the film that is at issue here.

In a recent interview, Gregory Nava indicated that he intentionally structured the story of Rosa and Enrique within a neo-Mayan framework, basing their narrative on the *Popol Vuh*.[26] Like the film, the Mayan origin myth rendered in the *Popol Vuh* recounts the beginnings of Mayan history through the struggles of two main subjects, a woman and a man. Yet, though *El Norte* follows the brother/sister couple in their prophesized/foretold journey through life, a closer examination of the narrative structure reveals that their narrative weight is not equivalent. Their differences are established in the first part of the film, in Guatemala. Even though brother and sister both flee from their village, they do so on different terms: Rosa's departure carries the greatest narrative weight, insofar as it is more invested with symbolism and the marvelous real.

The filmmakers visually embroider Rosa's farewell to her people, homeland, and, ultimately, to a way of life by focusing on ritual-based practices of the Maya-Quiché Indian community. Following her mother's tradition of prayer and ritual, Rosa enters a church to light three candles: "For my father; for my mother; for my village." As she exits to the town's streets, eerie supernatural images and sounds ac-

Rosa (Zaide Silvia Gutiérrez, center) walks through the streets of her village in Guatemala in the first part of *El Norte*.

company her final departure. Walking swiftly through dark streets of the village Rosa is bewildered by the ominous echoes of elderly Maya-Quiché women calling her name ("Rosa," "Rosa, where are you going?") and by the haunting force of the wind, flapping windows and doors. During her final trek out of the village, the hand of destiny intervenes: Rosa crosses an animal skull in her pathway, thereby prefiguring her death at the end of the film. This contrast in imaging strategy between the brother and the sister ultimately disturbs a univocal reading of *El Norte* as a film only about political repression and economic exploitation. The film does portray these themes, but it also grafts its story in terms of difference in gender, opening up a space for examining difference in subjectivities.

Rosa figures as the allegorical Maya-Quiché Indian, the embodiment of culturally specific codes of apprehending social reality that derive from an alternative logic to that of bourgeois reason. The film visually incorporates the blocked and prohibited realms of the subject, those manners in the individual that are usually regarded as "hallucinations" and "superstitions," but it does so only through the agency of Rosa. The tragic ending of each character has distinct causes. Military troops force Enrique out of Guatemala; he fails in the United States because a Chicano coworker envies his success and calls the *migra* to deport him.[27] Thus, the actions of men (Culture) impact the life of a man (Enrique). The cause of Rosa's tragedy resides in the domain of the nonhuman, either the "hand of destiny" (in apparitions such as the elderly Indian women), the dead skull in her path, or rat bites that give her typhus. Indeed, during the grueling scene where Rosa and Enrique cross into the United States through a sewer tunnel, rats attack both of them, infecting only Rosa with typhus. In Rosa's case, Nature (not Culture) impinges on her life.

As details of Indian nobility and cultural tradition are figured visually in Rosa's character as well as in her mother's, rather than in Enrique's, women then symbolize a distinct cultural system. Read allegorically, Rosa's death represents the impossibility of the survival of culturally distinct modes of apprehending social reality within another cultural system. The burden of cultural reproduction thus resides in the woman, in her spirituality and existence. Rosa symbolizes a "peoples" tradition. This Western (Enlightenment) distinction between men, as agents of their own individual story, and women, as agents of cultural reproduction and tradition, is maintained and emphasized by the parallel structure of the narrative. Whereas the filmmakers intended to render a neo-Mayan (alternative) vision of an indigenous worldview, *El Norte*'s representation follows the conventional Western division of Nature/Culture, positing female subjectivity in the unknown, Mystery, Nature, and woman as the ground for cultural reproduction and maintenance.

La Ofrenda: Coding Gendered Subjectivity

The scene of *La Ofrenda* (1989) that bears the same name as the title of the film demonstrates perfectly the filmmakers' preference for a coded mode of expression. This documentary by Lourdes Portillo and Susana Muñoz offers a scene of a man dressed as a widow for the Day of the Dead parade in a small town in Mexico. The man performs "her" grief for public spectacle, before multiple spectators—those on the parade route and those before the screen. There for public display is the image of a man, pacing his walk to the tempo of the town's marching band. This man's voice offscreen describes his perfor-

In *La Ofrenda*, the Mexican cross-dresser/performer offers the apple he is holding.

mance, a performance of a widow dressed in solemn attire. Reenact-
ing the cultural archetype, he performs the "suffering Mexican
mother" (*la madre dolorosa*). At this point the film shifts from the exterior actuality shots of the public performance on the streets to an
interior space. The man continues his description of the widow, noting how the grieving woman soon changes her composure in order to
find a new husband. The widow is thus doubly textualized. As his
words make evident, she embodies two cultural archetypes, the "suffering mother" and the "lewd woman," simultaneously the virgin/
whore binary. However, de-emphasizing her stable essence as "suf-
ferer," this man observes the slippage in her performance of a role,
from "widow" to "libertine," that is, he plays the *"viuda alegre,"* another cultural archetype. Yet the visual figuration of this man hints
that his performance is more than an occasion to reenact patriarchal
visions about Mexican women. With markedly "feminine" gestures,
the man carefully removes his wig and continues his on-camera and
offscreen didactic interpretation of the significance of various rituals
associated with the Day of the Dead.

This "native" informant we have observed is someone besides a participant/performer/actor. He is also a cross-dresser who uses this public occasion to perform his private fantasies. In a culture strictly driven by Catholicism, with its deeply embedded religious and social prescription of strict gender roles, the public domain of the streets and special festive occasions figure as the few socially sanctioned spaces where a clearly identifiable cross-dresser may operate. On the Day of the Dead, the cross-dresser assumes a subject position by subjecting himself to public acknowledgment and ridicule. The spectacle we have observed is thus doubly inscribed, first because sexual transgressions can only be exhibited to elicit laughter and ridicule, and second, because his agency and subjectivity subvert official religious prescriptions about gender.

In the final shot of this sequence, the man describes the significance of "la ofrenda." The Day of the Dead is a time for love and giving. In a spontaneous gesture, almost as if in afterthought, the man turns directly to the camera, to his spectators, and, like Eve in the biblical story of origins, offers us the fruit of knowledge and desire: the apple. The scene we have looked at is itself doubly inscribed, figuring as a pivotal scene in *La Ofrenda*'s ethnographic account of the "Day of the Dead" celebration in Mexico. Its structural location in the documentary draws attention to an intimacy between religious ritual, gender, and sexuality. The scene represents the turning point in this documentary about the Day of the Dead.

The body of this man, on the border of two genders, and the location of this scene as the turning point between the festivity in Mexico and the United States, suggest that *La Ofrenda* is a documentary about more than the Day of the Dead. The film juxtaposes three distinct discourses: first, the documentary or literal discourse that is the vehicle for its theme; the formal structure of the film compels the discourse of identity politics; and coded images contain the discourse on gender/sexuality. The articulation of these various discourses stresses the process of locating one's relation to the world differently, to a world reconfigured, and to the process of cultural transformation figured aesthetically and thematically by the distinction established between ritual celebration in Mexico and its transformation in the United States. *La Ofrenda* is a film that complicates the production of fixed meaning, opting instead for contingencies, for the process of making sense. But these are not features commonly attributed to documentary films.

The Documentary Discourse[28]

La Ofrenda was first released in 1989. Since then it airs yearly on local public television stations in November, coinciding with the Day of the Dead celebration on November 1-2.[29] The film is featured as well in the public art circuit, Chicano studies classes, and gay and lesbian activist circles. In order to communicate with a public television audience, La Ofrenda deploys a pedagogical apparatus, providing factual information for noninitiates about a different cultural system's views on death. A festivity dating to pre-Columbian Mexico, the "Day of the Dead" continues as a vital cultural ritual in Mexico, despite centuries of effort by Catholic/colonial authorities to eradicate the practice. In the 1970s, under the direction of Ralph Maderiaga, Chicano and Latino artists and community activists revived the ritual as a public community "event" in the Mission district of San Francisco, organizing exhibitions in cultural art centers and museums and planning an annual parade on the streets of La Misión. By no means the only public display of the festivity in the United States, the San Francisco event is, however, the most publicized and therefore the most cross-culturally attended celebration.[30]

The film flows chronologically, maintaining a spatial contrast between the Day of the Dead celebrations in Mexico and San Francisco, California. This spatial division renders a difference between a ritual rooted in the micropractices of culture among native Oaxaqueños and its revival by artists/activists/intellectuals as part of the process of the reaffirmation of cultural identity. A realist aesthetics predominates in both Mexico and the United States, but the film pays an inordinate attention to ritual within the context of everyday life for scenes shot in Mexico.

Given the film's conventional format, genre criticism suggests that, beyond its documentary discourse, there is little of interest for students of cultural productions. Viewed within the documentary genre, the film leans heavily toward what Roland Barthes describes as a zero-degree film.[31] Indeed, its acceptance of documentary realism, its ethnographic style of hand-held camera and long shots and classic interviewing techniques, postulates a smooth flow toward intelligibility. Spectators have little difficulty understanding the film's major intention, which is, primarily, the celebration of alternative cultural practices and beliefs about "death." By representing an "actual event," said to exist in the social world rather than in the fictional world of the imagination, La Ofrenda privileges the transparency rooted in traditional documentary discourse. Yet, Trinh T. Minh-ha's observation about the fictional quality of documentaries forces us to examine those features that the generic overemphasis of film criticism disregards.[32] Long, lyrical shots and the distinct tempo of the film evoke a non-Western sense of time and space, suggesting that something else is at stake in this film. *La Ofrenda* spatially and temporally re-configures oppositional identities of origin, authenticity, and collectivity.

Gendered Identity Politics

In a documentary realism style that simulates a prefilmic reality, *La Ofrenda* provides spectators with a procession of "generic" nameless subjects (artisans, native informants, images of tourists ironically subtitled "American tourists"), lingering, almost lyrical long shots, tracking shots, seamless editing, filtered lenses for "sacred" effects, and depicts the array of micropractices of a community organically mobilized for the festivity, from cooking the traditional foods, scenes of marketplace transaction, artisans creating various *calaveras* to praying before home altars, from the visit to the cemetery to dining in honor of the dead. The filmmakers could be criticized for the effects this transparent filmmaking style elicits, particularly because the mimetic mode is predominant for the scenes in Mexico, positioning the Mexican subjects as the objects of an ethnographic project. Yet, voice-over narration subverts the closure of this particular ideological reading of the film. Rather than standing as the objects of the Western ethnographer/subject, the Mexican subjects are presented as the authenticating reference point for Others in the United States. Within the context of the United States, where ritual and cultural practices of Chicanos/Latinos are not legitimated within the dominant cultural system, Mexican subjects function as the origin and authenticity for an alternative cultural system and oppositional identities.

Retaining the emblematic moment of Chicano identity politics, *La Ofrenda* traces the authenticity of the "Day of the Dead" celebration to present-day Mexico, and to its origin in pre-Columbian Mexico. In contrast to films such as *I Am Joaquin*, the pre-Columbian subject of *La Ofrenda* is gendered. As the site of origin and authenticity, Mexico figures in the interplay between historical documents (images of indigenous gods and temples as well as voice-over accounts of the ritual dating to the Conquest) and actual footage taken in Oaxaca, Mexico, depicting the practices of an elderly woman. In so doing, the film appeals to a re-gendering of a traditional Chicano trope of "origin."

La Ofrenda arranges its temporal order in terms of a spatial contrast between the Day of the Dead celebration in Mexico and in San Francisco. The stylistic shift between the visual and verbal discourses, a lyrical camera style for Mexico and a more conventional TV-documentary format for the United States, derives from the use of three cinematographers. Also, given the English-language fluency of the Chicano subjects, on-camera interviewing predominates for the scenes shot in San Francisco.[33]

Much more pertinent for the understanding of the workings of identity politics in the film are the effects of voice-over narration. For the scenes shot in Mexico, the filmmakers could have opted for a third-person authoritative voice-over description of the events on screen; however, they chose instead the re-occurring first-person singular and plural, characteristic of the "testimonial" style of narration prevalent in Latin American literature.

More significant is the positioning of the image of the elderly woman as the authenticating subject for cultural tradition—a strategy we have already seen in Esperanza Vásquez's early film, *Agueda Martínez*. The interface between the image of the *abuelita* (grandmother) and the autobiographic, poetic feminine voice-over as the authority of the film also recalls *Agueda Martínez*. Yet in *La Ofrenda*, the filmmakers add a new twist, deploying the feminine voice as the spatial order of the film and the masculine voice as its temporal order.

The feminine voice is stereotypically associated with memory whereas the masculine voice is associated with history, authority, and linear time. In *La Ofrenda*, the authoritative voice-over of a man effects the linear progression of the film and provides spectators with historical information about the Day of the Dead. Yet, the impersonal third-person plural of the masculine that governs the temporal pace of the film is repeatedly interrupted by a disembodied first-person singular and plural female voice. Through the interplay of poetic meditations and autobiographical digressions, the woman's voice-over disturbs the temporal (linear) flow, opening up a spatial (circular) order within *La Ofrenda*. Coupled with the long, lyrical shots, the extended length of takes held past the functionality of television documentaries, that is to say, the film's meditative visual style, the female narrator disturbs the smooth transition between images and sounds.

Moreover, the interplay between the female and male narrations disrupts the course of discursive time, introducing the present time of

the filmmakers' work on the text, namely, their mapping of an identity politics. In contrast to Chicano cultural politics that revisions the
Chicano past in the Mexican pre-Columbian past, *La Ofrenda*'s filmmakers reconstitute present-day Mexico as the Chicano past. Rituals
in San Francisco have this authenticating reference point in Mexico.
Memory passages, poetic meditations, and lyrical camera style work
to reconfigure an identification with the motherland, where we can
fix and locate the origin and authenticity of rituals.

The logic of identity, its trajectory through the film, culminates in
its narrative closure—a scene that posits a collective subject rather
than the *I*. Segments shot in Mexico and San Francisco appear in a
collage scene of rituals around the Day of the Dead. Insofar as these
distinct locales appear indistinguishable, *La Ofrenda* proposes a collective identity based on similarity rather than on difference. The film's
departure from the cultural politics of nationalism resides in its concern with the "production" of cultural identity, as opposed to the "archaeology" of an identity politics. *La Ofrenda*'s nuanced attention to
images of children in its narrative closure locates Chicano present-day
identities not just in the past tense, but productively, at the intersection of the past with the present and, more important, in the future
tense of culture: children.

The Body of Gender Conflict

La Ofrenda is more than a film about different cultural practices or
about identity politics. Certain narrative excess or disturbances not
found in the typical documentary reveal the extent to which *La Ofrenda* also represents a different way of broaching the question of gender. The narrative's turning point, the parade scene preceding the
U.S. part of the film, demands a situated reading, that is to say, an
attention, from various subject positions, to its complex layers of
meaning.

The parade scene depicts a group of men dressed as women during
the Day of the Dead festivity. In the streets of a rural town in Mexico,
these cross-dressers perform comedy skits before the town's residents. A staple in the yearly celebration, the cross-dressers' parade
culminates in the interior scene described earlier where one of the
cross-dressers describes his performance of the widow and the meaning of the events.

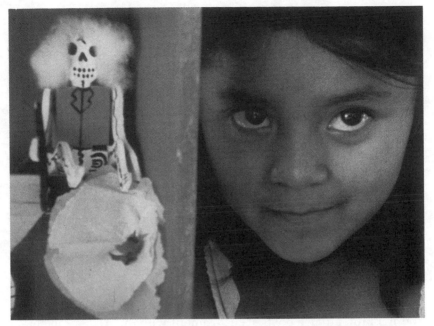

Image of a little girl next to a *calavera* in *La Ofrenda*. Courtesy of Lourdes Portillo.

To the extent that this man appears as the film's main informant in Mexico, the filmmakers position the cross-dresser as the master of language. His performance of the widow textualizes woman. As the film depicts images of the *abuela* performing her own rituals for the Day of the Dead, the disembodied voice of the cross-dresser (not the voice of the *abuela*) explains their significance, textualizing further woman's practices. Just as this man inhabits two genders, he also speaks for woman, for the widow and for the *abuela*. For the U.S.-situated reader, the cross-dresser colonizes both genders. He can have it both ways—be a woman yet not be a woman, be a man with male privilege: he is simultaneously the master of language (narration) and of gendered privilege.

Yet in the Mexican context, as well as in the United States, where Chicano gays have less male privilege than white homosexuals, the cross-dresser means something different. Within the context of Catholicism, his transgression is sacrilegious. As a figure who embodies two genders, his body also figures as the site of gender/sexuality conflict in contemporary rural Mexico. The cross-dresser's public enactment of private fantasies desecrates Catholic morals. Yet sexual trans-

gression is simultaneously contained by Catholicism, for cross-
dressers in rural Mexico have no other public venue for expressing
their private fantasies except for those spaces sanctioned by the Catholic church.

Thus, the body of this man on the border of two genders, the
meanings of this scene from a situated reading (my own) on the interstice of two cultural systems, the position of this scene in between
Mexico and the United States, open up a significant feature of the
film, namely, its submerged engagement with an urgent social problem: the "real issue" of AIDS in the Latino community. Recent studies
on Latino sexuality underscore the widespread phenomenon of bisex-
ual practices among heterosexual Mexican men.[34] Yet, because Catholicism does not sanction public discussions of sexuality, talking
about "sex" among U.S. Latinos is particularly difficult. Although
this is not the primary focus of the film, *La Ofrenda* has been used and
can be used in a discussion of Mexican/Chicano sexuality and AIDS,
and toward an understanding of culturally specific modes of confronting death through ritual. *La Ofrenda* proposes a "spiritual" encounter rather than a political engagement with the AIDS problem, in
the face of the state's indifference around the issue. For U.S. Latinos,
La Ofrenda opens up a space for talking about AIDS and for confronting death through the language of ritual.

Following in the tradition of using the body "as the site of struggle
to represent a Chicana lesbian desire,"[35] Lourdes Portillo and Susana
Muñoz "offer" their spectators a coded image of a cross-dresser, rendering visually what verbal discourse alone cannot.[36] Yvonne Yarbro-
Bejarano explains that the work of Chicana lesbian writers such as
Cherríe Moraga "embodies a sexual/textual project that disrupts the
dualism between mind and body, writing and desire."[37] Navigating
between memory-images and the scent of her childhood friend, Tiny/
Christina, Cherríe Moraga's poem "La Ofrenda" illuminates how a
single image embodies multiple levels of signification:

> ¿Donde 'stá ella
> que me regaló mi cuerpo
> como una ofrenda a mí misma?[38]

As in Moraga's poem, which opens Carla Trujillo's anthology on Latina sexuality, multiple levels of meaning implode onto the body of the
cross-dresser in the film *La Ofrenda*.[39]

The Mexican cross-dresser in the costume of a widow for the Day of the Dead parade in Oaxaca in a scene of *La Ofrenda*.

Conclusion: Experimenting with Gendered Subjectivity

Breaking with narrative conventions, the short films by Frances Salomé España re-vision questions of gender, desire, and subjectivity for Chicanas. España's experimental films are not narrative-driven, but insistently visual and poetic, re-defining a Chicana aesthetic politics. To the extent that España creates a new strategy and invents new texts, the filmmaker also conceives a new social subject: Chicanas "as speakers, readers, spectators, users, and makers of cultural forms, shapers of cultural process."[40]

In an earlier essay, I argued that España's film *Anima* (1989) marks a shift in Chicana aesthetic practices.[41] The short film alternates between three sequence spaces: the cemetery, images of women with painted faces characteristic of the Day of the Dead, and a negative shot of the cemetery in freeze-frame. The alternating movement, back and forth to each sequence, is rendered through time-distorted cinematic techniques, for instance, through jagged or abrupt pans of the cemetery or images of women with painted faces shot through reflection in chrome mylar. The effect of these distortions cannot be dismissed as simple gimmickry or film tricks. España lucidly captures, aesthetically, the ritual-based practices that in fact define the Day of the Dead. Images of women painting their faces, sitting around a kitchen table exhibiting their painted *calaveras*, are crosscut with eerie, surreal stills of tombstones. Through the film's infinite representational levels, España invents a new aesthetic language for depicting rituals in the interplay of form, content, and a Chicana cultural desire.

España's visual and symbolic space also renders the personal as theoretical in her experimental short *Espejo* (1991), which visualizes the thoughts/images of a young child growing up in the inner city, in a space where the rural and the urban intersect: the Chicano barrio ("It couldn't have been that bad; people survived"). The story is told from the point of view of a grown woman whose tone of narration evokes the stream-of-consciousness, dreamlike memories of a child ("I was always in the tree, so I was safe"). *Espejo* is intercut with surreal images, alternating from a desolate backyard, chickens, trains, fruits, bare feet hanging in the air, and a tight shot of the narrator's (filmmaker's) face. The richness of this autobiographic portrait derives from its "elliptic" mode of expression, navigating from projection to reflection. As Annette Kuhn explains, "ellipses offer the possibility of a rather different kind of pleasure, that of piecing together fragments of a story—the active pleasure, that is, of working on a puzzle."[42] The effects of *Espejo* linger on. Long after the film ends, we re-cognize this puzzle to be about desire and memory: the Chicano barrio ("the place had corazón"), on this side of the railroad tracks, where, as the narrator (España) tells us, "we drew our breath from the urban areas . . . yet so close to the homeland." España's short experimental film is thus akin to the writings of Chicanas whose short stories, according to Ramón Saldívar, "speak to the link between artistic creation and a kind of poetic self-creation that is not separated out as an individual imperative but is conditioned by its ineluctable tie to the community."[43]

Salomé España works toward experimenting with gender, subjectivity, and desire in a style that articulates oppositional form with oppositional content. Her recent film *Spit-Fire* (1992) plays with indigenous and religious iconic representations of womanhood, juxtaposing female cultural symbols with poetic passages. In entirely different ways, the narrative-driven films *El Norte* and *Después del Terremoto* experiment with gender, depicting other Latinos as central subjects of narrative discourse. Although the gender politics of each film differ sharply, the filmmakers of *El Norte* and *Después del Terremoto* work to critique implicitly the Chicano nationalist framework around Mexican identity. If Chicano cultural politics were to respond effectively to the everyday lives of urban barrios, the presence of other, non-Mexican Latinos could no longer be ignored. Both Gregory Nava and Lourdes Portillo identify themselves as part of the Chicano film movement, and their films capture the heterogeneity of the Latino population in this country. In an entirely different way Lourdes Portillo and Susana Muñoz's *La Ofrenda* experiments with gender by coding a male cross-dresser as the site of gendered subjectivity.

At the beginning of this chapter, I noted that *La Ofrenda, Después del Terremoto, Espejo*, and *Anima* center questions of subjectivity and gender in a new light, offering their spectators a different way of knowing and a different vision. This is a way of saying that these films address the spectator as female. Teresa de Lauretis makes it clear that what is at stake here is something more than the rhetorical question posed by Gertrud Koch of whether "the female look through the camera . . . will be an essentially different one."[44] As de Lauretis explains it, the question of addressing the spectator as female goes beyond the subversion of the camera's construction of the gaze:

> In saying that a film whose visual and symbolic space is organized in
> this manner, *addresses its spectator as a woman*, regardless of the
> gender of the viewer, I mean that the film defines all points of
> identification (with character, image, camera) as female, feminine,
> feminist.[45]

Después del Terremoto, La Ofrenda, Anima, and *Espejo* involve a shift toward the "aesthetics of reception" that de Lauretis makes reference to, "where the spectator is the film's primary concern—primary in the sense that it is there from the beginning, inscribed in the filmmaker's project, and even in the very making of the film."[46] The visual and symbolic spaces organized by Chicana filmmakers re-vision Chicano aesthetic and formal knowledge because they define their points of identification with characters, images, and camera as "female, feminine, feminist." Rather than addressing a universal subject (spectator/viewer/audience), these four films, each in its own unique manner of expression, articulate the sites and forms of visions for an alternative social subject, mapping feminist identities, subjectivities, and desires for U.S. Third World women of color.

6

Conclusion:
Eastside Story Re-visited

It seems quiet right now. But all of this could explode.
Anytime.
—Edward James Olmos, on East L.A.[1]

I am not in El Salvador, I tell myself. Those are not
soldiers down there, bursting through doors to ransack
the apartments of high school kids who participated in a
protest march . . . This is Los Angeles, not San Salvador,
this is 1991, not 1979, this is gang strife, not civil war.
—Rubén Martínez[2]

Shortly after the release of *American Me* (1992), Edward James Olmos's
directorial debut, I was talking on the phone with my good friend Iris
Blanco. Along with another longtime friend, Sylvia Lizárraga, Iris had
just seen *American Me*. "We were stunned," she said. "The film is so
hopeless. There's just no way out. Un callejón sin salida" (a tunnel
without an exit). A few weeks later, L.A.'s "long hot summer" faced
us on national television. Yet in this rerun of the 1965 Watts Rebellion,
and despite the arrogance of East-based media announcers and the
black leadership who repeatedly described the "black" rage un-
leashed after the Rodney King verdict while images on the screen
showed something quite different, it was Latinos (Mexicans, Salva-
dorans, Guatemalans) and not blacks who were doing most of the ri-
oting and looting.[3] Alvina Quintana called me from Delaware on the
second night of the Rebellion. We joked about the East Coast media
referring to the "rioters" as blacks, especially when they did so for the
news segment that showed a group of Latinos standing on top of an

overturned vehicle, raising the Mexican flag. "Chicanos re-claiming Aztlán!" we both chuckled. Was this the explosion (the exit at the end of the tunnel) Olmos prophesized?

The L.A. "rebellion," "uprising," "riot" evoked a *Blade Runner* scenario, a city gone "helter skelter." The explosion was long overdue. Residents of color in poor neighborhoods (where most of the riots took place) live under a constant state of siege, under the LAPD's "search and destroy" mission, making Los Angeles the sister city of Beirut and San Salvador. Perhaps the distopian vision of *American Me* makes more sense to barrio residents of East L.A. who are unrelentlessly besieged by what Mike Davis describes as the militarization of public space: "Even as the walls have come down in Eastern Europe, they are being erected all over Los Angeles."[4] But let's not be confused. *American Me* is not about how Chicano barrios weather the LAPD's *toque de queda* (martial law), even though the film is obliquely related. Rather, the film is about the depraved and ruined Chicano *familia*: a savage vision of Chicano gang life.

American Me takes its title from Beatrice Griffith's 1948 book about Chicano gangs. Based on a screenplay actually written in the early seventies by Floyd Mutrux (who also wrote *Up in Smoke* for Cheech and Chong),[5] *American Me* is the fictional adaptation of the lives of two friends, J. D. and Cheyenne. Cheyenne, a "real life" Chicano gang leader who died in prison in 1972, is the inspiration for *American Me*'s lead, Santana (played by Olmos), and also for Montana in the newest addition to the gangxploitation genre, *Bound by Honor* (1993), directed by Taylor Hackford. In the early eighties, Olmos and Robert Young secured the rights to the screenplay from Mutrux. Although Olmos rewrote the original script, along with Mutrux and Desmond Nakano, the Writer's Guild awarded screenplay credit only to Mutrux and Nakano.[6] In order to render a disturbing treatment of the psychotic dynamics of gang life, Olmos changed Mutrux's vision of Santana from an "Emiliano Zapata-like romantic hero" to the image of a cold and calculating prison lord.[7] Olmos explains his mission: "I want to show that there's a cancer in this subculture of gangs . . . They'll say, 'You've taken away our manhood with this movie.' I say to them, 'Either you treat the cancer or it'll eat you alive.' "[8]

In fact, what I like most about this movie is precisely its novel, unflinching treatment of Chicano masculinities, its shrewdly oblique refusal to romanticize the defiance of the masculine heroic figure (cholo, bato loco), as was done in the Pachuco character that Olmos himself had played in *Zoot Suit*. But there is a certain perversity to the way in which Olmos renders the underside of gang life in *American Me*. After all, there is a difference between treating the symptoms and liquidating the cause of a disease. The source of the "cancer in our barrios" is not the "subculture of the gang," as Olmos seems to believe.

With a fervor weirdly akin to an evangelist, Olmos is insistent about the correctness of his vision. I witnessed one of his sermons at the San Francisco screening of *American Me*. As much as he wanted to open our eyes to the "real issues" affecting our barrios, that night in San Francisco Olmos virulently derided any criticism of his film. Instead, he noted years of personal research into the "gang problem," insisting that his film shows (or "proves," if I may paraphrase) "how a dysfunctional family can ruin a youngster's life"—a claim that would certainly warm the hearts of Ronald Reagan, George Bush, and Dan Quayle.

The film's cinematographer, Reynaldo Villalobos, states, "Some people are going to love it, and some people are going to hate it. It's one of those movies. There isn't any in-between."[9] And here I sit, writing a conclusion to this book about a film, I must confess, "I hate to love," because I recognize an important shift in Chicano filmmaking. I find myself interpellated into contradictory subject positions, as academic parlance would say it, positioned in a welcomed-place of discomfort, yet also dis-appointed by this film text, and, most of all, having to account for this heterogeneity in myself as a spectator . . .

American Me tells the riveting story of Santana, an East L.A. Chicano who, after killing a fellow detainee in juvenile hall, ends up with a long-term sentence in Folsom State Prison. There for the long haul, Santana sets up an underground economy of drug trafficking. Narrated in the style of the "great anti-myth usually known as *noir*,"[10] *American Me* opens in the final moments of the life of Santana, the prison-ward lord and head of the notorious Mexican Mafia. The film then unfolds through a series of flashbacks and flash-forwards, including his father's beating and mother's rape by U.S. servicemen during the infamous "Zoot Suit riots" of 1943, Santana's first bouts with gang life, the formation of the Mexican Mafia in prison, his release and brief romance with Julie (Evelina Fernández), and constant gang strife in East L.A. It ends with Santana's brutal execution in prison by members of his own gang, "la eMe."

The $20 million that Universal Studios gave Olmos to do the film makes *American Me* the most expensive studio production by a Chicano filmmaker. What made this film possible is best summed up by Mike Davis's comments about gang films in general: "Hollywood is

Edward James Olmos as prison-ward lord Santana in *American Me*. Courtesy of Universal Studios.

eager to mine Los Angeles barrios and ghettos for every last lurid image of self-destruction and community holocaust."[11] That studios are more eager to finance films about gangs (sex-drugs-violence) than about, for instance, the militant folk-hero Tuburcio Vasquez, a Californio who was hanged by whites in the nineteenth century, says a lot about the industry's racism. As we know, the image of Mexicans as "inherently violent" is part of western America's racial imaginary. In this part of the nation, constructing Mexicans (and Indians) as savages is one of the ways white Americans can view themselves as civilized. Yet, *American Me* is not your typical gangxploitation film like *Boulevard Nights* or *Colors*, even though it does quote from other films in the gang/urban violence genre.[12] While exploring the darkest secrets of Chicano prison culture, unlike most gang or urban violence films, the violence in *American Me* is not gratuitous. The film is brutally realistic, providing gruesome details about prison life, which is probably why two of the film's technical advisors, Ana Lizarraga and Charles Manriquez, were fatally shot, execution-style, shortly after the release of *American Me*.[13]

The chilling luminosity of this unflinching drama also makes *Amer-*

ican Me different from other films by Chicanos and Chicanas. The film
departs from its predecessors in marking a shift in cultural politics.
Eschewing celebration of the Chicano nation, *American Me* disturbs
and disrupts our (Chicanos and Chicanas) imaginary self-coherence.
(My daughter walked out of the film in desperation and pain, saying
"This is not the way our culture is.") No ma'am, there's no romanti-
cization of the cholo/pachuco here, only a pitch darkness surrounding
Olmos's vision of Chicano barrios and the gang life-style.

Consequently, people do not like the film for various reasons. After its screening in San Jose, Luis Valdez, for instance, had "strong
reservations about the film's overriding negativism." It comes as no
surprise that Valdez, whose films *Zoot Suit* and *La Bamba* tend to glo-
rify Chicano masculinity, would take offense to *American Me*'s tragic
and horrific portrait of Chicano male culture: "My response then was
that it was a diatribe against Latinos . . . This is a genre (street-crime
movies) that's been offered to me many times. It's not what I relate to.
I believe in the cinema of triumph."[14]

In fact, whereas Hollywood is willing to finance a broad range of
themes in black filmmaking, Chicanos are locked into the gang genre,
into "negative stereotypes." Anticipating the "negative stereotype"
attacks on his film, Olmos tried some "damage control" by sending
the script beforehand to the National Hispanic Media Association. No
deal. The association did not (or really, could not) stop the production, but its chair, Esther Renteria, publicly chided Olmos, stating
that the group's members "regret the making of the film."[15] Without
a doubt, the film's focus normalizes dominant culture's view of Chicanos as poverty-infested "gangs"—a slap in the faces of Chicano corporate multiculturalism types who are eager to sell (market) a different image of Chicana and Chicano consumers to their clients. Chicano
filmmakers in Hollywood are also upset because the film did not
make a profit, "running in the red" (at a deficit), thereby deflating the
hopes of Hollywood-bound Chicanos for future studio financing.

Others in the Chicano intelligentsia have not liked the film for different, more substantive, political reasons. The major objection raised
at the San Francisco screening had to do with the film's simplistic account of the gang phenomenon in the barrios. Eliding the economic
roots of youth violence, *American Me* emphasizes instead the dysfunctional relationship between Santana and his father. Near the end of
the film, Santana and his father accidentally meet at the mother's
grave, where papá painfully tells Santana: "I tried to love you. But I
would always wonder which of those sailors' blood ran through

your veins"—a reference to the mother's rape by U.S. sailors during the "Zoot Suit riots." The father's suspicion that his son is the off-spring of a white soldier conditions the father's emotional distance, spiraling Santana into juvenile delinquency, gang violence, crime, and sociopathology. And although this graveside confession makes great heart-wrenching drama, *American Me* perpetuates a popular myth: the absence of parental love and a strong male role model are the major ingredients of youth-gang deviance. Given the film's total disregard or mention of poverty and underemployment in barrios as major factors contributing to the appeal of gangs, this popular myth is particularly misguided, perhaps even dangerous, especially in light of the right wing's campaign against the so-called "welfare mothers" in barrios and ghettos.

Olmos has repeatedly used the "cancer in our barrios" response to critics who correctly point to the film's failure to address the material conditions of poverty and unemployment among young Chicanos. The religious zealousness in Olmos's plea is not unfounded. Substantiating his "cancer" metaphor are very "real" facts: youth violence is on the rise; 40 percent of the kids in juvenile hall are there for murder; 85 percent of the kids in Central Juvenile Hall in Los Angeles are Latinos; the equivalent (in numbers) of half of the nation's juvenile population is jailed in California alone.[16] Even so, Olmos practices a misguided paternalism in attributing Santana's brutal sociopath cruelty to the lack of fatherly love. Studies about the gang phenomenon in this country show something entirely different.

Martín Sánchez-Jankowski's recent book *Islands in the Streets* dismisses some of the popular myths about why boys join street-gangs. In a comprehensive ethnography of thirty-seven gangs across the country, including Chicano gangs in Los Angeles, Sánchez-Jankowski found just as many gang members from two-parent nuclear families as from absent-father homes, thereby countering the notion that young boys join gangs because they have "no male authority figures with whom to identify."[17] Along with the "broken-home" scenario his study shows the dysfunctional home environment to be another sweeping myth because, as he puts it, "I found as many gang members who claimed close relationships with their families as those who denied them."[18] Coincidentally, the author singles out the central role Hollywood films play in perpetuating the dysfunctional-home-environment myth: "The parents of gang members are presented as individuals who do not care and/or are negligent in their parental responsibilities."[19]

Young boys join gangs for various reasons, including material incentives (gangs provide jobs unavailable in the inner cities, even though these are mostly illegal), physical protection, and entertainment (hanging out at the clubhouse). Because gang members lucidly understand "the world in terms of rich and poor," they willingly participate in gang activities in order to avoid "dead-end jobs" like those of their parents: "Most gang members come from families whose parents are either underemployed and/or employed in the secondary job market."[20] Therefore, it is poverty, unemployment, underemployment (or, as Sánchez-Jankowski says it, "conflict" and "competition over resource scarcity") and not unaffectionate parents that account for the persistence of gangs in U.S. society for most of the twentieth century.

In all fairness, Olmos did not intend for *American Me* to be the definitive scholarship on the gang phenomenon. Stripping the romantic illusions of gang culture and showing the gruesome dementia of prison life, *American Me* is told in a brutally realistic fashion in order to shock young people. Olmos has screened the film before "high-risk" young men at various "gang service" centers and juvenile halls, hoping, first, to discourage young boys from ever joining a gang, and, second, to encourage current members to get out before it's too late.[21] Yet, in terms of the latter, Sánchez-Jankowski's observations are well worth noting:

> Gang members believe that the efforts of the authorities to rehabilitate them—to accept the premise that they are wrong in what they did and that they need to learn a skill and become productive members of society—are acts of indoctrination that must be resisted. They see rehabilitation as identical to government brainwashing or thought reform.[22]

However, the reason this film works as a Chicano film is precisely this return to the "aesthetics of reception," to the politics of spectatorship. Olmos states it quite clearly: "I couldn't care less what Siskel and Ebert say . . . This film is being seen by the people who are going to use it the most."[23] And it is the resonance between Olmos's words and those of film theorist Teresa de Lauretis that reaffirms my conviction that *American Me* (like films by Chicanas) marks a shift in Chicano cinema. This shift is well summed up in the words of de Lauretis that I cited at the end of the previous chapter: "The spectator is the film's primary concern—primary in the sense that it is there from the beginning, inscribed in the filmmaker's project, and even in the very making of the film."[24]

Feminist film theory has taught me that films address spectators as gendered individuals (subjects).[25] Besides gender, the viewer's (spectator, audience) identification is secured in a film by other codes of representation, such as race and class. Early Chicano films were clear about their spectators. Mostly using race codes of representation as forms of address, Chicano films inscribed Chicanos (and I emphasize the male) as their "ideal" audiences. Stated another way, in the early period Chicano films were made by Chicanos, about Chicanos, and fundamentally *for* Chicanos who were inscribed in the film text as the intended audience/spectators.[26] As I have noted throughout this book, one of the reasons Chicano cinema has not been recognized as a serious cultural movement by mainstream film theorists/critics (in academia and in commercial media) has to do with the fact that these critics assume the position of an "ideal" white middle-class spectator (which they cannot necessarily avoid). To fully grasp the play of, for instance, the film *Zoot Suit*, one has to be literate in certain race (cultural) codes. These films were not intended for the "ideal" white viewer.

After Luis Valdez's *Zoot Suit*, things began to change. The drive for "universal" themes and spectators (crossover audiences), for mainstream reviews, and so on, begins. Thus, cultural specificity as a mode of address takes a backseat in this quest for universality. Even cultural illiterates can grasp the meaning of such films as *The Ballad of Gregorio Cortez*, *Break of Dawn*, *Seguin*, *El Norte*, *La Bamba*, and even *Raíces de Sangre* (which, in fact, predates *Zoot Suit*). Subtitles are provided just in case you failed the bilingual test. But there is a lot more to culture than language.

The point to emphasize for my discussion of *American Me* is that this film returns us to this question of address that was so paramount to the cultural politics of Chicano filmmaking once upon a time. If I paraphrase de Lauretis's observation about feminist cinema, I do so because her insights are appropriate for what I believe *American Me* does: "Its concern with address (whom the film addresses, to whom it speaks, what and for whom it seeks to represent, whom it represents) translates into a conscious effort to address its spectator as [Chicano], regardless of the gender [race and class] of the viewer . . . "[27] I have substituted Chicano for female, and added race and class in brackets.

American Me constructs a picture of prison life that feels immediately, intimately, and unquestionably true. It should first be emphasized that Hollywood set designers had a hand in making this "true" effect possible. The film was shot on location in Folsom State Prison, where Olmos was granted an unprecedented two-weeks shooting time, and in Chico State Prison. To obtain the kitchen-sink realism feel, lighting was a "pre-production mandate," according to cinematographer Rey Villalobos, who diligently worked on this aspect. And, because Folsom looked "too good," its walls were repainted in medium gray and windows were aged, giving the prison its dirty, gritty, filmic feel.[28] But when I say that the film's prison-life experience feels "true" or "real," I mean something other than props and set design.

The film renders the Chicano male presence in the feeling of a gesture, in the rhythms of his walk and speech. There is a certain L.A.-ishness in its style that, as Carmen Huaco-Nuzum has noted, is reminiscent of film noir.[29] However, it is not just the noir style that informs the film, but more precisely the style of Chicano pinto poets (inmate poets) of the Movement. *American Me* captures the melancholia of such pinto poets as Raúl Salinas and Ricardo Sánchez, who, in the early seventies, gave us, for the first time, bleak testimonies of *la pinta* (the prison) in powerful poems. Writing in a highly stylized poetic prose/prosaic poetry, pinto poets wrote about prison life, providing its readers with, as the title of one of Raúl Salinas's poems says it, a "trip through the mind-jail." The lyricism in their works displays an open-ended elliptic tone. This pinto-poet sensibility is rendered by the letter-writing device framing the film *American Me*—the letters written by Santana from inside the prison walls.

One could argue that the filmmaker switches fact with poetics, in other words, that Olmos is merely parroting the poems of pinto poets rather than the reality of actual pintos. Or so I thought, until a good friend whose brother spent twenty years in California prisons pointed out to me that Santana's letters sounded painfully like her brother's: open-ended, elliptical—which made me wonder if this style does in fact reflect that sense of the loss of time, or of loss while doing time. Santana's prose may very well capture the interminable agony of what it must feel like, on a daily, hourly basis, to be locked up for years.

Besides rendering a Chicano pinto presence in the rhythms of speech, Santana represents it in the stylized walk and prose of a pinto, a stance honed in the corridors behind prison walls or in the barrios of East L.A. If something like the Chicano Academy Awards existed, then Olmos would win the Oscar for his brilliant performance of the pinto, for realizing the writing, talking, walking mode of

a Chicano inmate behind bars. It is this authenticity in his performance that touches the hearts of the *familias* of Chicano inmates, this
genuine realism that explains why a relative of a pinto would recognize "in those movements, those looks," those gestures, and "those
silences," "the ways of an experience previously unseen in film."[30]
Shortly after the San Francisco screening of *American Me* ended, I witnessed the power of the film in the theater's lobby when I saw an
older Chicana weeping in Olmos's arms. "She's probably lost a son
behind those prison bars or in gang strife," I remember thinking. And
perhaps Olmos had given her back something she knew was once
there: her son's humanity.

Yes, for all his sociopathology, Santana is not a psychopath à la
Charles Manson (or even Hannibal Lector in *Silence of the Lambs*). Nor
is he demented, despite the dementia of his actions. Unlike the savage bestiality of antiheroes, Santana is rather an "emotionally stunted
human being" whose humanity pierces through his exterior brutality.
Olmos portrays not a cardboard antihero, but a human being who repents for his sins when it is too late, in the final moments of his life.

This tone of repentance, then, represents another feature worth
singling out in Santana's speech. For this tone of repentance evokes
the Catholic confession. The voice of Santana, detached from the
body (disembodied) and awaiting death, speaks to us with unquali-
fied authority, almost as if acknowledging the karmic precept "He
who lives by the sword, must die by the sword." *American Me* uses
the letter-writing device effectively, as a means for introducing the
radical notion of a contradicted human being. Santana repents, his
plea begs forgiveness. However, unlike in Catholicism's last rite of ab-
solution, no priest hears his final confession, granting him absolu-
tion, everlasting forgiveness for his sins. In the absence of a priest,
we, the spectators, stand in for God. There are inherent dangers to
this type of characterization, especially because Santana's audience
appeal derives from his final repentance (as in Catholicism, one can
sin and be forgiven). Yet there simply is no one-sided, fixed, final, or
univocal meaning attached to the image of Santana.

American Me, then, is not a film for "ideal" white middle-class
males (or females) like Siskel and Ebert (even though both gave the
film "thumbs up"). Its race and gender specificity speaks mostly to
young Chicano males, representing those unfortunate Chicanos
locked behind bars, the youth caught up in the urban East-bank of
Los Angeles where youth unemployment tops 30 percent and high-
school dropout rates are close to 80 percent.[31] The film also addresses

parents of these youth, rendering a dignity to children whose humanity has been stripped, not by their fathers, but by capitalism's inhu-
mane disdain for the poor and disempowered. These are the viewers
"inscribed in the filmmaker's project."

Yet while *American Me* speaks to the mother in me, it totally disregards the part in me that is not bound by motherhood: my self as a
feminist, a woman of color who is something else besides a mother.
Indeed, *American Me* "evokes the phantom of an anterior discourse"[32]
that Chicanas know all too well: Octavio Paz's metaphor/trope of
Conquest.[33]

Women appear in two ways in this film, as demonstrated by Santana's mother and by Julie. Santana's mother serves as the mythic origin of Santana's deviance. Like the Mexican philosopher Octavio
Paz's tale of Mexican pathos that underscores the mythic role of "La
Malinche," *American Me* traces Santana's downfall to a primal rape
scene: his mother's rape by U.S. servicemen during their invasion
(Conquest) of East L.A. Racial domination of East L.A. Chicanos is
here figured symbolically in the mother's rape, propelling Santana's
own criminality. For Paz, the culpability of "La Malinche" in the
downfall of the Aztec nation is the key to the Mexican inferiority complex. Hence, Chicanas inherit the legacy of "La Malinche," originat-
ing in this case the downfall of Chicanos in the barrio. Santana's
mother recalls "la Chingada" (the sexually violated Malintzín Tenépal) who, like "La Malinche" in Paz's shrewd account, bears illegitimate mestizo offspring: "los hijos de la Chingada." The effects of this
"original sin," the violation of a passive woman's sexuality, continue
to inform the internal logic of the film's narrative: rape, violations of
masculine sexuality, serves as the primary mechanism for shocking
retaliations on the part of Chicano males.

For example, Santana's arrest as a young boy lands him in juvenile
hall, where on the first night he is raped by a white teenager. Brutally
killing his rapist, Santana is subsequently sentenced to twenty years
in prison. Another especially horrifying moment occurs midway into
the film in the dual rape scene, rendered in parallel scenes of Santana
and Julie in bed and a prison murder. First a love scene, the lovemak-
ing between Santana and Julie turns violent, with Santana attempting
to sodomize Julie.[34] The scene's sexual tension is accentuated by in-
serts in parallel montage of a scene taking place inside the prison
where, on Santana's orders, Chicano inmates first sodomize and then
ram a "Christmas tree"-shaped knife into the rectum of the son of the

Italian mafia boss. The gruesome killing takes place exactly as Santana reaches an orgasm in the counterpointed bedroom scene.

Figured symbolically as the "Chingón" that Paz writes about, Santana "rips open the chingada, the female who is pure passivity, defenseless against the exterior world. The relationship between them is violent, it is determined by the cynical power of the first and the impotence of the second."[35] Even though Santana may figure as the symbol of "el Chingón" for his sexual violence against Julie and over the life of another man, the Chicana in *American Me* is neither passive nor impotent. Having also been a member of an East L.A. gang, Julie in this case fights back, terminating her love affair with Santana. She refused to be "la chingada."

At the threshold of the twenty-first century, *American Me* paints a portrait of hopelessness and despair in the barrios, telling the story of what Rubén Martínez calls "the inner-city black hole that threatens to swallow all the colors and deny every escape route."[36] Yet for Edward James Olmos, Chicanas represent the "glimmer of hope" in our barrios; Julie is the "only hero of the film."[37] Something about this flickering lantern we are expected to hold up at the end of the tunnel, about this burden bequeathed by Olmos to all Chicanas, makes me suspicious. Just as in the "real world," Chicanas in *American Me* carry more than their share of the responsibility for a man: first as origins of Santana's deviance, and second as vehicles for his salvation. This is a very old story indeed, "the mental habit of translating woman into metaphor," which Rosi Braidotti attributes to philosophers who "see in 'women' the privileged repository of 'the future of mankind.' "[38] It is this strange cusp of violation and salvation that contains Chicanas in the film.

In his final despair, Santana acknowledges a new possibility in the Chicana who shows him to love, who tries to teach him to dance. But like his repentance, his recognition comes too late. Too late for us and too late for her. Who is this new subject, this Chicana whom Edward James Olmos claims is the heroine of *American Me*, the hope in our barrios? His story ends before hers can begin. In the final close-up shot of a cross tattooed on Julie's hand resides her untold story. It is the history of Chicana membership in gangs that unfolds not on the screen, but in my mind. The final weathered look in Julie's eyes sparks the painful silent memory of the female gang members I have known: Chicanas surviving and resisting *la vida dura* (the hard life). I often wonder why the story of Julie's oppression and resistance, why the pain of her rape, is not up there, on the Hollywood screen, looking at me.

Notes

Introduction

1. Francisco X. Camplis, "Towards the Development of a Raza Cinema," in *Chicanos and Film*, ed. Chon A. Noriega (Minneapolis: University of Minnesota Press, 1992), 284-302, pp. 299-300.

2. Gloria Anzaldúa, "Speaking in Tongues: A Letter to Third World Women Writers," in *This Bridge Called My Back: Writings by Radical Women of Color*, ed. Cherríe Moraga and Gloria Anzaldúa (New York: Kitchen Table/Women of Color Press, 1983), 165-73, p. 172.

3. Rubén Martínez, *The Other Side* (New York and London: Verso, 1992), 146. The writer is paraphrasing Father Luis Olivares, who is in turn quoting from the Bible— Simeon's statement to the Virgin Mary: "Behold. This child is destined to be a sign that shall be contradicted." See Martínez's essay "La Placita," in *Sex, Death and God in L.A.*, ed. David Reid (New York: Pantheon Books, 1992), 225-58.

4. Teresa de Lauretis, *Alice Doesn't* (Bloomington: Indiana University Press, 1984), 69.

5. See the introductions to these anthologies: Gary D. Keller, "The Image of the Chicano in Mexican, United States and Chicano Cinema: An Overview," in *Chicano Cinema: Research, Reviews, and Resources*, ed. Gary D. Keller (Binghamton: Bilingual Review/Press, 1985), 13-58 and Chon A. Noriega, "Introduction," in *Chicanos and Film*, ed. Chon A. Noriega, xi-xxvi.

6. Carlos Muñoz, Jr., *Youth, Identity and Power* (London and New York: Verso, 1989). The Chicano Power Movement served as an umbrella, grouping the labor movement of the United Farmworkers' Union, headed by César Chávez; community-based politics in civil rights; and youth radicalism in high schools and colleges. Muñoz writes: "The Chicano Movement was a historic first attempt to shape a politics of unification on the basis of a nonwhite identity and culture and on the interests of the Mexican American working class. The movement rejected all previous identities and thus represented a counterhegemonic political and cultural project" (12).

7. See Keller, "The Image of the Chicano in Mexican, United States and Chicano Cinema"; Harry Gamboa, Jr., "El Barrio en la Pantalla," *La Opinión* (November 16, 1980): 6-7; and Jesús Salvador Treviño, "Chicano Cinema," *New Scholar* 8 (1982): 167-80, and "Form and Technique in Chicano Cinema," in *Chicano Cinema*, ed. Gary D. Keller, 109-15.

8. Treviño, "Chicano Cinema," 167.

9. Gamboa, "El Barrio en la Pantalla," 6.

10. See Teresa de Lauretis, "Guerrilla in the Midst: Women's Cinema in the 80s," *Screen* 31, no. 1 (Spring 1990): 6-25; B. Ruby Rich, "In the Name of Feminist Film Criticism," in *Issues in Feminist Film Criticism*, ed. Patricia Erens (Bloomington: Indiana University Press, 1990), 268-87; and Clyde Taylor, "We Don't Need Another Hero," in *Black*

Frames: Critical Perspectives on Black Independent Cinema, ed. Mbye B. Cham and Claire Andrade-Watkins (Cambridge and London: The MIT Press, 1988), 80-85.

11. Camplis, "Towards the Development of a Raza Cinema," 284-302.

12. The various manifestos written by Latin American filmmakers are compiled in *Cineaste* 4, no. 1 (Summer 1970), and *Cineaste* 4, no. 3 (Winter 1970-71).

13. Jason C. Johansen's "Notes on Chicano Cinema" was first published in the Chicano Cinema Coalition's newsletter and later in *La Opinión*. It is reprinted in *Chicanos and Film*, ed. Chon A. Noriega, 303-7.

14. Johansen, "Notes on Chicano Cinema," 305-6.

15. Quoted in the anonymous essay "Ya Basta con Yankee Imperialist Documentaries!" published in *Cine-Aztlán* (1974), and reprinted in *Chicanos and Film*, ed. Chon A. Noriega, 275-83.

16. Camplis, "Towards the Development of a Raza Cinema," 297.

17. Ibid., 293.

18. Noriega, "Introduction," xix.

19. Ibid.

20. Keller, "The Image of the Chicano in Mexican, United States and Chicano Cinema," 47.

21. Noriega, "Introduction," xxiii.

22. Allen L. Woll, "Latin Images in American Films," *Journal of Mexican History* 4 (1974): 28-40; Arthur G. Pettit, *Images of the Mexican American in Fiction and Film* (College Station: Texas A & M University Press, 1980); Carlos E. Cortés, "Chicanas in Film: History of an Image," in *Chicano Cinema*, ed. Gary D. Keller.

23. Kid Frost, "These Stories Have To Be Told," *East Side Story* (Virgin Records America, Inc., 92097-4, 1992); emphasis added. Used with permission. Translations: "cholito" = young cholo (urban Chicano); "plaqueazo" = signature (graffiti); "guero" = light-skinned; "batos quieren pedo" = guys looking for trouble; "filero" = switchblade. I have been told by students in my Chicano studies classes that young Chicanos and Chicanas of mixed (Anglo/Chicano) parents are not accepted by some members of Chicano student organizations because they are "too light-skinned"—a dead giveaway of one's white parent. My sense is that Kid Frost's lyrics respond to this phenomenon of mixed-race kids.

24. Patricia Zavella, "Reflections on Diversity among Chicanas," *Frontiers* 12, no. 2 (1991): 73-85; and José E. Limón, "The Folk Performance of '*Chicano*' and the Cultural Limits of Political Ideology," in "*And Other Neighborly Names*': Social Process and Cultural Image in Texas Folklore*, ed. Richard Bauman and Roger D. Abrahams (Austin: University of Texas Press, 1981), 197-225.

25. Frances Salomé España communicated these ideas to me in the context of a discussion in the spring of 1992 about her vision as a visual artist/filmmaker. Similar arguments are taken up by Kobena Mercer's discussion of black British filmmaking; see Kobena Mercer, "Recoding Narratives of Race and Nation," *ICA Documents*, no. 7 (1988): 4-14.

26. Paul Willeman, "Introduction," in *Questions of Third Cinema*, ed. Jim Pines and Paul Willeman (London: British Film Institute, 1989), 1-29, p. 12.

27. Fernando Birri, "For a Nationalist, Realist, Critical and Popular Cinema," *Screen* 26, nos. 3-4 (May-August 1985): 89-91, p. 90.

28. de Lauretis, "Guerrilla in the Midst: Women's Cinema in the 80s," 17.

29. Raymond Williams notes the relation between "project" and "social formation" as the "central theoretical point" that informs the cultural studies approach to the study of art and society; see Williams, *The Politics of Modernism* (London and New York: Verso, 1989), 151-52.

30. Carlos Blanco's dictum "historicize, always historicize" still rings through my head, as does Rosaura Sánchez's rigor for semiotics, contextual specificity, and class analysis; Herb Schiller's for the privatization of the public domain; Susan Kirkpatrick's for feminism and the nuances of discursive formations; Michel de Certeau's for the politics of resistance; Jaime Concha's for intellectual genealogies and Latin American philosophical discourse; Susan Davis's for popular culture and public space. To them I owe my "academic" formation.

31. For further discussion of the limitations of the postcolonial framework, see Ruth Frankenberg and Lata Mani's excellent essay, "Crosscurrents, Crosstalk: Race, 'Postcoloniality' and the Politics of Location," in *Cultural Studies* 7, no. 2 (May 1993): 292-310; and Ella Shohat's call for historical specificity in postcoloniality in "Notes on the 'Postcolonial,' " *Social Text* 10, nos. 2-3 (1992): 99-113.

32. Benedict Anderson, *Imagined Communities* (London and New York: Verso, 1991), 6.

1. *Actos* of "Imaginative Re-discovery"

1. Rolando Hinojosa-Smith, in a conference paper delivered at the Modern Language Association meeting in 1982 and published as "*I Am Joaquín*: The Relationships between the Text and the Film," in *Chicano Cinema*, ed. Gary D. Keller (Binghamton: Bilingual Review/Press, 1985), 144.

2. Stuart Hall, "Cultural Identity and Cinematic Representation," *Framework*, no. 36 (1989): 68-81.

3. *I Am Joaquin*, director Luis Valdez; *Agueda Martínez*, director Esperanza Vásquez; *Chicana*, director Sylvia Morales; *Yo Soy Chicano*, director Barry Nye, writer and producer Jesús Salvador Treviño.

4. The notion of the "documentary impulse" in Chicano film is taken up by Chon Noriega in his "Introduction," in *Chicanos and Film*, ed. Chon A. Noriega (Minneapolis: University of Minnesota Press, 1992), xi-xxvi.

5. For example, the poem "I Am Joaquin" was written in 1967 and distributed throughout the Southwest to Chicano student organizations by La Causa Publications in Oakland, California. It was printed in book form in 1972. Prior to its distribution in the 1960s, the only book available on Mexican-American history had been *North from Mexico*, by Carey McWilliams, but it was out of print during the early period of Movement activism. See Carlos Muñoz, Jr., *Youth, Identity and Power* (London and New York: Verso, 1989), 60-61.

6. Fernando Birri, "For a Nationalist, Realist, Critical and Popular Cinema," *Screen* 26, nos. 3-4 (May-August 1985): 91.

7. Chronologies (such as Keller's and Treviño's) dealing with the corpus of Chicano cinema are informed by an evolutionary paradigm. In other words, the genre's development is measured through a chronology that posits an evolution from "unsophisticated" (poor) to more "sophisticated" (better) filmic qualities. See Gary D. Keller, "The Image of the Chicano in Mexican, United States and Chicano Cinema: An Overview," 13-58, and Jesús Salvador Treviño, "Form and Technique in Chicano Cinema," 109-15, in *Chicano Cinema*. In writing about the evolution of Chicano cinema, Tomás Ybarra-Frausto, for instance, outlines the following stages: the experimental phase (1969 to the midseventies); the documentary phase (mid- to late seventies); and the feature-length or Hollywood phase (late seventies to the present). According to Ybarra-Frausto, the first phase is characterized by limited or virtually no filmmaking experience; the second, by the professionalization of filming; and the final by an entry into the Hollywood industry. Ybarra-Frausto correctly points out that the experimental

style predominates in the first phase, but his outline does not adequately account for "instances" of experimental cinema (in the second phase or even in the third) within the documentary and fictional modes (for example, in the films by Cheech Marin, which were all "Hollywood" films, or in Lourdes Portillo's documentary *La Ofrenda*, released in 1989). See Tomás Ybarra-Frausto, "The Chicano Alternative Film Movement," *Centro de Estudios Puertorriqueños Bulletin* 2, no. 8 (Spring 1990): 44-47.

Thus, evolutionary explanations fail to address adequately departures from the model, as in the case of Sylvia Morales, who, by the time she made *Chicana* in 1979, had amassed several years of experience in television documentary production. Moreover, it does not follow that improvisational or experimental techniques derive from a lack of "professional" training, for many experienced imagemakers, especially Frances Salomé España and Willie Varela, continue to experiment with style well into the nineties.

8. Eliud Martínez, "*I Am Joaquin*, as Poem and Film: Two Modes of Chicano Expression," *Journal of Popular Culture* 13, no. 3 (Spring 1980): 505-15, p. 507.

9. Ybarra-Frausto, "The Chicano Alternative Film Movement," 45.

10. See Treviño, "Form and Technique in Chicano Cinema," 111.

11. Hinojosa-Smith, "*I Am Joaquin*," 143.

12. Rodolfo Gonzales, *I Am Joaquin, Yo Soy Joaquín* (Toronto/New York/London: Bantam Books, Inc., 1972), 1.

13. Rudy Acuña, *Occupied America: The Chicano's Struggle toward Liberation* (San Francisco: Canfield Press, 1972), 241.

14. Ibid.

15. Rosa Linda Fregoso and Angie Chabram, "Introduction: Re-framing Alternative Critical Discourse," *Cultural Studies* 4, no. 3 (1990): 203-12.

16. Martínez, "*I Am Joaquin* as Poem and Film," 511.

17. See Gonzales, *I Am Joaquin, Yo Soy Joaquín*, 19, (40).

18. Rosaura Sánchez, "Chicana Prose Writers: The Case of Gina Valdés and Sylvia Lizárraga," in *Beyond Stereotypes*, ed. María Herrera-Sobek (Binghamton: Bilingual Press, 1985), 62.

19. Gonzales, *I Am Joaquin, Yo Soy Joaquín*, 70.

20. Ibid., 98.

21. Ibid., 42, 77.

22. See Yolanda Broyles-González, "What Price 'Mainstream'? Luis Valdez' *Corridos* on Stage and Film," *Cultural Studies* 4, no. 1 (1990): 281-93.

23. Originally published as "Tale of La Raza," *Bronze* 1, no. 1 (November 25, 1968); quoted in Muñoz, *Youth, Identity and Power*, 63.

24. Martínez, "*I Am Joaquin* as Poem and Film," 512.

25. Pierre Nora, "Between Memory and History: *Les Lieux de Mémoire*," *Representations* 26 (Spring 1989): 13. For further discussion of the relation between memory and "official history," see Michel de Certeau, *Heterologies* (Minneapolis: University of Minnesota Press, 1986). I have also taken up the relation of Chicano films to memory in "Re-membering the Border through Chicano Cinema," in *Rearticulations: The Practice of Chicano Cultural Studies*, ed. Mario García and Ellen McCracken (Los Angeles and Berkeley: University of California Press, forthcoming).

26. Gonzales, *I Am Joaquin, Yo Soy Joaquín*, 122.

27. John R. Chávez, *The Lost Land: The Chicano Image of the Southwest* (Albuquerque: University of New Mexico Press, 1984), 129-55.

28. Genaro Padilla, "Myth and Comparative Cultural Nationalism," in *Aztlán : Essays on the Chicano Homeland*, ed. Rudolfo A. Anaya and Francisco Lomelí (Albuquerque: Academia/El Norte Publications, 1989), 113.

29. Chávez, *The Lost Land*, 131.

30. Padilla, "Myth and Comparative Cultural Nationalism," 126.

31. The program was funded by a grant from the Corporation for Public Broadcasting, Public Broadcasting System, and KCET.

32. See Chávez, *The Lost Land*, 130. Chicano historians have traced the "universal acceptance" of the term among Chicanos to the 1969 Denver Youth Conference, where Chicano activists drafted the "Plan Espiritual de Aztlán" in the spring of 1969. Chávez writes that "Corky" Gonzales was the person most responsible for popularizing the term, whereas, in an interview I conducted for National Public Radio, the poet Alurista stated he first used the term within the context of Chicano nationalism. The following interesting detail is included in Chávez's account of the term: "In modern times the term was first applied to the Chicano homeland in 1962 by Jack D. Forbes, a Native-American professor who argued that Mexicans were more truly an Indian than a mestizo people; his mimeographed manuscript, 'The Mexican Heritage of Aztlán (the Southwest) to 1821,' was distributed among Mexican Americans in the Southwest during the early 1960s" (141).

33. I am always struck by the responses of audiences who view this film, either in public forums or in my classes. There is always someone who comments to the effect, "That's the way my grandmother is" or "Agueda reminds me of my grandmother." Hence, the appropriateness of the film's full title: *Agueda Martínez: Our People, Our Country*.

34. Alvina Quintana, "Politics, Representation and the Emergence of a Chicana Aesthetic," *Cultural Studies* 4, no. 3 (October 1990): 258.

35. Rosaura Sánchez, "The History of Chicanas: Proposal for a Materialist Perspective," in *Between Borders : Essays of Mexicana/Chicana History*, ed. Adelaida R. Del Castillo (Encino, Calif.: Floricanto Press, 1990), 13.

36. Sylvia Morales is credited as one of the camera operators of *Yo Soy Chicano*.

37. Quoted in Treviño, "Form and Technique in Chicano Cinema," 112.

38. *Chicana* was produced with a $5,000 grant from the Institute of American Cultures at UCLA while Morales was a film student. The Film Fund provided a $10,000 grant for the Spanish version of the film. All persons involved in its production volunteered their services. See Sylvia Morales, "Como se hizo *La Chicana*," *La Opinión* (1980): 13.

39. Ybarra-Frausto, "The Chicano Alternative Film Movement."

40. For a comprehensive survey of Chicana feminist critiques of cultural nationalism, see Denise A. Segura and Beatriz M. Pesquera, "Beyond Indifference and Antipathy: The Chicana Movement and Chicana Feminist Discourse," *Aztlán* 19, no. 2 (1988-90): 69-92.

41. Padilla, "Myth and Comparative Cultural Nationalism," 121.

42. A comprehensive critique of the oppression of women in Aztec society is provided by Iris Blanco, who bases her study on the chronicles of an indigenous historian; see Iris Blanco, "Participación de las Mujeres en la Sociedad Prehispanica," in *Essays on La Mujer*, ed. Rosaura Sánchez and Rosa Martínez Cruz (Los Angeles: UCLA, Chicano Studies Center Publications, 1977), 48-81.

43. In a personal conversation, Sylvia Morales told me that the credit for the film needs to be given primarily to Ana Nieto-Gómez. Morales first saw the slide show in the summer of 1977 at a seminar dealing with minority women and advertising held at the Inner City Cultural Center of Los Angeles. Morales was so impressed that she approached Nieto-Gómez about making it into a film. Interestingly, a ten-year span separates Nieto-Gómez's slide show from "Corky" Gonzales's poem, just as a decade separates the production of both films.

44. Two examples of Ana Nieto-Gómez's intervention in this regard are Nieto-Gómez, "La Feminista," *Encuentro Feminil* 1 (1974): 34-47; and Adelaida Del Castillo, Ana Nieto-Gómez, and Elizabeth Martínez, "La Chicana," in *Third World Women* (San Francisco: Third World Communications, 1972), 130-32.

45. Ana Nieto-Gómez was one of the first Chicana feminists of the movement to critique cultural nationalism for its sexism and for the lack of attention to gender oppression within the Chicano Movement. In the midseventies, she became the first woman in a Chicano studies department to be denied tenure. This incident took place at California State University-Northridge, at a time when the noted Chicano historian Rudy Acuña was the chair of the Chicano studies program. Her dismissal from the Chicano studies department, according to Carlos Muñoz, "accelerated demands by some feminists within the student movement for the establishment of a *Chicana* studies program" (Muñoz, *Youth, Identity and Power*, 160; emphasis in the original).

46. Norma Alarcón, "Chicana's Feminist Literature: A Re-vision through Malintzín; or, Malintzín: Putting Flesh Back on the Object," in *This Bridge Called My Back: Writings by Radical Women of Color*, ed. Cherríe Moraga and Gloria Anzaldúa (New York: Kitchen Table/Women of Color Press, 1983), 182.

47. Ibid., 188.

48. See especially Adelaida R. Del Castillo, "Malintzín Tenépal: A Preliminary Look into a New Perspective," in *Essays on La Mujer*, ed. Rosaura Sánchez and Rosa Martínez Cruz, 124-49.

49. Alarcón, "Chicana's Feminist Literature," 182.

50. Cherríe Moraga and Gloria Anzaldúa, eds., *This Bridge Called My Back*, 195.

51. For an extensive list of Chicano and Chicana films, see the two anthologies on Chicano cinema: *Chicano Cinema*, ed. Gary D. Keller, and *Chicanos and Film*, ed. Chon Noriega.

52. Notably absent from this discussion is a body of work that is also paradigmatic of Chicano cinema: the experimental films by Willie Varela.

53. Hall, "Cultural Identity and Cinematic Representation," 70.

54. The birth of the mestizo nation, based on the sixteenth-century interracial mixture between *conquistadores* from Extremadura, Spain, and the Aztec nation, ignores the ongoing waves of European migrations into the Americas well into the twentieth century, ignoring as well the heterogeneity and various nation backgrounds of the European immigrants to Mexico. My own ancestry complicates the lineage traced by Chicano Movement intellectuals. On my father's side, we are Italian immigrants to Mexico who came from Genova, Italy, in the nineteenth century. Hence my Italian family name, Fregoso. On my mother's side, the paternal ancestry is traced to Basque immigration to Puebla. Yet these immigrants, to my knowledge, intermarried by the time my grandfather was born. My maternal grandmother always said she was an "indian," even though she never specified the group. All we ever knew was that her family had lived in the Brownsville-Matamoros (Nuevo Santander) region of Texas, well before Anglo immigrants came into the region. As a child growing up in Corpus Christi, I learned that the Indians of the region were known as the Karankawa. Hence I am a Chicana of Karankawa/Basque/Italian origin.

2. Intertextuality and Cultural Identity in *Zoot Suit* and *La Bamba*

1. These comments are the Pachuco's response to Hank's accusation, "You're doing this to me."

2. Stephen Heath, *Questions of Cinema* (Bloomington: Indiana University Press, 1981), 132.

3. In conventional realism, according to Colin MacCabe, films appear transparent or hide their modes of articulation, hence the difficulty of determining the narrative discourse. As MacCabe explains: "The narrative discourse cannot be mistaken in its identifications because the narrative discourse is not present as discourse—as articulation. The unquestioned nature of the narrative discourse entails that the only problem that reality poses is to go and look and see what *Things* there are. The relationship between the reading subject and the real is placed as one of pure specularity. The real is not articulated—it is" (Colin MacCabe, *Tracking the Signifier* [Minneapolis: University of Minnesota Press, 1981], 39). In this respect, *Zoot Suit* draws attention to the mechanism of discourse.

4. Paul Willeman, "Introduction," in *Questions of Third Cinema*, ed. Jim Pines and Paul Willeman (London: British Film Institute, 1989), 7-8.

5. Kobena Mercer, "Diaspora Culture and the Dialogic Imagination: The Aesthetics of Black Independent Film in Britain," in *Black Frames: Critical Perspectives on Black Independent Cinema*, ed. Mbye B. Cham and Claire Andrade-Watkins, (Cambridge and London: The MIT Press, 1988), 50.

6. See Ramón Saldívar, *Chicano Narrative: The Dialectics of Difference* (Madison: University of Wisconsin Press, 1990).

7. The following historical events frame the film. In August 1942, twenty-four members of the 38th Street Club were arrested in connection with the death of José Díaz. Díaz's body was found near a swimming hole that Chicano/a youth called "Sleepy Lagoon," a name taken from the popular Henry James tune and movie. Because segregation barred Chicanos and blacks from using public pools, Sleepy Lagoon was popular among Chicano/a youth (Mauricio Mazon, *The Zoot Suit Riots: A Psychology of Symbolic Annihilation* [Austin: University of Texas Press, 1985], 20). In connection with the alleged murder of José Díaz, six hundred Chicano/a youth were rounded up and questioned by police. The mass trial of members of the 38th Street Club took place in the context of a "highly sensationalized press coverage." The Sleepy Lagoon trial also led to the conviction of seventeen Chicano/a youth: three on first-degree murder, nine on second-degree murder, and five others on lesser charges. In October 1944, the Second District Court of Appeals reversed the lower court convictions, citing lack of evidence. Yet, the Sleepy Lagoon defendants spent over two years in prison. For a full account of this event, see Rudy Acuña, *Occupied America: A History of Chicanos*, 2d ed. (New York: Harper and Row, 1981); Carey McWilliams, *North from Mexico* (New York: Greenwood, 1973); Mazon, *The Zoot Suit Riots: A Psychology of Symbolic Annihilation*; Dale McLemore and Ricardo Romo, "The Origins and Development of the Mexican American People," in *The Mexican American Experience*, ed. Rodolfo O. de la Garza et al. (Austin: University of Texas Press, 1985), 3-32.

The "Zoot Suit riots" of the summer of 1943 are less central to the narrative's plot than the Sleepy Lagoon incident, although this disturbing event in Los Angeles history also frames the film's narrative. Indeed, the events surrounding the "Zoot Suit riots" are crucial for a fuller understanding of the film's antiracism stance, particularly because the incident strained relations between the Mexican community and racist dominant institutions of law enforcement, media, and justice for decades afterward.

In June 1943 a group of pachucos allegedly beat several sailors in an east-side barrio of Los Angeles. Accompanied by off-duty policemen, servicemen responded to the beating with a series of mob attacks against Chicano/a youth who were wearing zoot suits. For ten days, servicemen systematically "invaded" and terrorized east-side barrios. They were also joined by thousands of Angelenos (whites), who were concerned about eradicating the so-called Mexican "crime wave." Law enforcement officials also participated in the "Zoot Suit riots" by indiscriminately arresting Chicano/a youth wearing zoot suits.

8. See Daniel Solorzano's account of his activism with students in 1979 in "Teaching and Social Change: Reflections on a Freirian Approach in a College Classroom," *Teaching Sociology* 17 (April 1989): 218-25, p. 222.

9. See Tomás Ybarra-Frausto, "The Chicano Alternative Film Movement," *Centro de Estudios Puertorriqueños Bulletin* 2, no. 8 (Spring 1990): 44-47.

10. Yolanda Broyles-González, *El Teatro Campesino: An Oral History of the Ensemble* (Austin: University of Texas Press, forthcoming).

11. See my article "*Zoot Suit* and *The Ballad of Gregorio Cortez*," *Crítica* 1, no. 2 (1985): 126-31.

12. See Jane Feuer, *The Hollywood Musical* (Bloomington: Indiana University Press, 1982), 35.

13. Ibid., 35-36.

14. See Mercer, "Diaspora Culture and the Dialogic Imagination," 51.

15. Broyles-González, *El Teatro Campesino*.

16. Kobena Mercer, "1968: Periodizing Postmodern Politics and Identity," in *Cultural Studies*, ed. Lawrence Grossberg, Cary Nelson, and Paula Treicher (New York and London: Routledge, 1992), 424-37, p. 424.

17. Susan E. Keefe and Amado M. Padilla, *Chicano Ethnicity* (Albuquerque: University of New Mexico Press, 1987); Felix M. Padilla, "On the Nature of Latino Ethnicity," in *The Mexican American Experience*, ed. Rodolfo O. de la Garza et al., 332-45; José E. Limón, "The Folk Performance of '*Chicano*' and the Cultural Limits of Political Ideology," in "*And Other Neighborly Names*": *Social Process and Cultural Image in Texas Folklore*, ed. Richard Bauman and Roger D. Abrahams (Austin: University of Texas Press, 1981), 197-225.

18. Patricia Zavella, "Reflections on Diversity among Chicanas," *Frontiers* 12, no. 2 (1991): 73-85; Maxine Baca Zinn, "Gender and Ethnic Identity among Chicanas," *Frontiers* 5, no. 2 (1981): 18-24.

19. Stuart Hall, "Cultural Identity and Cinematic Representation," *Framework*, no. 36 (1989): 71.

20. Cited in Carlos E. Cortés, "Who is Maria? What is Juan? Dilemmas of Analyzing the Chicano Image in U.S. Feature Films," in *Chicanos and Film*, ed. Chon A. Noriega (Minneapolis: University of Minnesota Press, 1992), 74-93, pp. 84-85.

21. Quoted in Solorzano, "Teaching and Social Change," 219. For further discussion about the "gang problem" in the Chicano community see Celia Heller, *Mexican American Youth: Forgotten Youth at the Crossroads* (New York: Random House, 1966); Larry Trujillo, "La Evolución del 'Bandido' al 'Pachuco': A Critical Examination and Evaluation of Criminological Literature on Chicanos," *Issues in Criminology* 9 (1974): 43-67; U.S. Commission on Civil Rights, *Window Dressing on the Set* (Washington, D.C.: U.S. Commission on Civil Rights, 1977); Octavio I. Romano, "Social Science, Objectivity and the Chicanos," *El Grito* 4, no. 1 (Fall 1970): 4-16; Nicolas C. Vaca, "The Mexican-American in the Social Sciences, 1912-1970. Part I: 1912-1935," *El Grito* 3, no. 3 (Spring 1970): 3-24, and "The Mexican-American in the Social Sciences, 1912-1970. Part II: 1936-1970," *El Grito* 4, no. 1 (Fall 1970): 17-51.

22. Rosa Linda Fregoso, "Cultural Identity in *Zoot Suit*," *Theory and Society* (forthcoming). On April 26, 1991, at a talk for the seminar "Popular Culture and Latino Identity in the United States" at Northeastern University, I gave a presentation on Chicano cultural identity and its representation in film. After my talk an African-American student from New Jersey approached me with a great deal of confusion. He thought that "Latino" was the self-designation for "Hispanic," whereas "Chicano" meant "gang."

Thus everytime I used the word Chicano, the term evoked for him the image of a gang member.

23. I have made this argument in my article "Cultural Identity in *Zoot Suit*." Bob Connell's research on masculinities examines the extent to which the expressive forms of gender (masculinity and femininity) regulating the substantive category of the modern subject (biological sex) acquire hegemony in different historical moments. In other words, what the dominant order defines as masculine, or manliness, has changed through time. As Connell's critical genealogy on masculinities reveals, hegemonic masculinity, namely, the dominant attributes that constitute the subject "man" of the dominant class, and race in the "Western" context, is far from stable. For the past two hundred years, hegemonic masculinity, in Connell's words, is rather a "history of displacement, splitting, and remaking of this cultural form." Masculine identities normalized as gender difference of the privileged Euro-American classes and manifested in various historical moments for the past two hundred years, re-emerge in other forms of masculinities. Their vestiges are re-fashioned or re-made into contemporary variations of hegemonic masculinities, for example, the militaristic individualism of Sylvester Stallone, Clint Eastwood, and Arnold Schwarzenegger, the masculinity of technocratic rationality associated with the recent Persian Gulf War, and the frontiers masculinity rendered in the Western film genre. However, the mobilization of various forms of masculinities underscores the extent to which multiple, often contradictory, masculine identities are available to members of the dominant culture. As part of a heterogeneous body of masculine identities, each may be positively or negatively valorized, depending on the social and cultural configurations. See Bob Connell, "The Big Picture—A Little Sketch," *Theory and Society* (forthcoming).

24. Connell, ibid. cites the *conquistador* as the first masculine type in European history. He mentions the subsequent *conquistadores* of other European ethnic groups (i.e., of Portugal, Holland, England, and France), but it is nonetheless interesting that the Spanish empire serves as the model for the first manifestation of a violent and unruly masculinity. One wonders to what extent this is not a wholly external view of masculine identities imposed from the outside onto Spain. Internal to the Spanish empire, other masculinities were available; for instance, the type embodied in religious figures such as Fray Bartolomé de Las Casas. Although he is cited by Connell as protesting the treatment of the *conquistadores* toward the indigenous population in the Americas, one has to wonder why Las Casas does not qualify as an alternative masculine type to that of the *conquistador*. Moreover, other masculinities were operative in Spain at the time of the Conquest, particularly those figured in Miguel de Cervantes's *Don Quixote*—a brilliant parody of chivalry and *conquistador* masculinities.

25. For example, the Northern European saying "Europe begins at the Pyrenees" calls attention to the racial (African) influence in Spain, particularly prior to the sixteenth century. Arnoldo de Leon and Raymund Paredes trace Anglos' negative view of Mexicans in nineteenth-century Texas to the British racism against Spain during wars between the empires. See Arnoldo de Leon, *They Called Them Greasers* (Austin: University of Texas Press, 1983); Raymund Paredes, "The Origins of Anti-Mexican Sentiment in the United States," in *New Directions in Chicano Scholarship*, ed. Ricardo Romo and Raymund Paredes (Santa Barbara: UCSB, Center for Chicano Studies, 1984), 139-66.

26. In Spanish, the term *macho* literally means "male." Its gender equivalent for female is *hembra*. Given that as a Romance language Spanish is an explicitly gendered language, *machismo* refers to the male domination of females. Although the word *sexismo* exists in Spanish as a synonym for *machismo*, the equivalent English translation for *machismo* would be "maleism"—a term I would urge those of us working in critical feminist tradition to adopt. For, as a signifier, I am convinced that *machismo* does not nec-

essarily slide, but stops at the signified, Chicano, Latino, perhaps even male of color, *content*. Such embodiments, in this critically discursive age, are entirely problematic. Furthermore, this is an objection that does not at all minimize the problems Chicanas do have with sexism.

27. Denise Segura, "Familism and Employment among Chicanas and Mexican Immigrant Women," in *Mexicanas at Work in the United States*, ed. Margarita B. Melville (Houston: University of Houston Press, 1988), 31. For some time now, Chicano and Chicana researchers have called attention to the problematic use of the term *machismo*. Chicana feminist writers have problematized the convenient way in which *machismo* positions Chicanos as the epitome of patriarchy. Feminists, particularly those working within the discipline of sociology, are always having to distinguish in their critical essays between patriarchy, or "male authority over women," and *machismo*. Critical of early fictional and anthropological texts that construct " 'machismo' as inherent in Chicano culture," according to Segura, critics since the early 1970s have refuted the existence of "exaggerated masculinity and excessive patriarchy in Chicano families" (31). The emphasis has been to single out that patriarchy is no more violent for Chicanas than for other women, but also to contest the positioning of Chicano and of "Latin" culture in general, as structure/model/system for the pathological transgressions of that order.

28. Carlos Muñoz, Jr., *Youth, Identity and Power* (London and New York: Verso, 1989), 76.

29. Partha Chatterjee, *Nationalist Thought and the Colonial World* (London: Zed Books, 1986).

30. This quote is taken from Kobena Mercer's article "1968" (424), in which he applies to a different yet related problem: the loss of identity and authority among postmodern intellectuals.

31. Wlad Godzich, "Foreword: The Further Possibility of Knowledge," in Michel de Certeau, *Heterologies* (Minneapolis: University of Minnesota Press, 1986), vii.

32. Judith Butler, *Gender Trouble* (New York and London: Routledge, 1990), 16.

33. Trinh T. Minh-ha, "Not You/Like You: Post Colonial Women and the Interlocking Question of Identity and Difference," in *Making Faces, Making Soul/Haciendo Caras*, ed. Gloria Anzaldúa (San Francisco: Aunt Lute Foundation Books, 1990), 371.

34. Hall, "Cultural Identity and Cinematic Representation," 69.

35. Avery Gordon, "Masquerading in the Postmodern," in *Cross Currents*, ed. E. A. Kaplan and M. Sprinker (London and New York: Verso, 1990), 72.

36. Hall, "Cultural Identity and Cinematic Representation," 70-72.

37. Ibid., 69.

38. Valdez imputes onto the Pachuco three narrative functions: as cinematic technique, as narrator, and as Hank's unconscious. In his role as cinematic technique, the Pachuco supplants traditional film editing devices. For instance, rather than resorting to the more conventional techniques of dissolves or slow-motion shots to signal respectively transitions in time or memory/dream effects, Valdez employs the Pachuco as a literal visual marker of time passages. With a snap of his fingers, the Pachuco freezes narrative action, particularly action involving violence. The Pachuco is also used to signal transitions in narrative space. In an early jail scene, the Pachuco marks a transition to a previous narrative event. As Hank begins to tell the defense lawyer about the events leading up to the Sleepy Lagoon incident, the camera cuts to a medium shot of the Pachuco, who snaps his fingers. The camera then cuts to the dance scene. Although the Pachuco's figuration is, according to Valdez, inspired by cinematic techniques, his function as the film's narrator is taken from Brechtian theater. The opening

segment of the film establishes the Pachuco's function as the narrative voice of *Zoot Suit*.

39. Hall, "Cultural Identity and Cinematic Representation," 80.

40. See Broyles-González, *El Teatro Campesino*.

41. In fact, this intelligibility was only accessible to those schooled in neo-Mayan philosophy. As Genaro Padilla writes, Valdez's "drama became increasingly esoteric and philosophical, a form of drama that required an audience schooled in pre-Columbian mythology, however much it had been adapted to the modern temper as well as to the iconographic needs of the political movement" [Genaro Padilla, "Myth and Comparative Cultural Nationalism," in *Aztlán: Essays on the Chicano Homeland*, ed. Rudolfo A. Anaya and Francisco Lomelí (Albuquerque: Academia/El Norte Publications, 1989), 121].

42. See Broyles-González, *El Teatro Campesino*. For further discussion of Mayan neo-myth in Valdez's work, see Víctor Fuentes, "Chicano Cinema: A Dialectic between Voices and Images of the Autonomous Discourse Versus Those of the Dominant," in *Chicanos and Film*, ed. Chon A. Noriega, 207-17.

43. This journey of the mind recalls pinto poet Raúl Salinas's poem "Trip through the Mind Jail."

44. Angie Chabram-Dernersesian, "I Throw Punches for My Race, but I Don't Want to Be a Man: Writing Us—Chica-nos (Girl, Us)/Chicanas—into the Movement Script," in *Cultural Studies*, ed. Lawrence Grossberg et al., 82.

45. It is part of the "nativist" mythmaking enterprise noted in the previous chapter. Yet, it had a certain popularity on the part of whites, especially those involved in the hippie countercultural movement. For instance, the popularity of Carlos Castañeda's novels among whites and Chicanos was part of this "New Age" metaphysical/mystical phenomenon.

46. Chabram-Dernersesian, "I Throw Punches for My Race," 82.

47. My translation of this passage is as follows: "And one must not forget / that according to ancient prophecy / QUETZALCOATL is soon to return / to earth / (Tezcatlipoca, his evil twin / came in the figure of [Hernan] Cortés / the last time in 1519) / But there comes / the day and year of the birth / of the FEATHERED SERPENT / (according to ancient calculations) in / the YEAR OF CE ACATL IN THE DAY / CE ACATL / and it falls on the 16th of August of 1987 / the prophecy says that the / entire world will be / enlightened / and so it is." This poetic essay was originally published in 1973 as *Pensamiento Serpentino* by Cucaracha Publications, El Centro Campesino Cultural. It was recently reprinted in *Luis Valdez—Early Works: Actos, Bernabé, and Pensamiento Serpentino* (Houston: Arte Publico Press, 1990), 168-99.

48. I first saw this film in August 1987 in Madrid. The connection with the date cited in his poem was not made until much later.

49. The eighties witnessed a conservative turn in the nation's political climate. Reaganomics was well under way. As the right-wing offensive chipped away at the social and educational gains of the previous decade, political mobilization sharply declined as well. Popular commercial culture appeared to capitalize on the uneasy social climate, seeking inspiration and refuge in earlier times. That this regression to a past responded to a general conservatism is evident in commercial media's revival of its "Happy Days" as the 1950s—a period of the most aggressive right-wing assaults on civil democracy. In the context of this climate, *La Bamba* was released.

50. Five percent of the film's advertising budget targeted the Latino audience; however, Latino moviegoers represented 10 percent of the audience [*Hispanic Business* (July 1988): 8-13].

51. See George Lipsitz, *Time Passages* (Minneapolis: University of Minnesota Press, 1990), especially chapter 6, on Chicano music. This quotation is taken from page 144.

52. Ibid., 145.

53. Tony Curiel, "Introduction," in *Luis Valdez—Early Works: Actos, Bernabé, and Pensamiento Serpentino*, 4.

54. For an introduction to "New Age" thought, see Elliot Miller, *A Crash Course on the New Age Movement* (Grand Rapids, Mich.: Baker Book House, 1989).

55. *Luis Valdez—Early Works: Actos, Bernabé, and Pensamiento Serpentino*, 198-99.

56. A common folk practice is to go to a card reader in order to ask for spiritual advice. The psychic usually "reads" one's future by using a tarot card deck or a poker deck.

57. Padilla, "Myth and Comparative Cultural Nationalism," 122.

58. Connell, "The Big Picture—A Little Sketch," 17.

59. See my essay "The Mother-motif in *La Bamba* and *Boulevard Nights*," in *Building with Our Hands: Issues in Chicana Studies*, ed. Beatriz Pesquera and Adela De La Torre (Berkeley: University of California Press, forthcoming).

60. Renato Rosaldo, "Assimilation Revisited," in *In Times of Challenge: Chicanos and Chicanas in American Society*, ed. Juan R. Garcia, Julia Curry Rodriguez, and Clara Lomas (Houston: Mexican American Studies, 1988), 43.

61. Ibid., 49.

62. Kobena Mercer, "Recoding Narratives of Race and Nation," *ICA Documents*, no. 7 (1988): 10.

63. See my article "*Seguin*: The Same Side of the Alamo," in *Chicano Cinema*, ed. Gary Keller, (Binghamton: Bilingual Review/Press, 1985), 146-52.

64. Mercer, "1968," 424.

65. Chabram-Dernersesian, "I Throw Punches for My Race," 83.

66. Ibid., 82.

67. Hall, "Cultural Identity and Cinematic Representation," 68.

68. Ibid., 68.

69. Ibid.

3. Humor as Subversive De-construction

1. Each time I discuss this film with audiences, I am asked about the meaning of this scene.

2. For further details about Marin's other films and for discussion about his split with Thomas Chong, see Christine List, "Self-Directed Stereotyping in the Films of Cheech Marin," in *Chicanos and Film*, ed. Chon A. Noriega (Minneapolis: University of Minnesota Press, 1992), 183-94.

3. For documentation of the massive deportation of Chicano U.S. citizens to Mexico throughout the twentieth century, see Rudy Acuña, *Occupied America: A History of Chicanos*, 2d ed. (New York: Harper and Row, 1981).

4. Ryan and Kellner also find this tendency among white leftist filmmakers whose emphasis on making "politically correct" films, according to the authors, leans toward "enjoining pleasure while privileging cinematic techniques that punish audiences" [Michael Ryan and Doug Kellner, *Camera Politica* (Bloomington: Indiana University Press, 1988), 286].

5. List, "Self-Directed Stereotyping in the Films of Cheech Marin," 185.

6. Details of this interview were published in Chon Noriega's article "Café Oralé: Narrative Structure in *Born in East L.A.*," *Tonantzin* 8, no. 1 (February 1991): 17-18.

7. Not only is she dressed in red, white, and green, but she interrupts a Cinco de Mayo parade, the public symbol of Chicanismo, and she is depicted walking directly in between a Mexican flag and an American flag of a mural in the background.

8. See Noriega, "Café Oralé," 17-18.

9. One could argue that injecting subliminal messages onto opaque images is a common practice in complex narratives; however, this problematically conflates author's intentionality with cinematic effects. Marin may have intended that the French woman function allegorically, but the visual language used in her depiction (i.e., close-ups of fragmented body parts) forecloses a univocal reading of the French woman as allegory for the Statue of Liberty.

10. D. Emily Hicks, *Border Writing: The Multidimensional Text* (Minneapolis: University of Minnesota Press, 1991), xxviii.

11. Ibid.

12. Mikhail Bakhtin, *Rabelais and His World* (Bloomington: Indiana University Press, 1986), 394.

13. Ibid., 20.

14. Ibid., 25.

15. Stephen Heath, *Questions of Cinema* (Bloomington: Indiana University Press, 1981), 107.

16. Bakhtin, *Rabelais and His World*, 433.

17. My strategy is to register a genealogy and not the "origins" of this tradition; see Michel Foucault, *Language, Counter-Memory, Practice* (Ithaca: Cornell University Press, 1977), 139-64. Certainly humor is one of the skillful weapons of the "underdogs" and thus is not the sole purview of Mexicans-Chicanas/os. Parody and satire are among the many tactics (or "oppositional practices of everyday life") of *lo popular*.

18. In some performances, Cantinflas mistakenly assumes the identity of a wrestler or a politician, and this reversal of identity would function as the space for critical commentary on class inequality or state corruption.

19. According to the Larousse, the term *cábula* is an Americanization of the argot *cabalá*, which means *trampa* or trap. There is some connection here with the Hebrew Kaballah: a text with hidden or cryptic meaning. I have been unable to locate any source that explains how the meaning has been transformed by this so-called Americanization. In current popular usage, *cábula* means to create an entanglement or entrapment through willful acts or through the use of words with double meaning—which is exactly the effect Cantinflas achieves against his verbal opponents, and hence its subversive and pleasurable moments.

20. This practice, according to Cantinflas's own account, appears to have come about spontaneously and as a result of the comedian's own nervousness during a performance. The audience's response was so positive that Cantinflas repeated and perfected the practice. This would merit him the creation of a Mexican word in his honor, the term *cantinflismo*, another way of saying *"puro palabrerio."* See Carlos Monsiváis, *Escenas de Pudor y Liviandades* (Mexico City: La Edición, 1988). A more recent example of *cantinflismo* is found in the popular joke about former Mexican president Luis Echeverría Alvarez, who in a famous speech was said to have explained the PRI's political ideology with the following words: "Ni somos de la izquierda, ni de la derecha, sino todo lo contrario" ("We are neither of the left, nor of the right, but entirely the opposite"; my translation).

21. When Tin-Tan performed for Mexico City audiences, he was forced (censored) to tone down the class critique within his parodic and satirical style; see Gary D. Keller, "The Image of the Chicano in Mexican, United States and Chicano Cinema: An Overview," in *Chicano Cinema*, ed. Gary D. Keller (Binghamton: Bilingual Review/Press,

1985), 13-22. For an overview of Mexican comedians, see Miguel Angel Morales, *Cómicos de México* (Mexico CIty: Panorama Editorial, 1987).

22. Octavio Paz, *The Labyrinth of Solitude* (New York: Grove Press, 1961). For an excellent critique of Paz's discussion of Chicanos, see Carlos Blanco Aguinaga, "El Laberinto Fabricado por Paz," *Aztlán* 3, no. 1 (1973): 1-12.

23. The role of Mexican comedians Viruta y Capulina and Palillo was pointed out to me by Lauro Flores of the University of Washington.

24. Jefferson Morley, "Bruce Springsteen. Made in the USA. The Phenomenon," *Rolling Stone* (October 10, 1985): 20.

25. See, for instance, Michael Rogin, *Ronald Reagan: The Movie* (Berkeley: University of California Press, 1987).

26. Marin deliberately created this enigmatic image of the French woman, arguing that her "cartoonish" aspect allowed him to slip in and out of humor/seriousness throughout the film; see Dennis West and Gary Crowdus, "Cheech Cleans Up His Act," *Cineaste* 16, no. 3 (July 1988): 37.

27. Latinos are these kinds of objects of representation, for example, in the daily intoxication of dark-skinned shots about the Medellín cartel connection on the nightly news.

28. The film also avoids what Stuart Hall terms a "simple set of reversals" in that *Born in East L.A.* does include a white businessman who comes to Rudy's aid in Mexico. The film also includes parodied images of problematic Chicanos/Mexicans, particularly in the jail sequences. See Stuart Hall, "New Ethnicities," *ICA Documents* 7 (1988): 27-31.

29. The connections of this scene to Chicano music culture were first pointed out to me by George Lipsitz, who notes that "Summertime Blues" was based on a riff by Bo Diddley, the black musician most connected to Afro-Cuban and Mexican musics. Diddley was a hero to Eddie Cochran and Ritchie Valens.

30. I am indebted to George Lipsitz for pointing out that "Twist and Shout" was written by whites imitating Puerto Rican music. The song was made a hit by a black group, the Isley Brothers, and a white group, the Beatles.

31. Ryan and Kellner, *Camera Politica*, 280.

32. Ibid., 286; emphasis in the original.

33. Kobena Mercer, "Recoding Narratives of Race and Nation," *ICA Documents*, no. 7 (1988): 4-14.

34. See my article *"Born in East L.A.*: The Politics of Representation," *Cultural Studies* 4, no. 1 (Spring 1990): 264-80.

35. See Fernando Birri's discussion of this shift in "For a Nationalist, Realist, Critical and Popular Cinema," *Screen* 26, nos. 3-4 (May-August 1985): 89-91. My use of *lo popular* has a different meaning or content from that of Euro-American notions of "popular culture," which are usually opposed to Kantian aesthetics or to "mass" and "elite" culture, and also differs from some strands of anthropological/folkloric usages where the "popular" signifies the "authentic," the "primitive," the "rural," the "simple folk" — in other words, the "other" outside of history. In the context of my essay I draw from Jesús Martín-Barbero's definition of *lo popular* as a notion that refers to "the reevaluation of the articulations and mediations of civil society, the social meanings of conflicts beyond their political formulation and synthesis, the recognition of collective experiences that are not encompassed by party political forms" [Jesús Martín-Barbero, "Communication from Culture: The Crisis of the National and the Emergence of the Popular," *Media, Culture and Society* 10 (1988): 453]. The author was in turn influenced by Michel de Certeau's brilliant formulation of this concept as "the oppositional practices of everyday life"; see Michel de Certeau, *The Practice of Everyday Life* (Berkeley and Los Angeles: University of California Press, 1984).

36. Birri, "For a Nationalist, Realist, Critical and Popular Cinema," 90. Realism in new cinema differs from dominant meanings of the term principally because a central problem for Latin American aesthetics is the epistemological one. Much closer to the new Latin American tradition is Silverman and Torode's concept of "real-ism." As the authors explain: "In contrast to realism which presupposes the reality of a world prior to its documentation, we have proposed a strategy of 'real-ism' which permits discovery of the ways in which 'reality' is constituted as an appearance in the language of social life" [David Silverman and Brian Torode, *The Material Word* (London: Routledge and Kegan Paul, 1980), 16].

37. Martín-Barbero, "Communication from Culture," 459.

38. For the formulation of the "internal colony" paradigm, see Rudy Acuña, *Occupied America*; and Mario Barrera, Carlos Muñoz, and Charles Ornelas, "The Barrio as an Internal Colony," in *People and Politics in Urban Society*, ed. Harlan Hahn (Beverly Hills: Sage Publications, 1972), 465-98. For critiques of the model, see Fred Cervantes, "Chicanos as a Post-Colonial Minority: Some Questions Concerning the Adequacy of the Paradigm of Internal Colonialism," in *Perspectives in Chicano Studies* 1, ed. Reynaldo Flores Macías (Los Angeles: UCLA, 1975); and Gilbert G. Gonzales, "A Critique of the Internal Colony Model," *Latin American Perspectives* (Spring 1974): 154-60.

39. Trinh T. Minh-ha, *When the Moon Waxes Red* (New York and London: Routledge, 1991), 18.

4. From Il(l)egal to Legal Subject

1. Laleen Jamayane and Anne Rutherford, "Why a Fish Pond? An Interview with Trinh T. Minh-ha," *The Independent* 14, no. 10 (December 1991): 20-25, p. 24.

2. James Clifford, "Borders/Diasporas," paper presented at the "Borders/Diasporas" conference, University of California-Santa Cruz, April 1992.

3. Renato Rosaldo, *Culture and Truth* (Boston: Beacon Press, 1989), 217.

4. Henry Giroux, *Border Crossings* (New York and London: Routledge, 1992), 151.

5. See Michael Rogin, *Ronald Reagan: The Movie* (Berkeley: University of California Press, 1987), especially pp. 169-89. Rogin notes the following: "The end of the frontier symbolized, for the country's political and cultural elite, the disappearance of the virgin land that had given the nation its identity" (183).

6. Américo Paredes, "On Ethnographic Work among Minority Groups: A Folklorist's Perspective," in *New Directions in Chicano Scholarship*, ed. Ricardo Romo and Raymund Paredes (Santa Barbara: UCSB, Center for Chicano Studies, 1984), 1-32; and Gloria Anzaldúa, *Borderlands/La Frontera* (San Francisco: Spinsters/Aunt Lute, 1987). That this territory was a contested terrain even before Anglo immigration into the area is clearly evident in the following observation made by Paredes: "The Nuevo Santander people [lower Rio Grande valley] . . . committed their daily affairs and their history to the ballad form: the fights against the Indians, the horse races, and the domestic triumphs and tragedies—and later the border conflicts and the civil war" (15).

7. Ibid.

8. Sonia Saldívar-Hull, "Feminism on the Border: From Gender Politics to Geopolitics," in *Criticism in the Borderlands*, ed. Hector Calderon and José David Saldívar (Durham, N.C.: Duke University Press, 1991), 211.

9. Guillermo Gómez-Peña, "The Multicultural Paradigm: An Open Letter to the National Arts Community," *High Performance* 12, no. 3 (Fall 1989): 17-27, p. 20.

10. Clifford, "Borders/Diasporas."

11. Jamayane and Rutherford, "Why a Fish Pond," 24. Chicana cultural critics and writers such as Chela Sandoval, Sonia Saldívar-Hull, and Gloria Anzaldúa apply the

notion of borders as a space "between and among" political, cultural identities and discourses. See Chela Sandoval, "U.S. Third World Feminism: The Theory and Method of Oppositional Consciousness in the Postmodern World," *Genders*, no. 10 (Spring 1991): 1-24; Saldívar-Hull, "Feminism on the Border"; Anzaldúa, *Borderlands/La Frontera*.

12. Genaro Padilla, "Myth and Comparative Cultural Nationalism," in *Aztlán: Essays on the Chicano Homeland*, ed. Rudolfo A. Anaya and Francisco Lomelí (Albuquerque: Academia/El Norte Publications, 1989), 111-34.

13. The fact that Ritchie was raised hearing his relatives playing Mexican music, as I have noted, was totally absent in Luis Valdez's account of Ritchie's life. I would like to focus nonetheless on the suggestive aspects of this border crossing as it relates to countermemory. See George Lipsitz, *Time Passages* (Minneapolis: University of Minnesota Press, 1990) for further discussion of this subject.

14. As I have noted in chapter 2, the film is recounted from Bob's point of view.

15. See, for instance, Néstor García Canclini, *Culturas Híbridas* (Mexico City: Grijalbo, 1989).

16. Clifford, "Borders/Diasporas."

17. Giroux, *Border Crossings*, 28.

18. Américo Paredes, *With His Pistol in His Hand: A Border Ballad and Its Hero* (Austin: University of Texas Press, 1958).

19. Tatcho Mindiola, "*El Corrido de Gregorio Cortez*," *Southwest Media Review* 3 (Spring 1985): 52-56; Guillermo Hernández, "*The Ballad of Gregorio Cortez*," *Critica* 1, no. 3 (Spring 1985): 122-31; and R. L. Fregoso, "*Zoot Suit* and *The Ballad of Gregorio Cortez*," *Critica* 1, no. 2 (Spring 1985): 126-31.

20. Carl Gutiérrez-Jones, "Legislating Languages: *The Ballad of Gregorio Cortez* and the English Language Amendment," in *Chicanos and Film*, ed. Chon A. Noriega (Minneapolis: University of Minnesota Press, 1992), 195-206, p. 197.

21. Lauren Berlant, "National Brands/National Body: Imitations of Life," in *Comparative American Identities*, ed. Hortense J. Spiller (New York and London: Routledge, 1991), 110-30, p. 113.

22. Giroux, *Border Crossings*, 56.

23. Hayden White, *The Content of Form* (Baltimore and London: The Johns Hopkins University Press, 1987), 9.

24. My earlier article on this film deals with the historical development of the discourse of objectivity in journalism; see Fregoso, "*Zoot Suit* and *The Ballad of Gregorio Cortez*."

25. Gutiérrez-Jones, "Legislating Languages," 198.

26. Ibid.

27. Ibid., 199.

28. The notion of "infantilized Indian"/other is taken from Michael Rogin's chapter on "Liberal Society and the Indian Question," in *Ronald Reagan*, especially pp. 141-53.

29. See José Limón, "Américo Paredes: A Man from the Border," *Revista Chicano—Riqueña* 8 (1980): 1-5; Ramón Saldívar, *Chicano Narrative: The Dialectics of Difference* (Madison: University of Wisconsin Press, 1990).

30. Giroux, *Border Crossings*, 30.

31. Mindiola, "*El Corrido de Gregorio Cortez*," 55.

32. Hernández, "*The Ballad of Gregorio Cortez*," 125.

33. Ibid., 122.

34. Ibid., 123.

35. Limón, "Américo Paredes: A Man from the Border," 1.

36. Saldívar, *Chicano Narrative*, 26.

37. Mindiola, "*El Corrido de Gregorio Cortez*," 53-54.

38. Slavoj Zizek, *Looking Awry: An Introduction to Jacques Lacan through Popular Culture* (Cambridge and London: The MIT Press, 1991), 89.

39. David Silverman and Brian Torode, *The Material Word* (London: Routledge and Kegan Paul, 1980), 16.

40. Giroux, *Border Crossings*, 33.

41. Rosaldo, *Culture and Truth*, 151.

42. Saldívar, *Chicano Narrative*, 41.

43. The film's contribution along these lines is echoed by Chon A. Noriega, "Chicano Cinema and the Horizon of Expectations: A Discursive Analysis of Film Reviews in the Mainstream, Alternative and Hispanic Press, 1987-1988," *Aztlán* 19, no. 2 (Fall 1988-1990); Carl Gutiérrez-Jones, "Legislating Languages"; and Michael Ryan and Doug Kellner, *Camera Politica* (Bloomington: Indiana University Press, 1988).

44. Olmos's comments are quoted in Hernández, "*The Ballad of Gregorio Cortez*," 123.

45. Ella Shohat, "Gender and Culture of Empire: Toward a Feminist Ethnography of the Cinema," *Quarterly Review of Film and Video* 13, nos. 1-3 (1991): 45-84, p. 56.

46. See Michael Rogin, *Ronald Reagan*, 134-68.

47. Michael Kennedy, "Medicine Bordering on Crisis," *Los Angeles Times* (July 3, 1992): 1 +. For a painful look at the rise of cholera among Chicano and Mexicano border residents in Texas, see the recent article by Roberto Suro, "The Cholera Watch," *The New York Times Magazine* (March 22, 1992): 32 +.

48. D. Emily Hicks, *Border Writing* (Minneapolis: University of Minnesota Press, 1991), xxv.

49. Ibid., xxiv.

50. I was first struck by this during James Clifford's talk at the "Borders/Diasporas" conference, when he referred to coyotes as shamans.

51. Hicks, *Border Writing*, xxxi.

52. The film was released in Mexico in 1977 and in the United States in 1979. It was the first and only film directed by a Chicano that has been financed and produced by the Banco Nacional Cinematográfico and Conacine in Mexico. An extensive analysis of the film is beyond the scope of this paper, particularly because I have not been able to obtain the film for a more detailed examination. Azteca Films went out of business, so the film is no longer available for U.S. distribution. I have attempted several times to obtain a copy from the filmmaker, Jesús Salvador Treviño, who has to this date not sent me a copy. For an extensive treatment of the film, see Alejandro Morales, "Expanding the Meaning of Chicano Cinema: *Yo Soy Chicano, Raíces de Sangre, Seguin*," in *Chicano Cinema*, ed. Gary D. Keller (Binghamton: Bilingual Review/Press, 1985), 121-37; and Guadalupe Ochoa Thompson, "*Raíces de Sangre*: Roots of Lineage, Sources of Life," ibid.

53. I was living in South Texas during the time this event actually took place. It was reported extensively by the media and dominated the conversation of Chicanos in South Texas.

54. Clifford, "Borders/Diasporas."

55. Tim Golden, "Mexico Is Now Acting to Protect Border Migrants from Robbery and Abuse," *New York Times* (June 28, 1992): 3.

56. Mary G. Dietz, "Citizenship with a Feminist Face: The Problem of Maternal Thinking," *Political Theory* 13, no. 1 (February 1985): 19-37, p. 32.

57. Quoted in Saldívar-Hull, "Feminism on the Border," 218.

58. Dietz, "Citizenship with a Feminist Face," 33.

59. Kathleen Newman, "Latino Sacrifice in the Discourse of Citizenship: Acting against the 'Mainstream,' 1985-1988," in *Chicanos and Film*, ed. Chon A. Noriega, 59-73, p. 60.

60. See Berlant, "National Brands/National Body," 112.

61. This quote is taken from a talk Mouffe and Laclau presented at University of California-Davis during the spring of 1992.

62. I was convinced to include this film in this chapter after my nine-year-old son, Sergio, who was viewing the film with me, said, "I like the way they [the filmmakers] use the borderline."

63. The film was based on the extensive research of historian Lorena Parlee.

64. This observation was made for the problem of translation in *The Ballad of Gregorio Cortez*, but it is equally applicable to the narrative terms that *Break of Dawn* sets up; see Gutiérrez-Jones, "Legislating Languages," 198.

65. Berlant, "National Brands/National Body," 112.

66. Michael Rogin writes: "Although American states abolished property qualifications for voting, they did not thereby overcome propertied distinctions among men" (*Ronald Reagan*, 178).

67. For an extensive account of land-grant families in California prior to white immigration, see Albert Camarillos, *Chicanos in a Changing Society: From Mexican Pueblos to American Barrios in Santa Barbara and Southern California, 1848-1930* (Cambridge: Harvard University Press, 1979); and John R. Chávez, *The Lost Land: The Chicano Image of the Southwest* (Albuquerque: University of New Mexico Press, 1984), especially pp. 43-49.

68. Rosaldo, *Culture and Truth*, 216.

69. Ibid.

70. Saldívar-Hull, "Feminism on the Border," 216.

71. Hicks, *Border Writing*, 15.

72. Trinh T. Minh-ha, cited in the epigraph to this chapter.

73. Jamayane and Rutherford, "Why a Fish Pond," 24.

5. *Nepantla* in Gendered Subjectivity

1. Chela Sandoval, "U.S. Third World Feminism: The Theory and Method of Oppositional Consciousness in the Postmodern World," *Genders*, no. 10 (Spring 1991): 3.

2. Tey Diana Rebolledo, "The Politics of Poetics; or, What Am I, a Critic, Doing in This Text Anyhow?" in *Making Face, Making Soul/Haciendo Caras*, ed. Gloria Anzaldúa (San Francisco: Aunt Lute Foundation Books, 1990), 352.

3. The *pastorela* is a traditional Christmas play performed in the Southwest and in Mexico during the Christmas holidays.

4. *The Trouble with Tonia* (Juan Garza, 1990) also features a woman, yet this film, though shown in the Chicano/Latino festival circuits, has been described as a showcase film, that is, one designed for funding purposes.

5. For discussion of stereotypes of Chicanas, see Cordelia Candelaria, "Social Equity in Film Criticism," Sylvia Morales, "Chicano-Produced Celluloid Mujeres" and Carlos E. Cortés, "Chicanas in Film: History of an Image," which appear in *Chicano Cinema*, ed. Gary D. Keller (Binghamton: Bilingual Review/Press, 1985).

6. This is especially accurate as most stories are about male historical figures.

7. Devon Peña, "Lucha Obrera en las Maquiladoras," *Aztlán* 11, no. 2 (Fall 1980): 159-230.

8. See Michel Foucault, *The Archaeology of Knowledge* (New York: Pantheon Books, 1972), especially pp. 199-211.

9. Quoted in Julianne Burton's interview with Humberto Solás in Burton, *Cinema and Social Change in Latin America* (Austin: University of Texas Press, 1988), 151.

10. Tomás Ybarra-Frausto's essay on Chicano poetry gives an important account of differences in ideological orientation among Chicano poets, particularly those differences based on contextual factors. Poets of the San Francisco Bay Area, for example, linked Chicano struggles within the United States to international revolutionary movements. In his examination of the journal *Pocho Che* published in the Bay Area, Ybarra-Frausto writes that Chicano poets "integrated an international political perspective" to reflect "the cultural fusion of the people of 'La Misión.'" As Ybarra-Frausto explains: "Perhaps it was natural that the Bay Area, with its kaleidoscopic array of Central Americans, West Indians and Mexican people, should inspire poetry which sought to express their diverse temperaments, speech patterns and world views"; see Tomás Ybarra-Frausto, "The Chicano Movement and the Emergence of a Chicano Political Consciousness," in *New Directions in Chicano Scholarship*, ed. Ricardo Romo and Raymund Paredes (Santa Barbara: UCSB, Center for Chicano Studies, 1984), 101. For further accounts of Chicano student activist connections with international revolutionary movements, see Carlos Muñoz's discussion of the San Francisco State University and University of California-Berkeley's "Third World Student Strike" in 1969, published in his book *Youth, Identity and Power* (London and New York: Verso, 1989).

11. In a conversation, Lourdes Portillo told me that the Sandinistas living in the Bay Area who first viewed the film did not appreciate its emphasis on gender, and refused to be associated with the film.

12. Sandoval, "U.S. Third World Feminism," 9.

13. Ibid., 4.

14. Ibid., 14; emphasis in the original.

15. Ibid., 11; emphasis in the original.

16. Sonia Saldívar-Hull, "Feminism on the Border," in *Criticism in the Borderlands*, ed. Hector Calderon and José David Saldívar (Durham, N.C.: Duke University Press, 1991), 203-20.

17. Herbert Schiller, *Communication and Cultural Domination* (New York: International Arts and Sciences Press, 1976).

18. Norma Alarcón, "The Theoretical Subject(s) of *This Bridge Called My Back* and Anglo-American Feminism," in *Making Faces, Making Soul/Haciendo Caras*, ed. Gloria Anzaldúa, 366.

19. Cora Kaplan, "Deterritorializations: The Rewriting of Home and Exile in Western Feminist Discourse," *Cultural Critique* 6 (Spring 1987): 197.

20. Sandoval, "U.S. Third World Feminism," 15.

21. Alarcón, "The Theoretical Subject(s)," 365-66.

22. To this date, the repression of Guatemalan Indians by the government continues, making the civil war in this country the longest in Latin American history; see Tim Golden, "Guatemala Rivals in Rights Accord," *New York Times* (August 9, 1992): 7.

23. For a critique of the politics of the film, see Chris List, "*El Norte*, Ideology and Immigration," *Jump Cut*, no. 34 (1989): 27-31; and Richard Allen, "Hollywood Corner," *Framework*, nos. 26-27 (1985): 86-89.

24. Julio Cortázar, "Neruda among Us," in *Cultures: Cultural Identity in Latin America* (Paris: UNESCO, 1986), 162.

25. Michael Ventura, "*El Norte*: Beautiful Nightmares," *Sundial News and Review* (May 24-31, 1984): 13+.

26. See Mario Barrera, "Story Structure in Latino Feature Films," in *Chicanos and Film*, ed. Chon A. Noriega (Minneapolis: University of Minnesota Press, 1992), 218-40.

27. The complexity of human action is explained away by the filmmakers' resort to troubling reductionism. For example, Enrique's good job at a chic L.A. restaurant ends with the INS visit that is prompted by a call from the Chicano waiter who had been working in the restaurant prior to Enrique's hiring yet did not receive the promotion to headwaiter's assistant that was given to Enrique. The film overly emphasizes the Chicano waiter's motivation for his call in terms of the cultural code *envidia* (envy).

28. My analysis of the documentary thrust of this film was informed by Bill Nichol's account of the mechanism operating in documentary films; see Nichol's excellent study *Representing Reality* (Bloomington: Indiana University Press, 1991).

29. Since its 1989 production, the film airs on some PBS stations; however, PBS refuses to air the film on its national network.

30. The filmmakers dedicated this film to the memory of Ralph Maderiaga, who died in the 1980s and who first started the annual parade and exhibition at the Centro Cultural de la Raza in San Francisco during the seventies. I have attended the Día de Los Muertos festivity in Santa Barbara's Centro Cultural de la Raza, where a few Chicanos, gathered by local Chicano musician Francisco Gonzalez, paint faces and parade around the block. Chicano studies departments also set up altars in their conference rooms to introduce students to cultural traditions.

31. See Roland Barthes, *S/Z* (Boston: Hill and Wang, 1974).

32. See Trinh T. Minh-ha, *When the Moon Waxes Red* (New York and London: Routledge, 1991), especially pp. 29-52.

33. The use of "authority" figures in the scenes shot in San Francisco is also related to the fact of public funds (National Endowment for the Arts, Paul Robeson, and so on), as most funding sources require the use of consultants or "experts" in the topic.

34. See, for example, Ana Maria Alonso and Maria Teresa Koreck, "Silences: 'Hispanics,' AIDS, and Sexual Practices," *Differences: A Journal of Feminist Cultural Studies* 1, no. 4 (Winter 1989); and Tomas Almaguer, "The Cartography of Homosexual Desire and Identity among Chicano Men," *Differences* 3, no. 2 (Summer 1992).

35. Yvonne Yarbro-Bejarano, "De-constructing the Lesbian Body: Cherríe Moraga's *Loving in the War Years*," in *Chicana Lesbians*, ed. Carla Trujillo (Berkeley: Third Women Press, 1991), 144.

36. During her talk "Ofrendas y esperanzas de la América Nuestra: Chicana Film," at Crossing Borders: First International Conference of Mexican and U.S. Latina Film and Video Makers (Baja California, Mexico) in December 1990, Kathleen Newman referred to the scene where the cross-dresser offers the apple to spectators as the "parodic offering."

37. Yarbro-Bejarano, "De-constructing the Lesbian Body," 144.

38. Cherríe Moraga, "La Ofrenda," in *Chicana Lesbians*, ed. Carla Trujillo, 8. My translation: "where is she / who gave me my body / as an offering to myself?"

39. Emma Perez's essay on Chicana sexuality also deploys the concept of the offering, investing the body of her textual/sexual project with the following: "I give these words to you now. Like a gift. I tell you who and what I am. This is the gift I offer. Do you understand? Ya no me van a robar mi sitio y mi lengua. They live inside my soul, with my mother, my sisters, mis hermanas del tercer mundo" (Emma Perez, "Sexuality and Discourse: Notes from a Chicana Survivor," in *Chicana Lesbians*, ed. Carla Trujillo, 179).

40. I have adopted this quote from Teresa de Lauretis's illuminating essay, "Rethinking Women's Cinema," in *Technologies of Gender* (Bloomington: Indiana University Press, 1987), where the author uses it to reference the films by women (135).

41. Rosa Linda Fregoso, "Chicana Film Practices: Confronting the 'Many-Headed Demon of Oppression,' " in *Chicanos and Film*, ed. Chon A. Noriega, 168-82.

42. Annette Kuhn, "Textual Politics," in *Issues in Feminist Film Criticism*, ed. Patricia Erens (Bloomington: Indiana University Press, 1990), 261.

43. Ramón Saldívar, *Chicano Narrative: The Dialectics of Difference* (Madison: University of Wisconsin Press, 1990), 184.

44. de Lauretis, *Technologies of Gender*, 134.

45. Ibid., 133; emphasis in the original.

46. Ibid., 141.

6. Conclusion

1. Stated as he rode through East L.A. with reporter Guy Garcia, and quoted in Guy Garcia, "A Tale of Two Cities," *Premier* (April 1992): 38-42.

2. Rubén Martínez, *The Other Side* (London and New York: Verso, 1992), 165.

3. See Paul Lieberman, "51% of Riot Arrests Were Latino, Study Says," *Los Angeles Times* (June 18, 1992): B11. The figures are taken from a study of those arrested: 51 percent Latinos, mostly males of ages 18 to 24; 36 percent black. For further analysis, see Mike Davis, "In L.A., Burning All Illusions," *The Nation* (June 1, 1992): 743-46.

4. Mike Davis, *City of Quartz* (London and New York: Verso, 1990), 228. For an account of the militarization and privatization of public space, see especially pp. 223-63.

5. Garcia, "A Tale of Two Cities," 42.

6. For more details, see Garcia, "A Tale of Two Cities"; Lawrence Christon, "Breaking the Chains," *Los Angeles Times Calendar* (September 1, 1991): 4+.

7. Christon, "Breaking the Chains," 7.

8. Ibid., 4.

9. Nora Lee, "*American Me* Explores Mexican Mafia," *American Cinematographer* (May 1992): 32.

10. Davis, *City of Quartz*, 27. For a great exposition on the centrality of literary and film noir in the "promotion" or "hype" of Los Angeles, see pp. 36-46.

11. Ibid., 87.

12. Like Chuco, the lead character in *Boulevard Nights* (1978, directed by Michael Pressman), Santana grew up in East L.A., yet had never been to the beach. There is also a certain stylized defiance in Santana's stance, reminiscent of the Pachuco in *Zoot Suit*. Finally, I would like to mention the "godfatheresque" quality of the film.

13. Lizarraga was a counselor with the Community Youth Gang Services in Los Angeles. She was shot on May 14, 1992. The other technical advisor, Charles Manriquez, was a reputed member of the Mexican Mafia when he was in prison. He was shot to death on March 25, 1992. See Stephanie Chavez and Greg Braxton, "Anti-Gang Crusader Slain in Driveway," *The Sacramento Bee* (May 15, 1992): B8.

14. Glenn Lovell, "Hispanic Film's Brutality Stirs Praise, Outrage," *San Jose Mercury News* (February 29, 1992): 1+.

15. Quoted in Garcia, "A Tale of Two Cities," 41.

16. Some of these figures are from a radio program, "Justice Blinded," which aired over KZYX-FM, the Pacifica affiliate in Mendocino, California, in September 1992. Others come from the various articles cited in this chapter about *American Me*.

17. Martín Sánchez-Jankowski, *Islands in the Streets* (Berkeley and Los Angeles: University of California Press, 1991), 39.

18. Ibid.

19. Ibid., 300.

20. Ibid., 41.

21. See Terry Pristin, "Olmos Puts a Warning Out to Gang Members," *Los Angeles Times* (February 24, 1992): F1+. Also see articles published in two Catholic weeklies:

Victor Alemán, "Olmos Recomienda Superacción a los Hispanos," *Vida Nueva* (June 18-July 1, 1992): 1+; "Edward James Olmos: A Movie Star with a Mission," *Tidings* (June 19, 1992): 12-13.

22. Sánchez-Jankowski, *Islands in the Streets*, 274.

23. Pristin, "Olmos Puts a Warning Out to Gang Members."

24. I would like to note that in this passage on the aesthetics of reception, de Lauretis is talking about the shift in women's cinema; see Teresa de Lauretis, *Technologies of Gender* (Bloomington: Indiana University Press, 1987), 141.

25. See, for example, de Lauretis, *Technologies of Gender*, especially pp. 1-30.

26. At the Latino Film Festival at the University of California-Santa Cruz in May 1992, I had occasion to sit on a panel with Chicano filmmaker (now mainly producer) Moctezuma Esparza. When I mentioned this "by, for, about" thesis, Moctezuma made it a point to emphasize that he did not buy into this early definition, or rather that he disagreed with the project as it was defined by the early filmmakers. If I may paraphrase what he said to me and the audience: "I give the studios a story about Chicanos that they (executives) want to see on the screen."

27. de Lauretis, *Technologies of Gender*, 119.

28. Lee, "*American Me* Explores Mexican Mafia," 26-32.

29. Carmen Huaco-Nuzum, "*American Me* (Despair in the Barrio)," *Jump Cut* (forthcoming).

30. de Lauretis, *Technologies of Gender*, 132.

31. These figures are for major urban centers and were reported by the media in March 1992. In a more recent article, national dropout rates for Latinos showed an increase in the years between 1972-92, from 34.3 to 35.3 percent, whereas the dropout rates for blacks decreased from 21.3 to 13.6 percent, and among whites from 12.3 to 8.9 percent. See Nanette Asimov, "Dropout Rate in U.S. Schools Falls to 11.2%," *San Francisco Chronicle* (September 17, 1992): 1+.

32. de Lauretis, *Technologies of Gender*, 109.

33. For Chicana critiques of Octavio Paz, see Norma Alarcón, "Tradductora, Traidora: A Paradigmatic Figure of Chicana Feminism," *Cultural Critique*, no. 13 (Fall 1989): 57-87; and Adelaida R. del Castillo, "Malintzín Tenépal: A Preliminary Look into a New Perspective," in *Essays on La Mujer*, ed. Rosaura Sánchez and Rosa Martínez Cruz (Los Angeles: UCLA, Chicano Studies Center Publications, 1977), 124-49. For a critique of Paz's views on *pachuquismo*, see Marcos Sánchez-Tranquilinos, "Mano a Mano: An Essay on the Representation of the Zoot Suit and Its Misrepresentation by Octavio Paz," *Journal of the Los Angeles Institute of Contemporary Art* (Winter 1987): 34-42.

34. According to Olmos, Universal executives changed only forty seconds in the film, the scene where Santana actually sodomizes Julie; see Lovell, "Hispanic Film's Brutality Stirs Praise, Outrage."

35. Octavio Paz, *The Labyrinth of Solitude* (New York: Grove Press, 1961), 77.

36. Martínez, *The Other Side*, 122.

37. Lovell, "Hispanic Film's Brutality Stirs Praise, Outrage." Olmos also made this claim at the San Francisco screening.

38. Rosi Braidotti is quoted in de Lauretis, *Technologies of Gender*, 24.

Index

Compiled by Eileen Quam and Theresa Wolner

Rosa Linda Fregoso is a native Tejana who lived in Corpus Christi, Texas, until 1979. A former secretary, and radio and television producer, she now teaches in Chicana/o studies and women's studies at the University of California-Davis. She is the coeditor of *Cruzando Fronteras* (1993) and of a special issue of *Cultural Studies* (1990). She has two children and lives in the former home of the L.A. Raiders and the current home of the Oakland A's.